The Limits of Reform
in the Enlightenment

The Limits of Reform in the Enlightenment:

Attitudes toward the Education of the Lower Classes in Eighteenth-Century France

Harvey Chisick

Princeton University Press
Princeton, New Jersey

Copyright © 1981 by Princeton University Press
Published by Princeton University Press, Princeton, New Jersey
In the United Kingdom: Princeton University Press, Guildford, Surrey

ALL RIGHTS RESERVED

Library of Congress Cataloging in Publication Data will be
found on the last printed page of this book

This book has been composed in VIP Baskerville

Clothbound editions of Princeton University Press books
are printed on acid-free paper, and binding materials are
chosen for strength and durability.

Printed in the United States of America by
Princeton University Press, Princeton, New Jersey

For Tammy

Contents

Tables and Graphs

Acknowledgments

I SHOULD first like to thank the Canada Council for the generous financial support it extended to me in the form of a doctoral grant from September 1971 to December 1973, and again as a postdoctoral grant for the summer of 1976. Without the support of the Council it would not have been possible for me to begin, let alone complete, the present study. I am also indebted to the Leverhulme Foundation for a Commonwealth Postdoctoral Fellowship it conferred on me for the academic year 1975-76.

In the course of research for this work I have benefited from the advice and help of many others. M. François Furet allowed me to attend his seminar in the VIe Section of the Ecole Pratique des Hautes Etudes during 1971-72. Dr. John F. Bosher and M. Dominique Julia helped initially to orient me in the archives, an invaluable service, as only those who have worked in the French archives can know; and M. Julia has in the years since my first stay in France often provided constructive criticism and encouragement for my work on the history of education under the old regime. To M. Daniel Roche I owe a special debt for taking time from his own busy schedule to guide me through the chaotic world of the archives of provincial academies, and for generously directing my attention to materials relevant to my subject. In a number of stimulating discussions Mr. Michael Meiselman and M. Eric Walter suggested new approaches and avenues of investigation. Robert Forster, who supervised my doctoral dissertation, impressed on me, though not without some effort and considerable patience, the importance of social history in general and of a social basis to the history of ideas in particular. Richard Kagan was a conscientious critic of my dissertation, on which the present study is in part based. Harry C. Payne was kind enough to let me see his doctoral dissertation on the attitudes of the *philosophes* toward the people before it was published and, moreover, read and criticized mine, offering many useful suggestions on how it might be improved. I would also like to express my appreciation to my friend Gabor Mate, who without being an historian had the interest to read a rather weighty doctoral thesis in history, and the goodness to offer encouragement, not untempered by criticism, to the author. Another friend, Stan Wallach, has been extremely generous in lending me books from his library, and in providing moral support. Harvey Mitchell read the entire manuscript of the book and offered, as usual, a meticulously thorough criticism of it. Thanks are also due to David Bien for bringing to my attention the work of Melvin Edelstein.

I find it difficult adequately to express my appreciation to M. René Vaillant, *archiviste adjoint* of the Department of the Somme and his entire staff, and to Mlles. Bruno and Le Courtoise and other members of the staff of the Municipal Library and Archives of Amiens for their constant good will and helpfulness. Thanks are likewise due to the archivists, librarians and staffs of the Archives Nationales, the Bibliothèque Nationale, the Bibliothèque de l'Arsenal, the Bibliothèque Mazarine, the Bibliothèque Historique de la Ville de Paris, the Bibliothèque Sainte Geneviève, the Library of the Sorbonne, the Departmental Archives of the Marne and Rhone, the Municipal Libraries and Archives of Angers, Rouen, Toulon, Metz, Nancy and Lyon, the British Museum, the Library of the London School of Economics and the Library of Cambridge University. I am further indebted to the Academies of Amiens, Châlons-sur-Marne, Lyon, Metz and Rouen for permission to consult documents in their archives or under their control.

In the course of preparing this book I have received invaluable assistance from a number of people whose expertise far exceeds mine in their particular fields. Mr. A. W.

Eagling of Cambridge kindly agreed to translate the Latin essay on popular education submitted to the Academy of Amiens in 1790 when it became clear that my attempt to put it into English would yield no very good result. Jordan Goodman advised me how to organize material for the computer, and Rachel Britten, Research Assistant in the Department of Economics at the University of Essex, was generous in the extreme with her time and energy in programming a computer study of the *Année littéraire* and the *Journal encyclopédique* on which chapter four is in part based. Valerie D'Angelo proved the most efficient and accurate, as well as good natured, typist I have yet encountered.

I would also like to thank Ms. R. Miriam Brokaw, Associate Director and Editor at the Princeton University Press, and Ms. Margot Cutter, Editor, for their courtesy, understanding and efficiency in dealing with my manuscript. Such inelegances and infelicities of style as are still to be found in the text cannot be laid to the account of the editors.

Finally, special thanks are due my wife for her consistent and single-minded criticism of the book ("It's too long") through the various stages of its preparation, and for her support, and sometimes ironic toleration of it and me during the time it was in the making. I am pleased to be able to say that she was not greatly inconvenienced by the writing of this book, for this allows me to dedicate it to her from motives other than an uneasy conscience.

It is customary in concluding the acknowledgments of one's debts to exonerate those from whom one has received help or derived ideas or information from responsibility for any inaccuracies, errors or shortcomings in what follows. Which thing I do.

Vancouver, B.C.
14 September, 1979

Note on Usage

In quoting from eighteenth-century sources, original spelling, punctuation and use of accents have been respected. As literary conventions, especially for manuscript documents, seem to have been extremely fluid at that time, the designation *sic* has not been used to indicate every variation from today's standards, but only where the sense of the passage has been called into question. For the convenience of the reader, words that were joined in a manuscript have been reproduced separately. Thus, for example, the phrase, "quepersonnenepeut," which is found in the *Examen* of the Abbé Terrisse, p. 7, is rendered, "que personne ne peut."

Generally, longer quotations have been left in the original, and shorter ones translated into English. Though I would have preferred to keep all quotations in the original, this would have resulted in the text becoming excessively choppy. Hence this rather pragmatic compromise. All translations from French to English are my own unless otherwise indicated.

Abbreviations

ARCHIVES AND LIBRARIES

A Ac.	Archives of an Academy
AD	Archives Départementales
A Mun.	Archives Municipales
AN	Archives Nationales
B Mun.	Bibliothèque Municipale
BN	Bibliothèque Nationale

DICTIONARIES, ENCYCLOPEDIAS AND PERIODICALS

AESC	*Annales: économies, sociétés, civilisations*
AHRF	*Annales historiques de la Révolution française*
AL	*Année littéraire*
CH	*Cahiers d'histoire*
DM	*Dictionnaire des moeurs*
DMP	*Dictionnaire de morale philosophique*
DSP	*Dictionnaire social et patriotique*
DUM	*Dictionnaire universel, historique et critique des moeurs, loix, usages et coutumes civiles, militaires et politiques*
DUS	*Dictionnaire universel des sciences morales, économiques et diplomatiques*
EM	*Encyclopédie méthodique*
ESR	*European Studies Review*
FHS	*French Historical Studies*
GVF	*Grand vocabulaire françois*
JE	*Journal encyclopédique*
JHI	*Journal of the History of Ideas*
JMH	*Journal of Modern History*
P&P	*Past and Present*
PDCV	*Petit dictionnaire de la cour et de la ville*
RH	*Revue historique*

RHMC	*Revue d'histoire moderne et contemporaine*
RIE	*Revue internationale de l'enseignement*
RP	*Revue pédagogique*
VS	*Studies on Voltaire and the Eighteenth Century*

The Limits of Reform
in the Enlightenment

—not but the planet is well enough, provided a man could be born in it to a great title or to a great estate; or could any how contrive to be called up to public charges, and employments of dignity or power;—but that is not my case;—and therefore every man will speak of the fair as his own market has gone in it;—for which cause I affirm it over again to be one of the vilest worlds that ever was made. . . .

Tristram Shandy, vol. i, chap. 5.

Introduction

THE PROBLEM: ENLIGHTENMENT VALUES AND THE
UNENLIGHTENED MASSES

"Enlightenment" and "lower classes" are, if not antag-
onistic, at least mutually exclusive terms. The *menu peuple,
petit peuple* pejoritavely the *canaille* or *racaille*, or simply "the
people" did not share in the Enlightment; they existed outside it. But this is not all. If the people did not take an active part in the movement, neither were they ignored by it.
The people posed a problem to the generally affluent
members of the world of the Enlightment, and this problem is of particular interest, for it focuses our attention on
a conflict between an ideology and the society that produced that ideology.

The Enlightenment was of course an extremely complex
movement, and its thought correspondingly varied and
rich. Certain *philosophes* questioned or denied propositions
that are regarded as characteristic of the movement as a
whole. Yet it cannot be denied that the enlightened community shared certain beliefs which bound it together and
gave coherence to its thought. Carl Becker once paradoxi-
cally referred to these beliefs as "the essential articles of the
Religion of the Enlightenment" and defined them as follows:

(1) man is not natively depraved; (2) the end of life is life
itself, the good life on earth instead of the beatific life
after death; (3) man is capable solely by the light of reason and experience of perfecting the good life here on
earth; and (4) the essential condition of the good life
here on earth is the freeing of men's minds from the
bonds of ignorance and superstition, and of their bodies

from the arbitrary oppression of the constituted social order.[1]

Certainly no thinker who systematically rejected reason, or who argued that ignorance was an unqualified good, can be regarded as part of the Enlightenment, for faith in reason, guided, to be sure, by a prudent empiricism, is the hallmark of Enlightenment thought.

The *philosophes* and thousands of literate, and for the most part unknown, members of the aristocracy and middle classes who thought like them adhered to these values. Their world view rested upon the empiricism of Bacon, the great mathematical and scientific achievements of Newton, and the sensationalist psychology of Locke. They generally gave little credence to any form of supernaturalism. Indeed, never before had the universe seemed so demystified. Pope's couplet in praise of Newton catches the intellectual mood of the early eighteenth century well: "all was light." The advances of science and common sense, the potential ability of reason to explain the physical world and to reform society seemed to the men of the Enlightenment good cause for optimism. And on the whole, optimists they were.[2]

Yet, what was to become of this rationalist optimism, founded on a new science and a new epistemology, when confronted with the very incarnation of superstition and unreason in the ignorant masses? Was the faith of the men of the Enlightenment in reason, in humanity and in their society strong enough to allow them to assert that the ignorance of the people could and should be dissipated, and that all men should be educated to the limits of their ability; or was the logic of Enlightenment thought turned aside

[1] C. L. Becker, *The Heavenly City of the Eighteenth Century Philosophers* (New Haven, 1959), pp. 102-03.

[2] There is also a strong undercurrent of pessimism in the Enlightenment, but its source is aesthetic theory, contemplation of human nature, and history, not the sciences. See H. Vyverberg, *Historical Pessimism in the French Enlightenment* (Cambridge, 1958).

at contemplation of the dirty, often hungry, sometimes res-
tive, but always economically indispensable masses? To
what extent could the people, who were obliged to labor
ten or twelve hours a day or more, be educated? And if
they could be educated, would this benefit society, or
would it disrupt the social order? In answering these questions the men of the Enlightenment revealed the extent to
which they were ruled by the imperatives of their ideology
and influenced by the socioeconomic exigencies of the society in which they lived.[3]

[3] There are a number of previous treatments of Enlightenment attitudes to popular education. Roustan in *Les Philosophes et la société française
au XVIIIe siècle* (Paris, 1911; reprinted Geneva, 1970), pp. 319-33, argued
that the *philosophes* in general, and Voltaire in particular, ultimately favored educating the lower classes. Two articles on the physiocrats,
H. Gourdon, "Les physiocrates et l'éducation nationale au XVIIIe siècle,"
RP, xxxviii (1901), and B. Grosperrin, "Faut-il instruire le peuple? La réponse des physiocrates," CH, xxi (1976), emphasize the desire of these
economists to see the people instructed. Though for the most part concerned with nineteenth-century England, H. Silver devotes the first chapter of his book, *The Concept of Popular Education: A Study of Ideas and Social
Movements in the Early Nineteenth Century* (London, 1965), to the eighteenth
century and discusses arguments for and against popular education in
both England and France. Daniel Mornet, whose knowledge of eighteenth-century intellectual history and whose contributions in this field
remain unsurpassed, has pointed out that although their faith in reason
should have allowed the *philosophes* to advocate the extension of popular
education, they in fact did not do so (*La Pensée française au XVIIIe siècle*,
Paris, 1969, p. 119, and *Les Origines intellectuelles de la Révolution française*,
Paris, 1967, pp. 420-23). Similarly, in the sixth chapter of his book *The
Philosophes and the People* (New Haven and London, 1976), Harry C. Payne
finds that the *philosophes* had little or no inclination to enlighten the
people. Finally, James Leith, in his article, "Modernization, Mass Education and Social Mobility in French Thought, 1750-1789" in R. F. Brissenden, ed., *Studies in the Eighteenth Century*, vol. ii (Toronto, 1973), pp. 223-
38, emphasizes the unwillingness of contemporaries to see the lower
classes broadly educated, and the limitations they wished to impose on
popular instruction. Leith gives as satisfactory a treatment as one could
ask in the scope of a brief article, but is far from exhausting the subject. In
order fully to understand Enlightenment views on popular education it is
necessary to look more thoroughly and closely at the relevant contemporary literature, to put this literature into its social context, and to examine

SOME CONSIDERATIONS ON SOURCES IN THE HISTORY OF IDEAS

Since the bibliography contains a complete list of the works on which this study is based, it is hardly necessary to discuss each of them separately. Nevertheless, it may be useful to make some observations about sources in the history of ideas in general, and on certain of those that figure here in particular.

It is clear, for example, that a philosophical treatise, a propaganda pamphlet, an administrative report and a lyric poem are fundamentally different sorts of literature. Their levels of discourse, even their universes of discourse, are not the same. If an author were to treat the same subject in each of these genres, he would have to write in a completely different way and to emphasize different aspects of the problem. As a philosopher he would be concerned with abstract and absolute truths; as a propagandist he would argue a particular point of view with reference to certain groups or parties; as an administrator he would attempt to deal in the specifics of the case, and remain conceptually close to the outlook of the government; as a poet he would pay special attention to the aesthetics of language. Because the intention of the writer varies in each case, his rhetoric and the scope of his work must vary, too. One could, of course, enter into an extended discussion of the nature of various literary genres, but only two aspects of the question are of immediate relevance here. One concerns the completeness of a work, the other its representativeness.

For the men of the Enlightenment, popular education was a large and complicated issue, and one that they treated philosophically, propagandistically, literarily and, occasionally, even practically. As a result, they tended to hold somewhat inconsistent views on the subject, depend-

the way in which ideas on popular education were related to other key ideas of the time.

ing on the perspective from which they approached it. Voltaire, for example, once asserted that the children of peasants should remain illiterate.[4] But he did not believe that they should be left in superstition. Although he denounced popular education in his correspondence with La Chalotais, he built a school for the children of Ferney.[5] Moreover, can one seriously maintain that Voltaire, who in his historical works and elsewhere condemned the effects of ignorance and superstition on the masses, unreservedly wished that the greater part of mankind be kept ignorant? The crux of the matter lay in the particular aspect of the question he was treating at the time. Basing his opinion on economic criteria, the patriarch of Ferney regarded an illiterate peasantry as a good; considering the Saint Bartholomew's Day massacre, he underscored the evils of ignorance and superstition.[6] Failure to take into account the contexts of the two views makes them appear to be irreconcilably contradictory.

Similarly, Diderot, Helvétius and Holbach, as we shall see, all condemned ignorance. More specifically, they denounced the policy of systematically misleading the people and spoke of education as the dissipation of ignorance and superstition. Yet precisely by defining popular education as the freeing of the people from superstition and consequent oppression, they prejudged the question. Few authors consulted for this study would have objected to popular education so defined. But this fundamentally negative approach to popular instruction—which equates education with the elimination of patent ills—misrepresents the problem faced by the enlightened elite. In denouncing ignorance and superstition, Helvétius and Holbach expressed an

---

[4] See below, p. 94.

[5] Characteristically, however, Voltaire had misgivings about it. See Payne, *The French Philosophes and the People*, p. 97.

[6] See K. J. Weintraub, "Toward the History of the Common Man: Voltaire and Condorcet," in R. Herr, ed., *Ideas in History: Essays presented to Louis R. Gottschalk* (Durham, 1965).

ideological imperative of the Enlightenment; they spoke
philosophically and propagandistically. They failed, however, to discuss popular education positively, and to propose how much instruction the people should receive and
in what it should consist. Which is to say that they discussed
less than half of the question. It is imperative, therefore, to
pay close attention to context and to base any evaluation of
Enlightenment attitudes toward popular education on
more positive and complete statements on the subject.

For the most comprehensive treatments of popular education before 1789 we are indebted to the Academy of
Châlons-sur-Marne, which proposed as the subject of its
essay contest for 1779 the question, "What is the best plan
of education for the people?" The prize was awarded to
Goyon d'Arzac for his *Essais de Laopédie*, which survives
only in manuscript,[7] while Philipon de la Madelaine's book,
Vues patriotiques sur l'éducation du peuple, was said by a well-
informed contemporary to have been inspired by the
academy's contest.[8] Whatever the literary value of these
works, they present a full and rounded view of popular
education and of the scope and nature of this education,
based on explicit assumptions about the social and eco-

[7] *Essais de Laopédie ou Mémoire à l'Académie de Châlons-sur-Marne en reponse à cette question: Quel seroit le meilleur plan d'éducation pour Le Peuple*, BN,
ancien fonds français, mss. 22048 fols. 51-70. References will be given to the
pagination of the essay rather than to the folio into which it has been in-
serted. It may be noted that although Goyon had an agreement with a
bookseller for the publication of this essay, and though the academy also
asked for the right to publish it (AD Marne J 48[18]), the work did not, so
far as I have been able to determine, appear in print.

[8] F. A. Delandine, *Couronnes Académiques, ou Recueil des Prix proposés par
les Sociétés Savantes, avec les noms de ceux qui les ont obtenus, des Concurens distingués, des Auteurs qui ont écrit sur les mêmes sujets, le titre & le lieu de l'impression de leurs Ouvrages* (Paris, 1787), p. 253. Furthermore, one of the contestants in this contest signed himself La Madelaine (AD Marne J 48[18]),
and while there is no positive proof that this was Philipon, the likelihood
that it was is very great. The full reference to Philipon's work is, *Vues patriotiques sur l'éducation du peuple. Tant des villes que de la campagne; Avec
beaucoup de notes interéssantes* (Lyon, 1783).

nomic role of the lower classes. So, too, to a greater or lesser extent, do Père Gourdin's *De l'éducation physique et morale*, J. A. Perreau's *Instruction du peuple*, Jacques Sellier's "Lettre sur l'instruction des enfants du peuple," and the Count de Thélis' *Mémoires concernant les écoles nationales*.[9] These works examined not only matters of principle and the issue of whether the people ought or ought not to be educated, but also discussed such specific questions as: What was the purpose of popular education? Was religion to figure in the curriculum, and if so to what extent? Should the people be taught to read? To write? Should they be given occupational training, or would it be preferable to retain some sort of system of apprenticeship? What sort of moral education was fitting for the lower classes? How far should popular education extend? Which should be given precedence, the skills of literacy, occupational training or moral instruction? How was one part of the curriculum related to the others, and how was the whole to be structured? All these questions must be answered if one is to have a comprehensive and undistorted appreciation of attitudes toward the education of the lower classes in the Enlightenment, and it is because Goyon's and Philipon's works, and to a lesser but still considerable degree, those of Gourdin, Perreau, Thélis and Sellier do answer these questions comprehensively that they are so valuable. However, while the completeness of these works assures them pride of place, they will by no means be allowed to eclipse the views of other writers.

There are, on the whole, two methods of determining the attitudes of any group. One is to focus on its leaders

---

[9] Gourdin, *De l'éducation physique et morale considérée relativement à la place qu'occupent, et que doivent occuper les Enfans dans l'ordre de la Société* (1780). A Ac. Lyon, mss. 147, fols. 94-103. J. A. Perreau, *Instruction du peuple, divisée en trois parties* (Paris, 1786). Jacques Sellier, "Lettre sur l'instruction des enfants du peuple," AD Somme C 1547[2] (1783). C.A.P. de Thélis, A. J. de Charost et al., *Mémoires concernant les écoles nationales* (Paris, 1781-89).

and on the institutions and organs through which it expresses its collective opinion. This may be termed the elitist approach. For the Enlightenment, the recognized leaders are the *philosophes*, the representative institutions, the academies, and its organs, certain periodicals and journals. By definition, the statement of a recognized leader of a movement must be taken as representative of it, though one should avoid ascribing to the movement as a whole the opinions of its most advanced and most radical thinkers. The second way of gauging the attitudes of a group is to collect and analyze the views on a given issue of as many members of the group as possible. This may be called the democratic approach. If, for example, in a body of twenty texts, five favor a point of view and fifteen oppose it, the negative opinion is the more representative. Here the representativeness of a text is determined by its relation to other, generally independent texts.

Another, perhaps even more valuable, means of assessing the degree of representativeness of a given book or article is to examine the reactions of contemporaries to it. Works of literature generally undergo certain processes of differentiation which reveal a good deal about them, and allow us to ascribe a weight to the opinions they express. The simple fact that a book is published indicates that someone was convinced that there was advantage to be derived from its publication. Nevertheless, important as the step from manuscript to printed page may be, it is generally only after a work has been published that the real process of differentiation begins. It is then reviewed, criticized, cited, republished, banned, refuted, commented on, plagiarized or ignored. And it is precisely through this process of banning, criticizing and reediting that ideas are sifted and articulated. A book that goes through sixty editions or one that passes through the hands of the hangman has had some impact. Of course, most works published in the eighteenth century neither went through more than a few editions nor suffered condemnation. Still, most made some impact on the republic of letters, and the reaction of the educated public to a book or pamphlet usually provides a fair indication of its representativeness. While there is no need to discuss the degree of representativeness of each work appearing in this study, this being most suitably done, when it can be done at all, where the work is encountered below, it will perhaps be well to move from these general considerations to one or two specific examples.

A number of works drawn on here won essay contests proposed by academies. These, it seems fair to assume, would represent the views of the academy on a given subject.[10] But how closely an essay represented the collective opinion of the academy crowning it can be appreciated only by examination of the process of selection and of the nature of the control exercised by the academy over the work it endorsed. The contest proposed by the Academy of Châlons-sur-Marne for 1779 provides us with an example.

The first limitation to which participants in this contest were subject followed from the question itself. "What is the best plan of education for the people?" is not a proposition that admits of a negative answer. Should anyone nevertheless have been tempted to reply in the negative, the academy stated in the printed announcement of the contest that in its view, "an ignorant people can only be a vicious and consequently an unhappy people," and qualified the belief that the people should be left in ignorance as "a false . . . a barbarous policy."[11] More generally, the academy asked for entries to be practical and simple, and

---

[10] This statement holds true for political, religious or socioeconomic subjects, but less so for purely literary or speculative ones. For example, it is reasonable to assume that in crowning Rousseau's First Discourse, the Academy of Dijon indicated that it considered the piece the most original and eloquent, not that it believed that the arts and sciences were agents of corruption.

[11] "Prix proposés par l'Académie des Sciences, Arts & Belles Lettres de Châlons-sur-Marne, dans son Assemblée publique de 25 Août [1779]" (AD Marne J 48⁸, p. 1).

warned contestants against criticizing the government or religion.[12]

By the end of 1779 the academy had received at least fifteen entries to the contest,[13] of which three were considered superior. The first was criticized for neglecting the education of the urban poor, for including much superfluous material, and for containing views that "might harm the reputation and honor of the academy."[14] The second was more suitable but still failed to "fulfill entirely the views of the academy."[15] The last essay, Goyon's, was said to contain "excellent things, but drowned in a multitude of details, [and] presented in a manner scarcely agreeable."[16] In all three cases the plans proposed were said to leave much to be desired and to contain many things that should be suppressed.

Finding none of the 1779 entries worthy of the prize, and believing the subject of the contest to be an important one,[17] the academy proposed the question again, doubling

[12] Ibid., p. 2. The manuscript report of the commissioners of the academy also warns prospective contestants against employing either irony or satire (AD Marne J 48[1]).

[13] The essays submitted to the academy were numbered, and the highest number mentioned in the dossier on this contest is fifteen ("Rapport général" of the commissioners of the academy, AD Marne J 48[1]). The author of essay number 15 was Goyon d'Arzac, and his correspondence with the academy shows that he was given permission to send in his entry after the deadline (Letter of Goyon to academy, 7 March 1779, and answer of academy, 1 May 1779, AD Marne J 48[25] and [22]). Nevertheless, Delandine refers to an entry number 16, which received an honorary mention (*Couronnes académiques*, p. 252). Of the contestants, twelve can be identified from their correspondence with the academy. Seven stated their professions, and include three churchmen (a curate, an Oratorian and a *grand vicaire*) and four lawyers (an *avocat en parlement*, a *notaire*, a *lieutenant de baillage* and an *avocat général*) (AD Marne J 48[9-26]). The best-known contestant was Guyton de Morveau, on whom see below, chap. II. The rest, with the exception of Goyon and Philipon, are unknown to the present writer.

[14] AD Marne J 48[1].   [15] Ibid.   [16] Ibid.

[17] "Un sujet aussi interessant pour la partie la plus nombreuse & la plus utile de la Nation mérite sans doute d'être traité avec toute la maturité convenable . . ." ("Prix proposés . . ." p. 1).

the prize to six hundred *livres* and giving 1781 as the new deadline. On learning of this decision Goyon wrote the academy to ask why his entry had been rejected, and about the "qualities it lacked in order to fulfill the views of the academy."[18] It appears from a later letter that Goyon received the guidance he requested for reworking his essay, for he said of the revised version: "This work, entirely rewritten . . . presents, as you see and as the academy demands, a plan free from all unnecessary details."[19] Thus it would seem safe to assert that when Goyon's essay was awarded the prize in 1781, it was of a sort to "fulfill entirely the views of the academy" on the matter of popular education.

It is also possible to determine something of the representativeness of Philipon's *Vues patriotiques*, though by different means. The author's copious footnotes clearly reveal the sources on which he drew, and reviews of the work in the periodical press indicate how it was received by the literate public.

From the point of view of the historian of ideas, one of the principal virtues of the *Vues patriotiques* is that it is a remarkably unoriginal book. One reviewer observed somewhat caustically that it might have been preferable had Philipon "read the ancients less and observed the people more, and had he based his work on his own reflections, rather than on books."[20] It is clear from his notes that Philipon drew his ideas from three main sources: Greek and Roman classics, *philosophe* and related works, and travel literature. Among classical authors, Plato, Aristotle, Zeno, Plutarch, Quintilian and Cicero are cited, while frequent references are made to figures such as Lycurgus, Minos, Solon and Caesar. Philipon tended to admire the Spartans and Romans, and it was doubtless their example that inspired much of the patriotism in his book. Philipon's citations of *philosophe* literature include the *Encyclopédie*,

[18] AD Marne J 48[19] (11 September 1779).
[19] AD Marne J 48[15] (19 May 1781).
[20] *Mercure de France*, 1784 I, 201-02.

Voltaire, Montesquieu, Rousseau, Buffon, and Helvétius. Several theorists of physical education—Ballexerd, Fourcroy de Guillerville and Tissot—are also drawn upon. Travel literature, together with references to Montaigne, Locke, the Abbé St. Pierre and Rollin indicate that the author of the *Vues patriotiques* was deeply immersed in Enlightenment literature, and in the literature that helped create the Enlightenment.

How the enlightened community received Philipon's book may be judged by the half dozen reviews in the periodical press. Four of these were favorable, two critical. The mainstream *Journal des savants* gave the work unenthusiastic, but neverthless favorable, treatment. It observed that the subject was a new and important one, and likened the *Vues patriotiques* to *Emile*, pointing out that while neither work set forth a practicable program of studies, both were seminal.[21] The *Journal général* also reviewed the book briefly but favorably,[22] while a warmer treatment appeared in the pro-*philosophe Journal de Paris*.[23] Though this journal generally mentioned only the author, title and publisher of a work, it gave a reasonably detailed account of the *Vues patriotiques*. It referred to the book as "this excellent work," and to its author as an "estimable protector of the people."[24] The most enthusiastic review of Philipon's book, however, appeared in the *Journal encyclopédique*, a publication that expressed the views of the *philosophe* party.[25] The journalist noted that in contrast to the many books on education published since *Emile*, Philipon's was "truly an excellent book" and his views "as wisely perceived as they are

---

[21] *Journal des savants*, 1784, pp. 281-83.

[22] *Affiches, Annonces et Avis Divers ou Journal Général de France*, 1784, p. 103.

[23] ". . . ce quotidien reflète bien l'opinion moyenne du siècle des lumières." (C. Bellanger, J. Godeschot et al., *Histoire générale de la presse française* [Paris, 1969], I, 243.)

[24] *Journal de Paris*, 1784, pp. 254-55.

[25] Bellanger et al., *Histoire générale de la presse française*, I, 278.

well expressed."[26] He then went on to praise specific aspects of the author's program. Of the two critical reviews of the *Vues patriotiques*, one appeared in the noted anti-*philosophe* journal, the *Année littéraire*,[27] and the other in the *Mercure de France*, a review that cautiously favored the new spirit.[28] Thus, if, as a hostile critic alleged, Philipon was sometimes carried away by his patriotic views,[29] these views were for the most part inspired by *philosophe* literature, and by a broader literature common to the enlightened community, and his book was well received by most organs of that community. Moreover, the *Vues patriotiques* was not forgotten after 1789. In their cahier, the third estate of Marseilles asked that Philipon's views be adopted, and the Abbé Grégoire, while sitting on the committee of public instruction, praised the book.[30]

While we are fortunate to have been able to assess the representativeness of the two most comprehensive treatments of popular education under the old regime, in most cases such full information is lacking. Where no reference to a work can be found in contemporary literature, one can still examine the views it puts forth in relation to other statements on the same subjects, and consider the place of its author in the republic of letters. With these considerations in mind, we can now proceed to examine what is admittedly a rather disparate set of sources and hope to derive from them a reasonably coherent and comprehensive view of the problem we have set out to investigate.

[26] JE, 1784 II, 210.

[27] Bellanger et al., *Histoire générale de la presse française*, I, 264-68. AL, 1784 I, 217-35.

[28] Bellanger et al., *Histoire générale de la presse française*, I, 218. *Mercure de France*, 1784 I, 201-10.

[29] AL, 1784 I, 233.

[30] B. F. Hyslop, *French Nationalism in 1789 according to the General Cahiers* (New York, 1934), p. 109; Leith, "Modernization, Mass Education and Social Mobility," pp. 235-36.

CHAPTER I

The Elements of the Problem

WHOSE ATTITUDES? THE ENLIGHTENED COMMUNITY

The term "Enlightenment" is generally taken to designate
an intellectual movement which spread widely throughout
Europe during the eighteenth century. To speak of "Enlightenment ideas" does not, however, suppose that these
ideas had a disembodied and independent existence.
Rather, it is simply a shorthand way of saying, "ideas that
were commonly held by the men and women who shared
in this movement," or, as an influential school of French
historians represented by Daniel Roche and André Burguière have termed it, by members of the *communauté des
lumières*, or enlightened community. What is under study
here is a set of attitudes as they emerge from the essays,
books and articles of some sixty writers who can be identified by name (see Figure 1), and well over eighty, if
anonymous authors, journal articles and individual contributions to collective publications are taken into account.
These men, I will argue, belong to, and are representative
of, a larger community. If many of them are obscure and
some unknown, even to students of the Enlightenment,
this is due not to a taste for obscurity on the part of the
writer, but to demands imposed by the subject. The
philosophes, that small yet diverse and highly influential
group of thinkers about whom so much has been written,
seldom concerned themselves with popular education, so
that while they are not entirely neglected, they do not occupy a central place in what follows.

Twelve writers are of particular importance because of
the extent or nature of their contributions to the debates
on the lower classes and popular education. Of these, we

FIGURE 1. Professional and Cultural Standing of Principal Writers Consulted

Key:		
A	-	High status within profession[1]
B	-	Middle or low status within profession
X	-	Status within profession undetermined
*	-	Principal occupation
Ac	-	Member of one or more academies
Cont	-	Winner of contest proposed by an academy
En	-	Encyclopedist
J	-	Jansenist
L	-	Man of letters
Phys	-	Physiocrat
Reg	-	Régulier

	CH	LAW	MED	ARMY	ADM	ED	LETTERS	MISC
uffray							Ac Phys	
achelier						X		Painter
allexerd			X*					
astide						B	L*	
audeau	Abbé					A	L* Phys	
eguillet		B*					Ac	
erenger	Reg				B	A	Cont	
orelly						X	Ac	
antillon								Merchant
hantréau							L	
lément						B	L	
ondorcet							Ac	
oyer	Abbé					A B	L* Ac	
révier						A*	J	
elacroix	Abbé						Ac	
iderot						B	L* En Ac	
urosoy	Abbé					A		
erlus	Reg					A*		
ormey	X				A	A*	L Ac En	
urcroy/G.		X		A				
osselin							L Cont	
ourdin	Reg*					A	Ac Cont	
oyon/A.		A*					Ac Cont	
oyon/P.							En Phys	
ranet		B*						
rivel		B					L* Ac En	
uyton/M.		A*					Ac	Chemist
ubert	B						L Ac	

	CH	LAW	MED	ARMY	ADM	ED	LETTERS	MISC
Jaucourt			X				L Ac En	
Joly	Reg*					A	L Ac	
Helvétius					A		L Ac En	
Holbach							L En	
La Chalotais		A*						
Lefebvre/B.		X					L Ac	
Le Mercier/R.		A			A*		L Phys	
Lezay-Marnesia				A			Ac En	
Mathon/C.							Cont	
Mauduit						A*		
Meerman					A		Cont	.
Mercier		B				X	L*	
Montlinot	X		X				L Ac Cont	
Navarre	Reg					A*	Cont	
Necker					A*		L	
Pernetti	Abbé					B	L Ac	
Perrache							Ac	
Perreau						B	L	
Philipon		X*					L Cont	
Rivard						A*	L J	
Rolland		A*					Ac	
Rousseau						B	L* Count	
Sellier				B		X*	Ac	
Terrisse	A*						Ac	
Thélis				A*				
Thiebault	Reg	X				A	L Ac	
Thomas						A	L* Ac Cont	
Tissot			A*				Ac	
Tschudy							L Ac	
Turgot		A			A*		L Ac En Phys	
Vauréal				A*				
Verlac		B				X*		
Voltaire							L* Ac En	

[1] President or *avocat général* of a parlement, *professeur* of the higher classes in *collèges*, bishops and canons are considered to be positions of high status; *avocat* or notary, tutor, cu〉 and vicar are considered positions of low status.

shall first consider a number of men who did much to create a new image of the people.

Abbé Coyer's essay on the people unquestionably marks a turning point in the attitudes of the upper classes toward their social inferiors. François Gabriel Coyer (1707-1782) was one of thirteen children of a cloth merchant in the Franche-Comté. On completing his studies he became a Jesuit and for a time taught humanities and philosophy in one of the Jesuit *collèges*, but he left the order in 1736. He subsequently became the tutor of the future Duke de Bouillon, and apparently succeeded in winning his student's respect and affection, for the Duke became and remained his patron for life. Coyer also received pensions from the houses of Condé and Soubise, and enjoyed several ecclesiastical benefices, so that by the time of his death he had the considerable annual income of thirteen thousand *livres*. Like most leading men of letters of the eighteenth century, Coyer was able to supplement the income he derived from his pen with the fruits of patronage. As an author, the Abbé is best known today for a work entitled *La Noblesse commerçante*, in which he set forth the advantages that would accrue to France if the nobility could be dissuaded from its prejudices against commerce. He also wrote a series of brilliant satires which were collected and published under the title *Bagatelles morales*. This work proved popular and went through four editions by 1769. Neither Coyer's essay on the people nor his plan of education, however, were reprinted before his death.[1]

[1] Relatively little is known of Coyer's life. Apart from articles in the standard biographical dictionaries, one can consult Georges Malibran's unpublished doctoral thesis presented at the Sorbonne in 1953, "Un ami de la philosophie: l'abbé Coyer, 1707-1782. Sa vie, son oeuvre." Jean Fabre praises and draws on this dissertation for details concerning Coyer's life and fortune in his essay, "L'article 'Peuple' de l' 'Encyclopédie' et le couple Coyer-Jaucourt," in *Images du peuple au dix-huitième siècle*, J. R. Armogathe, G. Besse et al. (Paris, 1973). An old but still valuable study of Coyer as a writer and thinker is F. C. Green's "L'abbé Coyer—A Society in Transition," in his *Eighteenth-Century France: Six Essays* (New York, 1964).

Antoine Léonard Thomas was born in Clermont-Ferrand in 1732 and was intended by his mother for the bar. A brilliant student, he completed his secondary studies with distinction, then dutifully began to work toward a law degree. But his natural inclination for letters proved too strong for him, and he abandoned the lucrative profession of law for the uncertainties of literature. Unable to support himself by his pen, Thomas accepted a chair at the Collège de Beauvais in Paris and there combined teaching and writing until, having achieved fame by winning a series of contests proposed by the Académie Française, he was offered the position of private secretary to the Duke de Praslin. His patron secured for him a sizeable annuity, and in 1765 he was named historiographer of the King's buildings, a post that brought with it a further pension. Two years later Thomas was elected to the Académie Française and eventually became the director of that body. Though neither Coyer nor Thomas are today regarded as major figures in the intellectual history of the eighteenth century, Fréron included them, together with d'Alembert, Diderot, Marmontel and Saint Lambert, as prominent spokesmen of the *philosophe* school.[2]

The third writer who sought to change existing views of the lower classes was the Abbé Pierre Jaubert. Born in Bordeaux in 1715, Jaubert studied theology and was ordained a priest. He served as a curate for several years, but relinquished his benefice in order to devote himself to literature and writing. Jaubert achieved membership in the Academy of Bordeaux, and in addition to producing works of a purely scholarly nature also wrote on social and economic matters. Having edited a multivolume dictionary of arts and crafts and having translated the *Imitation of Christ*, he cannot be said to have been a man of excessively narrow interests.

A more recent study of Coyer is Leonard Adams' "Coyer and the Enlightenment," VS, CXXIII (1974).

[2] AL, 1773 II, 13.

The careers of Baudeau and Berenger recall that of Jaubert. Nicolas Baudeau (1730-1792) was the son of a peasant of the Touraine. He took orders, becoming a canon and prior of St. Lo in Normandy, and taught theology. But he soon came to devote most of his energies to writing plans of reform, and, after having been converted to physiocracy, to popularizing the ideas of that school. L. P. Berenger (1749-1822) entered the Oratory and taught rhetoric in the Oratorian *collège* of Orleans, but later left the order to combine the position of tutor in a noble household with that of royal censor.

It is striking that four of the five men who sought to change the prevailing attitudes of mistrust and hostility toward the lower classes began their careers in the church, then took up secular letters, while the fifth taught in a *collège* noted for its Jansenism.[3] Worth noting, too, is the fact that none of the five was noble, and none came from a wealthy family.

The two most thorough and comprehensive treatments of popular education during our period, the *Essais de Laopédie* of Goyon d'Arzac and the *Vues patriotiques sur l'éducation du peuple* of Philipon de la Madelaine were produced by men who were neither clerics nor teachers, but members of the legal profession. Goyon was born in 1740 in the town of Mezin in the present day Lot-et-Garonne. He died in 1800 in Berlin, but was not an *émigré*, for he had left France just before the outbreak of the Revolution. Goyon's social standing was partly determined by the fact that he was both a *parlementaire* and a nobleman (viscount), while his place in the enlightened community is adequately indicated by his participation in numerous essay contests and his membership in the Academies of Mountauban, Châlons-sur-Marne and Berlin.

Like Goyon, Philipon came from the Midi. He was born in Lyon in 1734, and as a younger son was intended for the

---

[3] See below, chap. ii, n. 61.

church. Having studied theology under the Jesuits, Philipon decided to abandon Augustine for Grotius and entered the law school of Besançon, where he completed his studies. Soon after, he contracted an advantageous marriage, and became an *avocat du roi* in the Chambre de Comptes of Dole. He served in this capacity until 1786 when he became the steward of the Count d'Artois. Parallel to a successful career in law, Philipon was able to indulge his taste for literature. During the 1760s he wrote manuals on epistolary style and translation from Latin, but by the 1780s he was drawn into many of the debates concerning legal, educational and other sorts of reform. Under the Convention, La Madelaine worked out a copyright system for which he received two thousand francs. In 1795, during the Thermidorian reaction, he was made librarian to the minister of the interior. A versatile man, Philipon adapted both to the Empire and the Restoration. When he died in 1816 he held the title of honorary steward of the Count d'Artois, and enjoyed a pension from his former employer.

Clerics were responsible for two other substantial contributions to the debate on popular education. During the first half of the century, the Abbé Terrisse, dean of the cathedral chapter of Rouen and a member of the academy of that town, read a memoir on the utility of educating the peasantry in a public session of the academy. In 1780 an associate of the academy of Lyon sent that body a memoir on the education of children relative to their social standing. This was the Benedictine, François Philippe Gourdin, who had entered the cloister because he was unable to pursue a career in literature outside it for lack of resources and patronage. If he cannot be said to have become another Mabillon, he by no means shamed an order renowned for its scholarship. Gourdin taught for a time in one of the *collèges* maintained by the congregation, served as librarian, and published a half dozen books on history and literature. He was also, like Terrisse, a member of the Academy of

Rouen as well as an associate of three foreign academies. During the Revolution this erudite monk spent his time peaceably collecting antiquities of Normandy and organizing the municipal library of Rouen.

Of lesser but still considerable importance is Bertrand Verlac, a friend of the mathematician Monge and a lawyer who made teaching his career. A large section of a plan of education he wrote "for all classes of citizens" was devoted to the people.

The views of two other men also deserve special attention, for in addition to writing on popular education, they founded and directed schools for children of the lower classes. Jacques Sellier was the guiding spirit behind the *école des arts* of Amiens, an engineer and a member of the academies of Amiens and a number of other towns. The Count de Thélis, a wealthy, liberal noble of the Forez, created and supervised the *écoles nationales militaires*. He devoted his professional life to the army, in which he was a captain, and was a socially conscious, reforming seigneur.

Taken as a group, the sixty writers who appear in Figure 1 show no more socioprofessional consistency than the twelve men just discussed. They belong to the legal and medical professions, the army, administration, church, and were both professional teachers and men of letters. A large proportion were what the English at the time would have described as gentlemen, which is to say that they cultivated polite company, the arts and sciences and their hounds, and were obliged to follow no special calling in order to live.

Together the learned professions of law, medicine and theology account for more than half the writers consulted. But not all those who had a qualification or degree in a field chose to practice in it. Whereas fifteen men had law degrees, only eight derived their livelihoods from the tortuous and convoluted legal system of the old regime. At the head of those actively engaged in legal practice were three magnates of the robe: La Chalotais, the *procureur général* of the Parlement of Rennes and correspondent of Voltaire; Guyton de Morveau, *avocat général* of the sovereign court of Dijon, and distinguished chemist and savant; and Rolland d'Erceville, a *Président* of the Parlement of Paris and organizer of the Collège Louis-le-Grand, who has been called the true minister of public education of the years following the expulsion of the Jesuits from France.[4] Both Goyon and Philipon made professional use of their legal training, and so too did Granet, an official of the *sénéchaussée* of Toulon, E. Béguillet and Fourcroy de Guillerville. By contrast, Turgot, G. Grivel, Louis Sebastien Mercier, Lefebvre de Beauvray, Le Mercier de la Rivière, Thiebault and Bertrand Verlac, though they had law degrees, did not practice or did not devote the greater part of their time to their practices.

Four of the men in Figure 1 had medical degrees, but only two of them, Tissot and Ballexerd, wielded the bleeding bowl and the clyster. The Chevalier Jaucourt, who is best known today for his heroic role in the production of the *Encyclopédie*, studied medicine in his youth, and wrote a medical dictionary all five volumes of which were lost on the way to the printer, but he never actually practiced as a doctor.[5] Similarly, the savant C.A.J.L. de Montlinot, though he had earned a degree in medicine, occupied himself in other ways. He had a degree in theology, wrote, served for a time as canon of a church in Lille, and was actively engaged in poor relief at Soissons.

If, as an eminent medievalist has observed, the monasteries were not always peopled with altogether willing acolytes during the Middle Ages,[6] how much more must this

[4] M. A. Silvy, "Les Collèges en France avant la Révolution," in *Bulletin de la Société d'économie sociale*, IX, 2e partie (1895), p. 4.

[5] See John Lough's article, "Louis, Chevalier de Jaucourt (1704-1780). A Biographical Sketch," in his book, *The Encyclopédie in Eighteenth-Century England and Other Studies* (Newcastle-upon-Tyne, 1970).

[6] R. W. Southern, *The Making of the Middle Ages* (London, 1967), p. 156.

have been the case in the eighteenth century. With fifteen men having taken orders of some sort, the clergy boasts as many representatives in Figure 1 as does the legal profession. But even fewer clerics than lawyers made the subject in which they had taken degrees their main field of endeavor. Only Terrisse, Gourdin and Joseph Romain Joly, a Capuchin monk, can be said to have been primarily concerned with either religious duties or ecclesiastical administration. The other twelve men who had clerical titles or degrees in theology left the orders they had entered, or pursued some occupation on which their clerical training had little bearing. We have seen that Montlinot took a degree in theology without devoting himself to a clerical vocation; that Jaubert was ordained a priest and served for a time in that capacity before retiring to devote himself to study and writing; and that Coyer, Baudeau and Berenger began their careers in the church, but opted for secular letters as soon as their fortunes permitted. Similarly, Thiebault became a Jesuit and taught in one of the *collèges* of the order until it was dissolved. But his clerical training and career seem to have marked him little enough, for he went on to write works that were approved by the *philosophes* and to become a confidant of Frederick II. He ended his career in the French bureaucracy. In some cases it was possible, by gaining a benefice without care of souls, to assure one's livelihood from the church without carrying out any priestly or ecclesiastical function. Thus the Abbé Pernetti of Lyon, after taking orders and serving as a tutor in an important household, was able to secure a benefice that allowed him to pursue his scholarly interests unhindered. Of the Abbé Delacroix of Lyon virtually nothing is known, and only his nebulous title allows us to place him among the churchmen. In the case of J.H.S. Formey, however, we are better informed. The scion of a French Protestant family that fled the country for Prussia in 1685, Formey became a pastor and professor of eloquence. His great energy and ability also enabled him to attain a leading

place in the Berlin academy and to become a privy counselor to Frederick II. If Formey's career was an unusually
successful one, his experience in beginning it in the church
and then moving into other fields of endeavor appears to
have been common at the time.

Three other clerics devoted their principal energies to
education, and though they did so within the framework of
the church, they should, nevertheless, be regarded primarily as educators and only secondarily as churchmen. They
are the Abbé Durosoy, a Jesuit who taught theology at the
collège of Colmar; Dom Ferlus, a Benedictine who directed
the celebrated *collège* of Sorèze; and the Father Navarre, a
member of the Fathers of the Christian Doctrine. In addition to these three clerics, five other writers consulted here
were primarily educators. F. D. Rivard and J. B. Crévier
were both highly distinguished professors at the Collège de
Beauvais in Paris, while François Mauduit taught at the
Collège d'Harcourt, and Verlac held a teaching position at
the naval school of Vannes. Sellier, as has been mentioned,
taught and directed the *école des arts* of Amiens.

Education, like the church, seems to have been a calling
that many followed from expediency rather than inclination. If eight of the men on whom this study is based were
content to spend their lives instructing the young, twice as
many taught temporarily or as an avocation. For J.M.B.
Clément, who taught at the *collège* of Dijon before becoming a writer and literary critic; for J. A. Perreau, who tu-
tored the children of a marquis after having failed in his
literary debut; for J. F. Bastide, who became tutor to the
children of a German Prince after a moderate success at
the writer's craft; for Thomas, Baudeau, Berenger, Coyer,
L. S. Mercier, Formey, Pernetti, Borelly, Rousseau and Diderot, teaching was a springboard to a literary career or a
means of supplementing a slender income. For Thélis, on
the other hand, and for J. J. Bachelier, a painter by profession who founded and directed the *école de dessin* of Paris,
education was a serious avocation.

Some thirteen men who concerned themselves with some aspect of popular education served in either the army or the administration, but these functions were the principal occupations of only five of them. Sellier fought in the ranks but soon left the army to make his career as an architect, savant and pedagogue. Fourcroy de Guillerville served as an artillery officer in the colony of Saint-Domingue, but eventually returned to France to buy the post of counsellor in a *baillage* of the Beauvaisis. Lezay-Marnesia, a *noble d'épée*, resigned his commission early in life and retired to his estate where he carried out such reforms as abolishing mortmain and the *corvée*, and wrote. Only the Counts Thélis and Vauréal, the latter an officer of the engineering corps, can be said to have made their careers in the army.

The royal administration is represented by three high officials. These were Le Mercier de la Rivière, a well-known physiocrat who served as Intendant of Martinique, and who had also sat in the Parlement of Paris; Turgot, the *philosophe* and physiocrat who served as an intendant of Louis XV and as minister to his successor; and finally, Jacques Necker, the Swiss banker, author and politician who was controller general of finance during the early stages of the Revolution. We have seen that Formey held an important position at the court of Berlin, and that Berenger exercised the minor office of royal censor. Before the Revolution Jean Meerman was primarily a wealthy amateur of letters but he was also an alderman of Leyden.

Since this study is based on written sources it is not surprising to find that almost half the men in Figure 1 may be described as writers or litterateurs. Yet if some twenty-nine of them fall into this category, only nine were dependent upon their pens for their livelihood. Bastide, Thomas, Baudeau, Coyer, Diderot, Grivel, L. S. Mercier, Rousseau and Voltaire are the only professional men of letters here. Even if such distinguished writers as the *philosophes* Helvétius, Holbach, Condorcet and Turgot are added to the group, less than a quarter of the men appearing in Figure 1 can be described as outstanding or professional men of letters. Many of the men already mentioned, however, found sufficient time away from their legal, administrative and other professional duties to make substantial contributions to the frequent debates on a whole range of issues in which the educated and leisured classes indulged during the eighteenth century. Certain others, such as Lezay-Marnesia, Mathon de la Cour, Meerman, Condorcet and the Baron de Tschudy were independently wealthy and thus able to use their leisure to explore the arts and sciences, both natural and political.

Two of the writers consulted do not fit into any of the above categories. Helvétius, well known for his materialist philosophy, was a farmer-general, and thus involved in tax collecting and finance. Cantillon was a merchant-banker who made a fortune speculating on Law's system, and who died in the first half of the century. It is not possible to say what the main professions of one third of the men in Figure 1 were because biographical information is either altogether lacking or not sufficiently detailed to allow us to determine which of a number of occupations a man practiced longest or most consistently. About one-quarter of the writers under consideration were nobles, and the majority were provincials.

Advanced thinkers are not lacking among those who wrote on the lower classes and their instruction, but they do not predominate (see Figure 1b). There are seven *philosophes* in the group, and with some overlapping, ten contributors to the *Encyclopédie* and five physiocrats. Of a more traditional cast of mind, but by no means untouched by Enlightenment thought, are two Jansenists. With half the men in Figure 1 formally associated with academies and another ten, again with overlapping, having participated in contests they sponsored, the learned societies and the milieu that they represent will necessarily hold a central place in this study. By contrast, no writer who can be iden-

FIGURE 1a. PROFESSIONAL BREAKDOWN OF FIGURE 1

	Number of Occupations Pursued	Principal Occupation
Church	15	3
Law	15	8
Medicine	4	2
Education	25	8
Army	5	2
Administration	8	3
Writers or Litterateurs	29	9
Independently Wealthy	-	5
Miscellaneous	-	2
	Total	42

FIGURE 1b. CULTURAL BREAKDOWN OF FIGURE 1

Philosophes	7
Encyclopedists	10
Physiocrats	5
Jansenists	2
Academicians	29
Competitors in Essay Contests	10

tified with Grub Street, so far as I have been able to discover, concerned himself with popular education. Thus, the group of men whose opinions and attitudes are under study here consists of a small minority of professional intellectuals (about twenty percent) and a large majority of respectable academicians, unaffiliated clerics, educators, lawyers and gentlemen. Whether or not there was continuity in their views will be seen as the discussion develops.

One of the most striking features to emerge from the preceding analysis is, to my mind, the number of changes from one occupation to another. This fluidity of profession suggests something of the instability and insecurity of intellectuals—or at least of intellectuals who were not independently wealthy—under the old regime.[7] Those men who owned a good deal of property, whether in land or in office, tended to follow only one profession, as, for example, higher officers in the sovereign courts, or wealthy seigneurs who made their careers in the king's service. Educated but unpropertied men showed no such single-mindedness. They seem to have aspired to the position of independent men of letters, but as the society of the time had little need and few outlets for men of this sort, they turned their hands to what they might. Most often this proved to be the church or some form of teaching; not infrequently it was both. Well over half the men in Figure 1 exercised either a clerical or a pedagogical function at some time in their lives. But for the great majority of them, these professions were only stopgaps, and when they could, they moved on to other more appealing callings. Still, one seldom loses a professional cast of mind once it has been acquired, and the fact that so many of the men who wrote on popular education practiced the inherently conservative professions of churchmanship and teaching is bound to have influenced their collective opinion.

A second, equally significant, feature of this group of writers is that professional men of letters remain a minority in it, and a small one at that. Professor Gay's "little flock" or "family" of *philosophes* formed a relatively tight-knit group of professional writers and publicists.[8] The men considered here did not. Rather, they were members of the

[7] On the place and role of intellectuals toward the end of the old régime, see R. Darnton's brilliantly researched article, "The High Enlightenment and the Low-Life of Literature in Pre-Revolutionary France," P&P, no. 51 (1971); the fourth part of G. Gusdorf's synthesis, *Les Principes de la pensée au siècle des lumières* (Paris, 1971), entitled "La condition de l'intellectuel"; and Eric Walter, "Sur l'intelligentsia des lumières" in *Dix-huitième siècle*, v (1973).

[8] Peter Gay, *The Enlightenment: An Interpretation* (New York, 2 vols., 1966-69), vol. 1, pp. 3-6.

sovereign courts, lesser legal functionaries, administrators, clerics, educators, army officers and other professional men. They come, on the whole, from those groups that shared what Norman Hampson has suggestively called the enlightened "attitude of mind."[9]

Summarizing the results in what is admittedly a new field of enquiry, Hampson points out that many great aristocrats, and even churchmen, especially in the upper echelons of the ecclesiastical hierarchy, looked favorably on the thought of the Enlightenment.[10] Within the third estate, participation in the collective life of the enlightened community seems to have been restricted to members of the liberal professions and the administration.[11] In a study on the social diffusion of the Enlightenment, André Burguière reaches similar conclusions about the limits of the enlightened community. He asks how far down the social scale the *société des lumières* reaches, and replies that it scarcely descends below the level of members of the liberal professions and *officiers*, and that on the whole it resembles a "society of notables."[12]

Those who can be said to have shared the enlightened

[9] Norman Hampson, *The Enlightenment* (Aylesbury, 1969), p. 146, states: "The Enlightenment was an attitude of mind rather than a course in science and philosophy." The point is well taken, but the fact that this attitude of mind ultimately rested upon the new science and philosophy should not be overlooked.

[10] Ibid., pp. 133-36.

[11] Ibid., p. 136.

[12] A. Burguière, "Société et Culture à Reims à la fin du XVIIIe siècle: la diffusion des 'lumières' analysé à travers les cahiers de doléances," in AESC, XXII (1967), p. 309. It should not, however, be assumed that all levels of the liberal professions were influenced to a significant degree by the new currents of thought. A French scholar has observed that the vocabulary of the *lumières* did not come easily to the pens of the rural lawyers and *officiers* who wrote the *cahiers de doléances* in 1789. Alphonse Dupront, "Formes de la culture des masses: de la doléance politique au pèlerinage panique (XVIIIe-XXe siècles)," in M. David, G. Duby et al., *Niveaux de culture et groupes sociaux* (Paris, 1971), p. 158.

attitude of mind were probably about five percent of the population.[13] It is generally agreed that the masses did not participate in the Enlightenment,[14] and that the movement was the affair of an elite. But if the enlightened community remains small in comparison to the rest of the population, it is all the same extremely heterogeneous. It does not descend low in the social scale, but it cuts across many social categories.

This heterogeneity of the enlightened community poses a problem for the study of its attitudes. Can the community be regarded as a whole? Can one speak of "enlightenment attitudes," or should one preferably deal with individuals and subgroups within the community? It is my view that though the enlightened community fails to exhibit monolithic consistency, there is adequate justification for treating it as a collectivity.

The enlightened community enjoyed the coherence imposed on it by its opposition to the unenlightened, unpos-

[13] Pierre Chaunu has put the "active and thinking elite of Europeans" as low as one twenty-fifth of one percent, or fifteen to twenty thousand out of an adult population of fifty million, for the period 1620-1760. *La Civilisation de l'Europe classique* (Mulhouse, 1970), p. 20. Gusdorf, rather more reasonably, it seems, estimates the "classe culturelle" at several hundred thousand individuals, or between 1.5 and 2 percent of the population (*Principes de la pensée*, p. 475). One's estimate of the size of the enlightened community of course depends on the criterion used to determine membership.

[14] Jean Dautry quotes Diderot to the effect that "The progress of enlightenment is limited; it scarcely reaches the suburbs; the lower classes [*peuple*] there are too stupid," and himself states that "In effect, in their general outlook on the world, as in the very simple thoughts that directed their political action . . . the working classes [*classes populaires*] were more or less strangers to the philosophy of the Enlightenment." ("La révolution bourgeoise et *l'Encyclopédie*" in *La Pensée*, nos. 38 and 39 [1951]; no. 38, p. 76.) Similarly, Albert Soboul affirms that, "Members of the lower classes [*gens au peuple*] who could read and think evidently constituted only a small number." ("L'Audience des lumières sous la Révolution: J. J. Rousseau et les classes populaires" in, *Utopie et institutions au XVIIIe siècle: Le Pragmatisme des Lumières*, P. Francastel, ed. [Paris and The Hague, 1963], p. 295.)

sessing and unperfumed masses. Leisured and relatively wealthy lawyers, doctors, administrators and other professionals had certain interests and opinions in common that they would not have shared with their servants or with manual laborers. The cohesiveness of the enlightened community, however, consists in far more than the awareness of the gulf that separated it from the people. For, as Maurice Agulhon has observed in the case of Provence, bourgeois and nobles shared not only a common attitude toward the masses, but also a common culture and life style.[15]

Most members of the enlightened community received the same sort of education. It can be said with certainty of only two of our writers (Sellier and Rousseau) that they did not attend *collèges*. The rest received a long classical education, the cultural heritage of the upper classes of Europe during the eighteenth century, and were thus provided with the requisite degree of literacy and the conceptual tools that gave them access to the world of the Enlightenment.

The education most of these men received at *collèges*, and often continued at universities, prepared them for responsible positions in public life, whether in the church, army, administration or legal system. It is true that the functions performed by churchmen, army officers and lawyers differ considerably, and that the fortunes of some depended primarily upon their professional skills, while others were wealthy landowners. Yet there is a loose occupational cohesion here. All these men were community leaders in some sense; though they did not share a common profession, they were all "public men" by vocation and all occupied responsible positions. Moreover, some socioeconomic diversity need not preclude cultural and intellectual community. The unity of the enlightened community was a function

<hr>

[15] M. Agulhon, *La Vie sociale en Provence intérieure au lendemain de la révolution* (Paris, 1970), p. 95.

less of its social composition than of its cultural and intellectual orientation.[16]

Members of the enlightened community shared more than an attitude of mind. They subscribed to, and financed, certain projects, such as the *Encyclopédie* and Thélis' schools, and they had a set of institutions that at once gave expression to their views and helped to crystallize and to form these views. It is the academies that were, par excellence, the spokesmen of the enlightened community. In social composition the learned societies reflected this community, and in their activities they expressed its concerns and interests.

In the Academy of Bordeaux, for example, thirty-one percent of the academicians were noble, eighteen percent clerics, and thirty-nine percent bourgeois.[17] The respective proportions for Dijon are twenty-nine, twelve, and fifty-five percent and for Châlons-sur-Marne twenty-one, twenty-five and fifty-three percent.[18] These figures, static as they are, give no hint of the progressive opening of the academies to the bourgeoisie which M. Roche traces.[19] Nor do they indicate that the social makeup of the orders differed from place to place; *parlementaires*, for example, predominated in the nobility of the Academies of Bordeaux and Dijon, but officers of the king, in Châlons. In the case of the bourgeoisie, however, the liberal professions and especially the medical profession predominate, whereas in none of the three academies studied by M. Roche was there a single *négociant* or *manufacturier*.[20] It might be mentioned

[16] Eric Walter has warned against identifying the intelligentsia of the eighteenth century with any one social group ("Sur l'intelligentsia des lumières," p. 174).

[17] Daniel Roche, "Milieux académiques provinciaux et société des lumières," in *Livre et société I* (Paris and The Hague, 1965), p. 118. Statistics on the social composition of the Academies of Bordeaux, Dijon and Châlons-sur-Marne are presented graphically in ibid., pp. 114-17.

[18] Ibid., pp. 132 and 147.

[19] Ibid., pp. 122 and 137-38.

[20] See the graph in ibid., p. 114.

in this connection also that no known encyclopedist was a businessman.[21]

Contemporaries recognized the elitist nature of the academies, and some who achieved membership in them prided themselves on it. For example, Dupré de Saint Maur, the Intendant of Guyenne and director of the Academy of Bordeaux, described that body as "a chosen assembly, which brings together an enlightened portion of the first classes of citizens."[22] Indeed, not only were the academies "chosen assemblies" of notables, but they tended to be run by an elite within an elite—the honorary members, who were generally noble.[23] Despite their exclusive membership, the academies did not wish to cut themselves off from the rest of the enlightened community. On the contrary, they sought to act as its leaders. In their public sessions, but especially in the essay contests they proposed,

[21] D. Roche, "Encyclopédistes et académiciens," in *Livre et société II* (Paris and The Hague, 1970), p. 85. It ought not to be assumed that because the *négoce* and certain other groups within the bourgeoisie were excluded from the academies and had no part in the production of the *Encyclopédie* that they were excluded from, or played no active part in, the enlightened community. There were literary societies less elevated than the academies to which *marchands*, *négociants* and the like might belong; for example, the museum of Bordeaux (ibid., p. 85); a literary society and masonic lodges in Reims (Burguière, "Société et culture à Reims," p. 311); and the Compagnie des Chevaliers de l'Arquebuse in Châlons-sur-Marne (D. Roche, "La Diffusion des lumières. Un exemple: l'Académie de Châlons-sur-Marne" in AESC, XIX [1964], p. 891). Evaluations of the enlightened community tend to be inordinately weighted in favor of the academies, and this for the simple reason that records from which the academies can be studied exist and are available. This is not the case for reading rooms, minor literary societies or simple reading circles. Yet if the extent of the role of such institutions in the diffusion of Enlightenment ideas cannot be determined for want of sources, their importance must nevertheless have been great.

[22] JE, 1783 IV, 251.

[23] There were generally three categories of academicians, though an academy might add another if it so chose. In order of diminishing status they were the *honoraires*, the *titulaires* or *ordinaires* and the *associés* or *correspondants*.

the academies did much to stimulate and direct enlightened opinion. Through these contests, which were commonly announced in the periodical press, the academies also involved in their activities strata of the enlightened community that were excluded from formal membership.

Given that men of property, status and power predominated in the academies, these societies were not so stodgy and conservative as one might have expected. To be sure, Rousseau claimed that a work such as his Second Discourse was not the sort of thing an academy would confer a prize on, and Helvétius denounced academies in general as tools of absolutism and obstacles to free thought.[24] Certainly they cannot be said to have been in any way radical. But neither were they backward-looking or blind adherents to the status quo. In their discussions on practical issues such as commerce and agriculture and their treatments of social problems such as poverty, education and legal reform, they showed that they were progressive and eager for reform. Far from giving the impression that they represented an elite in crisis or one that doubted its own ability, the academies reflect the views of men who had sufficient confidence in themselves and their society to recognize serious problems, to discuss them openly, and to seek far-reaching reform—though always within the framework of the existing order.

EDUCATION

Education occupied a doubly important place in the Enlightenment. On the one hand, it was an integral part of the thought of the period because sensationalist psychology, one of the distinguishing features and unifying ele-

---

[24] J. J. Rousseau, Les Confessions, B. Gagnebin and M. Raymond, eds. (Bruges, 1964), p. 389; C. A. Helvétius, "Letter to Lefebvre-Laroche," in Oeuvres complètes (Paris, 14 vols., 1795; reprinted Hildesheim, 1967), vol. XIV, p. 100.

THE PROBLEM · 39

ments of this thought, implied a theory of education. On
the other hand, education came to be looked upon by
many Enlightenment figures as a means both of reform
and of social control.

The basis for the Enlightenment theory of education was
laid by John Locke in his *Essay Concerning Human Understanding* (1689). In this seminal work, Locke denied that
man had any innate ideas whatever at birth. He described
the mind as a *tabula rasa*, and argued that it could gain
knowledge only from sensation and reflection. In the
course of the eighteenth century the category of reflection
was rejected by reductionist sensationalists and the working of the mind was explained exclusively in terms of sensation.

Sensationalist psychology has justly been called, "Proposition One of the whole philosophy of the Enlightenment,"
and it has been argued that it was "not only a psychology
but a metaphysics, and not only a theory of knowledge but
a theory of human nature."[25] It was, I submit, even more
than this: it also served as the basis of a theory of education. Extremely diverse thinkers agreed in so regarding it.
Helvétius asked: "At this time [infancy] what can the true
teachers of childhood be?" and answered, "the various sensations that it experiences."[26] Rousseau emphasized that
"the education of man begins at his birth; before speaking,
before understanding, he is already learning. Experience
precedes lessons. . . ."[27] Serious criticism of sensationalism
usually came from those critical of enlightenment
thought.[28] For Condillac, the chief.expositor of reduction-

[25] R. R. Palmer, *Catholics and Unbelievers in Eighteenth-Century France*
(Princeton, n.d.), p. 131.
[26] C. A. Helvétius, *De l'Homme, de ses facultés intellectuelles et de son éducation* (London, 2 vols., 1773), vol. 1, p. 13.
[27] J. J. Rousseau, *Emile ou De l'éducation*, B. Gagnebin and M. Raymond,
eds. (Dijon, 1969), p. 281.
[28] Palmer's assertion, "The assent of Diderot, Condillac, Helvétius, and
Raynal [to sensationalist psychology] was entire" (*Catholics and Unbelievers*,
p. 131), is not entirely accurate. Diderot had serious misgivings about the

ist sensationalist psychology, epistemology was in itself a system of education. He wrote:

> Pour savoir comment nous devons nous conduire avec eux [children to be taught] la première précaution à prendre est de savoir comment nous conçevons nous-mêmes, les choses que nous avons apprises. Il faut décomposer l'esprit humain, c'est à dire, observer les opérations de l'entendment, les habitudes de l'âme et la génération des idées. Aussitôt que cette analyse est faite, le plan d'instruction est trouvé; on sait du moins par où on doit commencer, et il n'en faut pas davantage.[29]

The assumption that one's mind is constituted by the sensations that are presented to it, and by the order in which they are presented, tends to endow education with considerable power to form its subject. Many *philosophes*, and others besides, did not fail to draw this conclusion and to apply it to the society around them.[30]

The *philosophes* were not alone in their interest in education. Many rulers, and especially enlightened despots, also turned their attention to the subject. In 1770, Catherine the Great asked Diderot to outline a plan for a university in Russia. The same year Frederick II of Prussia published a brief *Lettre sur l'éducation*. In 1775, Le Mercier de la Rivière

doctrine. See his "Réfutation suivie de l'ouvrage d'Helvétius intitulé *De l'Homme*," in the *Oeuvres complètes de Diderot* (Paris, 20 vols., 1875-77), vol. II, pp. 298-99 and 318. For an anti-*philosophe* criticism of sensationalist psychology, see the Jansenist Crévier's, *Difficultés proposées à Monsieur de Caradeuc de la Chalotais sur le Mémoire intitulé Essai d'éducation nationale ou Plan d'études pour la jeunesse* (Paris, 1763), objection v, pp. 50-61. Crévier asserted, for example, that La Chalotais' authorities (Locke, Condillac) were "tous égarés" (ibid., p. 50) and that Condillac especially has "prodigieusement & Grossièrement égaré dans ses derniers ouvrages" (ibid., pp. 54-55).

[29] E. B. Condillac, "Discourse préliminaire" to the *Cours d'études pour l'instruction du Prince de Parme*, in *Oeuvres de Condillac* (Paris, 23 vols., 1798), vol. v, p. v.

[30] The first chapter of book x of *De l'Homme*, for example, is entitled "l'Education peut tout." See below, pp. 239-42.

wrote a treatise entitled *De l'instruction publique* at the request of Gustave III of Sweden. The same year Turgot
submitted to Louis XVI a memoir on education. Helvétius,
meanwhile, had dedicated his *De l'Homme* (1773) to both
Catherine and Frederick. The common interest of
monarch and *philosophe* in education doubtless had its origin in the supposed power of education to reform—or to
conserve and strengthen—society, and in the assumption
that as a means of reform it would be both gradual and
peaceful.

Although it was an integral part of the philosophy of the
Enlightenment and drew attention from certain *philosophes*
and enlightened despots, was education a subject that
aroused the interest of the enlightened community as a
whole? If one is to judge by the volume of books written on
the subject, it seems to have been.

Thanks to the extensive article "bibliographie" in Buisson's *Dictionnaire pédagogique*, it is possible to determine the
quantity of works devoted to education in the eighteenth
century, and the rhythm at which they were produced.[31]
The list in the dictionary has certain shortcomings, however. First, it is not complete.[32] Secondly, it occasionally includes works that only tangentially touch on education.[33]
Finally, the Buisson article makes no attempt to examine

[31] F. Buisson, ed., *Dictionnaire de pédagogie et d'instruction primaire* (Paris,
4 vols., 1882-93), part I, vol. I.

[32] The subject catalogue of the *Bibliothèque Mazarine* shows some works
that do not appear in Buisson, as, for example, Louis Dumas' *Bibliothèque
des Enfants* (1763) or Fromageot's *Cours des jeunes demoiselles* (1772). Many
more such omissions could doubtless be found, but no attempt has been
made to do so. The difficulties involved in establishing a complete bibliography of works on education for France in the eighteenth century are
overwhelming, and it is highly unlikely that the results would repay the
effort. It should be kept in mind, therefore, that the figures used here are
only approximate, and rather lower than they would be if a complete list
were established.

[33] For example, Daniel Jousse's *Traité du gouvernement des paroisses* (1769)
is included, though only the fourth chapter ("Des écoles de charité") is directly relevant; similarly the Abbé Pluche's *Spectacle de la Nature* (1732-50),
of which only a part of the sixth volume treats education, is also included.

the periodical press. These reservations made, we may proceed to a rough quantitative analysis of books dealing with education in the eighteenth century based on the article cited.

The production of books on education between 1715 and 1789 falls into two distinct periods (see Figure 2). In the first, 1715 to 1759, few treatises or manuals on education were published. They total fifty-one works for a forty-four-year period, an average 1.1 books a year. In no year during this period were more than three books on education published, while in eighteen of these forty-four years no work on the subject appeared at all. By contrast, from 1760 to 1790 at least two works on education were published every year (except in 1761). During this thirty-year period a total of 161 books treating some aspect of education appeared, averaging 5.3 books or pamphlets a year.

Transition from the first to the second period was abrupt. In 1760, four works on education appeared, in 1761 only one; but in 1762 the highest total for the period under consideration, fifteen, was reached. This sudden upswing is readily explained. In 1762 Rousseau published his *Emile*, the greatest Enlightenment treatment of education, and of even greater significance, at least in the short run, the Jesuits were expelled from France. Rousseau's book called forth a dozen or so refutations and helped focus attention on education; but the expulsion of the Jesuits left France with hundreds of *collèges* without teachers or programs. It was to the practical and pressing issue of reforming the *collèges*, and providing a new program for them, that most writers on education addressed themselves during the 1760s. The people were mentioned incidentally, if at all, in the educational writings of this decade.

The interest in education did not subside after the *collèges* had been more or less reorganized, or after *Emile* had lost its novelty.[34] Fifty-five works were published on the

[34] Some ten books were written on *Emile* (mostly refutations) from the

subject in the decade of the 1760s, fifty-two in the 1770s, and fifty-four in the 1780s. In addition, provincial academies held a number of essay contests on the topic of education, and these give the impression that interest in education grew as the century wore on. Two contests were proposed on the subject in the 1760s, four in the 1770s, and nine in the 1780s (see Figure 2).

Whether or not a rough statistical analysis convinces the reader that education was a subject that sustained intense interest in France during the thirty years before the Revolution, contemporaries seem to have had few doubts on this score. In 1763 Grimm wrote that "since the fall of the Jesuits and the useless book of Jean Jacques Rousseau, entitled *Emile*, people have not stopped writing about education."[35] In 1769 an article in the *Journal d'éducation*—and the fact that a journal was devoted to the subject further indicates contemporary interest—asserted that "never, perhaps, have people spoken so much about education as they do today."[36] Five years later the *Journal encyclopédique* stated, "There is no country today, regardless of how little civilized it may be, in which people do not seriously give their attention to the important matter of education: from all sides new light is cast on this subject, which appears inexhaustible."[37] Nor did interest in pedagogy slacken in the 1780s. Writing in a work that was not directly concerned with education, the Abbé Durosoy observed:

> Aussi le mot d'éducation est-il dans la bouche de tout le monde aujourd'hui; il est devenu comme le cri général de toute l'Europe; on ne l'entend, on ne le repète qu'avec

time of its publication to 1770; between 1771 and 1790 only three appeared.

[35] F. M. Grimm, D. Diderot, G. Raynal et al., *Correspondance littéraire, philosophique & critique*, M. Tourneux, ed. (Paris, 16 vols., 1877-81), April, 1763, vol. v, p. 259. Future references will be given as *Correspondance littéraire*, with volume and page numbers.

[36] Abbé de Lille, "Discours sur l'éducation," in the *Journal d'éducation, Presenté au Roi* (January, 1769), p. 41.

[37] JE, 1774 III, 89.

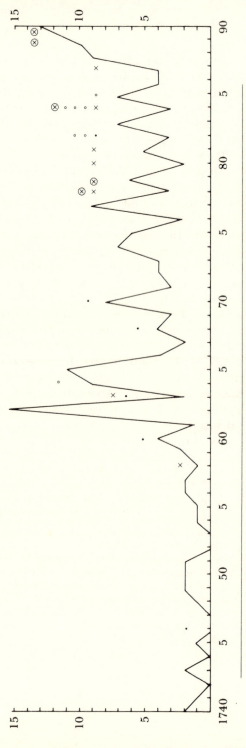

FIGURE 2. BOOKS CONCERNING EDUCATION PUBLISHED 1740-1790, AND ESSAY CONTESTS AND DISCOURSES OF ACADEMIES CONCERNING EDUCATION OR THE PEOPLE*

Key: ° = essay contest concerning education
x = essay contest concerning the people (*mendicité, fainéantise, enfants trouvés*)
⊗ = essay contest concerning education of the people
• = discourse read in an Academy on any of the above subjects

* I am indebted to Daniel Roche for the data concerning the academies. The source of the graph is F. Buisson, *Dictionnaire pédagogique*, part 1, vol. 1, art. "Bibliographie."

une sorte de transport: jamais tant d'ouvrages, jamais tant de systêmes sur cette matiere; elle a exercé la plume des particuliers & des hommes en place. Personne parmi nous qui ne préconise avec emphase la nécessité & le mérite d'une bonne éducation.[38]

It would seem, then, that education not only held an important place in the philosophy of the Enlightenment, but that it also aroused and sustained the interest of the enlightened community during the last decades of the old regime. Nor was education one of those issues that was obscured after 1789. The Revolution debated it with vigor, and legislated on it repeatedly.[39]

THE PEOPLE

Historians have little difficulty in identifying the *peuple* of seventeenth- and eighteenth-century France. It consisted of those who lived on the edge of subsistence and continually faced what has been called, "the anguished problem of daily bread—the fundamental problem before which all else recedes."[40] The people were those without reserves, those who lived from day to day and from week to week, and who were immediately vulnerable to the vagaries of the job market and to fluctuations in the price of basic foodstuffs.[41] They formed, too, the "floating population" of beggars, vagabonds and seasonal migrants typical of primitive demographic systems. Reduced in normal times to a diet of vegetables and cereals, the people were chronically undernourished; following a bad harvest or a

[38] Abbé J. B. Durosoy, *Philosophie sociale ou Essai sur les devoirs de l'homme & du citoyen* (Paris, 1783), p. 271.

[39] A good general treatment of education during the Revolution is H. C. Barnard's *Education and the French Revolution* (Cambridge, 1969).

[40] Pierre Goubert, *Cent mille provinciaux au XVIIe siècle: Beauvais et le Beauvaisis de 1600 à 1730* (Paris, 1968), p. 334.

[41] J. P. Gutton, *La Société et les pauvres en Europe (XVIe-XVIIIe siècles)* (Paris, 1974), p. 8.

series of bad years, they faced severe deprivation and often starvation.[42] They were the victims not only of extreme weather conditions, but also of less impersonal forces, such as the speculations of grain merchants or political conditions.[43] Generally quiescent, in times of crisis the people emerged as the authors of rural *jaqueries* and the pillage of bourgeois houses in the towns.[44] But when left to themselves, their violence was never sustained nor intended to achieve fundamental social change.[45]

The line dividing the people from the moderately well-off cut through the artisan-shopkeeper class in the towns, and in the countryside divided *fermiers* and *laboureurs* from *journaliers* and *manouvriers*. On the one side of this line, relative security; on the other, precariousness of existence, dependence, and the ever present specter of poverty. Because a great many factors, such as size of family, salary, food prices, availability of work and whatever property one owned all contributed to determining economic well-being, the threshold of poverty was extremely variable.[46] But in general, those without a special skill or sufficient property to support themselves were constantly in danger of being thrust beyond that threshold, for, "nowhere in the conditions of the *ancien régime* could a man expect to earn by the work of his hands more than sufficient to provide himself with food and shelter and possibly support a child."[47] Hence the people consisted not only of the poor and

[42] R. Mandrou, *Introduction à la France moderne (1500-1640): Essai de psychologie historique* (Paris, 1961), p. 22; Olwen Hufton, *The Poor of Eighteenth-Century France 1750-1789* (Oxford, 1974), pp. 44-46; and Jeffry Kaplow, *The Names of Kings: Parisian Laboring Poor in the Eighteenth Century* (New York, 1972), pp. 71-79.

[43] François Lebrun, *Les Hommes et la mort en Anjou aux XVIIe et XVIIIe siècles* (Paris, 1975), pp. 81-82 and p. 241.

[44] Mandrou, *Introduction à la France moderne*, pp. 153 and 161.

[45] François Furet, "Pour une définition des classes inférieures à l'époque moderne," in AESC, XVIII (1963), p. 470.

[46] Gutton, *La Société et les pauvres*, pp. 74-76.

[47] Hufton, *The Poor*, p. 19.

indigent, but also of those who might, as a result of accidents such as illness or unemployment, be reduced to want. And in this category we find skilled workers as well as day laborers.[48]

In every aspect of their lives, the people suffered the effects of the "acid" of poverty.[49] Economic pressures forced the children of the poor to beg, and their parents to take to the road in search of work or to resort to petty crime.[50] But to place too great an emphasis on the dependence and the poverty of the people obscures the fact that they were at the same time the economic mainstay of society. For as peasants and workers, they produced such wealth as their preindustrial society enjoyed. By 1789 the poor and indigent of France accounted for between a third and a half of the population, and in particularly disfavored provinces such as Brittany, Poitou and Auvergne, as much as two-thirds.[51] If one wished to characterize the conditions of the people during the old regime, he could do no better than to recall Pierre Léon's enumeration of the factors contributing to the unity of what he calls the embryonic working class of the eighteenth century: extreme precariousness, physical suffering and moral wretchedness.[52]

It is less the objective condition of the lower classes in eighteenth-century France than the way contemporaries perceived them that is my concern here. The subject has been singled out as an admirable one for the history of ideas,[53] and it has recently received a good deal of atten-

[48] M. Garden, *Lyon et les Lyonnais au XVIIIe siècle* (Paris, 1975), pp. 230-31.

[49] O. Hufton, "Begging, Vagrancy, Vagabondage and the Law: an Aspect of the Problem of Poverty in Eighteenth-Century France," ESR, II (1972), p. 108.

[50] See Hufton, *The Poor*, chap. 8 and 9, and Kaplow, *The Names of Kings*, chap. 6.

[51] Régine Robin, *La Société française en 1789: Semur-en-Auxois* (Paris, 1970), p. 190; Hufton, *The Poor*, pp. 22-24.

[52] F. Braudel and E. Labrousse, eds., *Histoire économique et sociale de la France*, vol. II (Paris, 1970), p. 661.

[53] Furet, "Pour une définition des classes inférieures," p. 446.

tion.[54] But it is no easy matter to determine how members of the enlightened community viewed their social subordinates. There are, to my knowledge, no books or pamphlets that deal specifically with the *peuple* before mid-century, and few enough after.[55] However, dictionaries were coming into use by the end of the seventeenth century and as some of these have entries under "people," they provide a starting point for our investigation.

The dictionary of the Académie Française, which was first published in 1694, distinguishes between a "people" as a collectivity, such as a national or religious group, and the

[54] In addition to those works cited in the Introduction, n. 3, one should mention in this connection Roland Mortier's articles, "Diderot et la notion du 'peuple,' " in *Europe*, January-February 1963, and "Voltaire et le peuple," in *The Age of Enlightenment, Studies Presented to Theodore Besterman*, Barber, Brumfitt et al. (Edinburgh and London, 1967); W. Bahner, "Le mot et la notion de 'peuple' dans l'oeuvre de Rousseau," VS, LV (1967); L. G. Crocker, "Rousseau and the Common People," in John Pappas, ed., *Essays on Diderot and the Enlightenment in Honor of Otis Fellows* (Geneva, 1974); I. Vissière, "Le peuple d'après Condorcet: classifications et images," in *Structure et fonction du vocabulaire social dans la littérature française* (Halle, 1970); K. Baker, "Scientism, Elitism and Liberalism: The Case of Condorcet," VS, LV (1967); R. Chartier, "Les élites et les gueux: quelques représentations (XVIe-XVIIe siècles), RHMC, XXI (1974); J. P. Gutton, "A l'aube du XVIIe siècle: idées nouvelles sur les pauvres," CH, X (1965); A. Geoffroy, "Le 'peuple' selon Saint-Just," AHRF, XL (1968); F. G. Healey, "The Enlightenment View of 'Homo Faber,' " VS, XXV (1963); R. I. Boss, "The Development of Social Religion: A Contradiction of French Free Thought," JHI, XXXIV (1973); H. C. Payne, "Elite Versus Popular Mentality in the Eighteenth Century," *Historical Reflexions*, II (1975) (see Payne's first note for several other relevant items not cited here); Maxime Leroy, *Histoire des idées sociales en France: de Montesquieu à Robespierre* (Paris, 1946); J. R. Poynter, *Society and Pauperism: English Ideas on Poor Relief, 1795-1834* (Toronto and London, 1969); J. G. Gagliardo, *From Pariah to Patriot: The Changing Image of the German Peasant 1770-1840* (Lexington, 1969); and *Images du peuple*.

[55] A. Cioranescu, *Bibliographie de la littérature française du dix-huitième siècle* (Paris, 3 vols., 1969), gives only two entries under "peuple" for the pre-revolutionary period. One of these is Coyer's *Essai sur la nature du peuple*, the other a reprint of the *Encyclopédie* article "peuple." Both will be treated below.

"people" in the sense of the lower classes. On the one hand, a people is defined as a "multitude of men of a same country, who live under the same laws," a "multitude of men who are of the same religion, whether they are of the same country or not," and all inhabitants of "a same city or . . . same town or village." On the other hand, the term "people":

> . . . se prend aussi quelquefois pour la partie la moins considérable d'entre les habitants d'une mesme ville, d'un mesme païs. *Il y eut quelque émotion parmi le peuple. Le peuple ne sçait ce qu'il veut la plupart du temps.* En ce mesme sens on dit, *Le menu peuple, le bas peuple, le petit peuple.*[56]

The dictionary also cites the proverb *vox populi*, explaining it to mean that "ordinarily the general feeling is founded on the truth."[57]

Another lexicographer of this period, P. Richelet, used Latin equivalents to give his definitions more precision. *Populus* or *gens* is taken to signify, "a multitude of persons who live in a same place, including gentlefolk (*gens de qualité*) and others." *Cives* or *paroeiciani* simply designate the residents of the same parish. Qualified as *vulgus* and taken figuratively, "people" was used in a new way: to distinguish the *bourgeois* from the *grands*. Penultimately, "people" without a Latin equivalent, "se prend dans un sens moins vague [than *Peuple: populus, gens*] pour dire, tout le corps du peuple, sans y comprendre ce qu'on appelle les gens de qualité & gens qui ont de l'esprit et de la politesse." Finally, as in the dictionary of the Académie, the *menu peuple* are treated separately:

---

[56] *Dictionnaire de l'Académie Françoise dédié au Roy* (Paris, 2 vols., 1694), art. "Peuple." In the case of dictionaries and encyclopedias, references will be given to the edition and article, except where an article is too long to make this method convenient. The emphasis is in the original unless otherwise indicated.

[57] Ibid.

> *Le petite* [*sic*] *peuple* (*Plebecula, plebs infima*). C'est toute la
> racaille d'une Ville. C'est tout ce qu'il a de gens qui ne
> sont pas de qualité ni bourgeois aisez, ni ce qu'on apelle
> [*sic*] honnêtes gens. (Le petit peuple de Londres est
> méchant.)[58]

Richelet has here provided graphic content to the clear but
colorless definition of the *menu peuple* in the dictionary of
the Académie.

The *Dictionnaire de Trévoux*, like Richelet, also had recourse to Latin synonyms in its definition of the people.
The *populus, gens, natio*, are the nation, *cives* the residents of
the same town and *multitudo* simply "a multitude of people
[*gens*]." On the *menu peuple*, however, Furetière cites several
authors and provides a much fuller definition than either
the Académie or Richelet. This section of the article de-
serves to be quoted in full:

> PEUPLE, se dit encore plus particulièrement par opposi-
> tion à ceux qui sont nobles, riches ou éclairez. *Plebs, vul-
> gus*. Qui dit peuple dit plus d'une chose; c'est une vaste
> expression. Il y a le *peuple*, qui est opposé aux Grands,
> c'est la populace & la multitude. Il y a le *peuple*, qui est
> opposé aux sages & aux habiles: ce sont les Grands,
> comme les petits. LA BR. Il y a bien de la difference
> entre *populus* en Latin, & peuple en François. Le mot de
> peuple ne signifie d'ordinaire parmi nous que ce que les
> Romains appelloient *plebs*. VAU. Il faut être bien *peuple*
> pour se laisser éblouir par l'éclat qui environne les
> Grands. S. EVR. Les gens de Cour méprisent le peuple,
> ils sont souvent peuple eux-mêmes. LA BRUY. En ce
> sens peuple, signifie les manières basses, & les sots pré-
> jugez du peuple. Tout le monde n'est pas *peuple*; c'est-à-
> dire, tout le monde n'est pas sot, ou duppe. Le *peuple* est
> *peuple* par tout, c'est-àdire, sot, remuant, aimant les

[58] P. Richelet, *Dictionnaire de la langue françoise ancienne et moderne* (Paris, 3 vols., 1728), art. "Peuple."

nouveautez. *Inconstans, varians, mutabilis.* Cet homme est gâté de toutes les erreurs & opinions du *peuple*. Il est de la lie du *peuple*. Le petit *peuple*, le menu *peuple*, le commun du *peuple* est malin & séditieux. Il y a bien du *peuple* au quartier des halles, c'est-à-dire, de la poplace, de la canaille.[59]

The dictionary of the Académie simply designates the *menu peuple* as the "least considerable part" of any community. Richelet refers to them as "racaille" (rabble, riff-raff), but defines them by a process of exclusion. They are neither titled (*gens de qualité*), nor well off (*bourgeois aisez*), nor well-bred or respectable (*honnêtes gens*), nor intelligent (*gens qui ont de l'esprit*). Furetière also begins by excluding the "noble, rich or enlightened" from the ranks of the people, and he too calls them by other names: "populace" and "canaille" (rabble, riff-raff). Furetière, however, also has at his command a colorful string of adjectives to describe the lower classes. They are "duppe," "sot" (used three times), "remuant," "malin," "séditieux," as well as *inconstans, varians, mutabilis.*

The three dictionaries consulted are in basic agreement about the nature of the *petit* or *menu peuple*, or simply the *peuple*. For all of them the lower classes are poor and ignorant, if not actually stupid. More than this, the people is not to be trusted, and may even be dangerous: "the people does not know what it wants"; "The common people of London is malicious"; "the common people, the rabble, the mob is malevolent and seditious." The note of fear and mistrust struck by the masses comes through with unequal force in each of the three dictionaries, but is present in all.

What these dictionaries choose to ignore in their discussion of the people is as indicative of their attitudes as what they include. None, for example, refers to the conditions in which the lower classes lived and died, or to their produc-

[59] *Dictionnaire universel de Furetière françois et latin, vulgairement appellé Dictionnaire de Trévoux* (Paris, 8 vols., 1732), art. "Peuple."

tive role in society.[60] Perhaps both were taken for granted. Certainly there is no trace of sympathy for the people to be detected in any of these articles.

A completely different spirit pervades a number of works on the lower classes published after mid-century. Coyer's *Dissertation sur la nature du peuple* appeared in 1755, Thomas' *Epître au peuple* in 1761, Baudeau's *Idées d'un citoyen sur les besoins, les droits et les devoirs des vrais pauvres* in 1765, Jaubert's *Eloge de la roture* in 1766, and Berenger's *Les Quatre Etats de la France* in 1789. The first of these works may best be described as a satire, while the second is a poem and the last three are essays in social and political theory. Despite their different forms and their very unequal literary value, these pieces share a common desire to assert the respectability and usefulness of the lower classes and to radically recast their image.

Coyer set the tone of satire at the outset of his essay by asking with apparent seriousness whether the people should be considered human.[61] He himself had always supposed that they were but, he admitted, consideration of the question raised doubts. Coyer returned to this theme later, but first, like the very able writer he was, took care to define his subject:

---

[60] The dictionaries do not appear to have been atypical in this regard. Healey asserts that the men of the later seventeenth century were "not apparently given to thinking very much at all about those who supplied its material wants by the labour of their hands" ("The Enlightenment View of 'Homo Faber,'" p. 839). Among those who did reflect on the economic role of the lower classes during the seventeenth century are Richelieu and La Bruyère. The Cardinal-Minister wrote of the people, "Il les faut comparer aux mulets, qui, étant accoutumés à la charge, se gâtent par un long repos plus que par le travail" (Richelieu, *Testament politique*, Louis André, ed., Paris, 1947, p. 254). For La Bruyère's celebrated description of the lot of the peasantry, see his *Les Caractères ou Les Moeurs de ce siècle*, G. Servois and A. Rebelliau, eds., Paris, 1901, pp. 332-33.

[61] Abbé F. G. Coyer, *Dissertation sur la Nature du Peuple*, in *Oeuvres Complètes de M. l'abbé Coyer* (Paris, 7 vols., 1782-83), vol. 1, p. 166.

. . . Le peuple fut autrefois la partie la plus utile, la plus vertueuse, & par conséquent la plus respectable de la nation. Il était composé de cultivateurs, d'artisans, de négocians, de financiers, de gens de lettres & gens de loix. Les gens de loix ont cru qu'il y avait bien autant de gloire à rendre la justice aux hommes qu'à les tuer, & ils se sont annoblis sans le secours de l'épée. Les gens de lettres, à l'exemple d'Horace, ont regardé le peuple comme profane, & ils lui ont tourné le dos. Les financiers ont pris un vol si élevé, qu'ils se font violence pour n'être qu'au niveau des grands. Il n'y a plus moyen de confondre négocians avec le peuple, depuis qu'ils rougissent de leur état, & qu'ils en sortent, même avant que d'en sortir. Il ne reste donc dans la masse du peuple que les cultivateurs, les domestiques, & les artisans; encore ne sais-je si l'on doit y laisser cette espèce d'artisans maniérés, qui travaillent le luxe: des mains qui peignent divinement une voiture, qui montent un diamant au parfait, qui ajustent une mode supérieurement, ne ressemblent plus aux mains du peuple. Le peuple ainsi reduit, ne laisse pas d'être encore la partie la plus nombreuse, peut-être même la plus nécessaire de la nation.[62]

Coyer implies that rightly considered the people were the whole third estate. It had been reduced to peasants, menial artisans and servants by the defection of professionals who were by right and ancestry "people" themselves. Even so it constituted the majority and "perhaps most necessary part of the nation."

Coyer goes on to describe the way of life of the masses. The *peuple* lives "under thatch, or in some corner which our towns abandon to it," works from sunrise to sunset, and has little to show for its labor. Unlike the nobility, the people marry for love, and leave inheritances of equal size for all the children of a family. A mode of existence such as this, Coyer observes sardonically, is based more on instinct

[62] Ibid., pp. 186-87.

than reason and is more fitted to animals than men. The
only virtue that the people are said to have is patience—
which is an animal virtue. Coyer does not deny that the
people have vices, but he compares them favorably to the
vices of polite society.[63] Yet it is precisely in the attitude of
the rich and educated that the author says he finds proof
that the people are not human. At this point Coyer's *Dissertation* takes on a tone which in power and restrained bitter-
ness is reminiscent of Swift's *Modest Proposal*. He writes:

> La plus belle, la plus noble partie de l'état, celle qui ré-
> unit l'esprit aux richesses & à la grandeur, n'y croit pas;
> qui suis-je pour contredire? Son jugement est écrit dans
> ses procédés avec le peuple. On a des porteurs comme
> on a des mulets. Le fouet est toujours levé sur un animal
> rétif; quel est le galant homme qui n'emploie pas sa
> canne sur un faquin, lorsque l'occasion le demande? Un
> seigneur élégant pousse devant son carosse un coureur
> & un chien. Dans une chasse il paraît assez égal de crever
> un cheval ou un piqueur; & après une bataille on ne
> nomme pas plus les soldats tués que les chevaux morts.
> Tous ces faits ne me présentent que des animaux dé-
> guisés en hommes.
>
> Les choses vont si loin, que le peuple lui-même ques-
> tionne sur son état: *sommes-nous des bêtes?* C'est un propos
> qu'on entend assez souvent dans les travaux publics:
> *sommes-nous des bêtes?* Peuple! cela se pourrait.[64]

Coyer's indignation is here aroused at what he considers
the dehumanization of the greater part of his fellow men.[65]
Yet the people, he marshals arguments to show, are indeed
human. A workman's head has more sound and useful

[63] Ibid., pp. 186-91.   [64] Ibid., p. 193.
[65] Fabre accuses Coyer of "bad taste" in his social criticism ("L'article
'Peuple,'" p. 17). It seems to me that the criterion of "taste" is as irrelevant
to a just evaluation of Coyer's essay as it is to an analysis of Jeremiah or
Marx. All three say things that are in appallingly bad taste; but that is not
the point.

ideas than a gentleman's;[66] Greek and Roman history shows that the people were at one time deemed worthy of political rights; and servants are often clever enough to govern their masters rather than be governed by them.[67] As his decisive argument, Coyer points out that a noble's family tree must begin somewhere, and that a rustic who had made his fortune was never considered to belong to the *peuple*.

Le [poor man become rich] voilà bien décidé homme: sa nature aurait-elle changé? Le singe est toujours singe, & l'homme toujours homme. Le peuple est donc composé d'hommes. Mais il est à propos qu'il l'ignore toujours, & je ne le dis qu'aux riches, aux grands & aux ministres, qui pourront comme auparavant abuser de l'ignorance du peuple.[68]

In contrast to most of those who wrote before him, Coyer showed great sympathy and compassion for the lower classes. He saw that they were subject not only to the rigors of the elements, but also to oppression by the rich and powerful, as in a legal system that had one set of laws for the rich and another for the poor.[69] Rather than fear of what their poverty might lead them to, he expressed indignation at the injustices they suffered, and instead of dismissing them as an inconsequential part of the state, he emphasized their importance and usefulness.[70]

[66] Coyer, *Dissertation sur le peuple*, pp. 195-96, Fabre again sees "bad taste" in Coyer's description of a "dissection" of the heads of a peasant and his seigneur, the complete absence of any anatomical details notwithstanding ("L'article 'Peuple,'" pp. 17-18). One might equally well see here a clever piece of satire based on, and in no worse taste than, Addison's letters nos. 275 and 281 in *The Spectator*, describing the dissection of a beau's head and a coquette's heart.

[67] Coyer, *Dissertation sur le peuple*, pp. 195-96, and 202.

[68] Ibid., p. 202.

[69] Ibid., p. 201.

[70] Coyer referred to the people as the "support of the state." *Bagatelles morales*, in *Oeuvres*, i, 68.

It is not hard to understand why the *Dissertation sur la nature du peuple*, despite its force and vigorous style, was not republished until after Coyer's death. It told truths that many did not wish to hear. Yet this pamphlet was not to be without influence in changing contemporary attitudes to the lower classes, for Jaucourt took it as the basis of his article "Peuple" in the *Encyclopédie*, and it passed from there into other reference works of the time.

Jaucourt, though writing for a dictionary as Richelet and Furetière had done, did not bother with five or six definitions of "people," but simply stated that the term was a "collective name difficult to define because different ideas of it are formed at different times and under various kinds of governments." He then picked up Coyer's definition: the "people" were formerly the entire third estate, but due to the defection of lawyers, financiers, intellectuals and craftsmen of the luxury trades, "there only remain in the mass of the people . . . workers [*ouvriers*] and peasants [*laboureurs*]." Jaucourt ignored a third class of the people—domestics—named by Coyer, but followed the Abbé in describing the harsh life of the working poor, and in some of his satire, as when he referred to financiers who ate "nobly in one meal enough food for a hundred families of the people." But Jaucourt did not make irony and moral indignation the substance of his article as Coyer had done. Rather he argued against a current view of the people that would have prevented any improvement in their condition on the theory that poverty was a necessary spur to industry. He wrote:

> Qui croiroit qu'on a osé avancer de nos jours cette maxime d'une politique infâme, que de tels hommes ne doivent point être à leur aise, si l'on veut qu'ils soient industrieux & obéissans; si ces prétendus politiques, ces beaux génies pleins d'humanité, voyageoient un peu, ils verroient que l'industrie n'est nulle part si active que dans le pays ou le petit *peuple* est à son aise, & que nulle

part chaque genre d'ouvrage ne reçoit plus de perfection.[71]

Jaucourt felt that men work best not when forced to, but
when following their natural proclivity to improve themselves. In his mind proverty was a hindrance, not an incen-
tive, to industry. He denied that the people were naturally
given to insubordination, or would be if their lives were
made easier: "it is an injustice to calumny in this way an infinite multitude of innocents." On the contrary, the people
conduct themselves, "with the natural respect of the humble [petits] for the great [grands]," and "kings have no more
faithful subjects." Jaucourt went so far as to assert that
"there is more love of the public good in this order,
perhaps, than in all the others."[72]

In Jaucourt's hands the people have become "innocents"; they are respectful, obedient, patriotic, attached to
the person of the king. In short, they are idealized, and
idealized in such a way as to make them acceptable to the
aristocracy and comfortable members of the third estate.
Jaucourt was not so intent upon showing the degradation
of the poor and the inhumanity of the rich as upon proving
that poverty was not a necessary spur to industry, that the
people were the opposite of dangerous, and that their lot
not only should but could be ameliorated without disrupting social order. Jaucourt was arguing for the improvement of the condition of the people, so that while he began
from Coyer's position, he went far beyond it.[73]

[71] Jaucourt did not acknowledge Coyer by name. He referred to him
only as, ". . . un homme de beaucoup d'esprit. . . ." See the article "Peuple"
in the Encyclopédie ou Dictionnaire raisonné des sciences, des arts et des métiers,
D. Diderot and J.I.R. d'Alembert, eds. (Paris, 28 vols., 1751-72). Henceforth Encyclopédie. The "infamous policy" to which Jaucourt refers is that
of Richelieu in his Testament politique, pp. 253-54.

[72] Encyclopédie, art. "Peuple."

[73] Fabre asserts that both Coyer and Jaucourt make a "properly political
claim" on behalf of the people ("L'article 'Peuple,' " p. 19) and implies that
both men were writing as democrats. I believe that Fabre is mistaken on

The article "Peuple" in the *Encyclopédie* can well be regarded as an important statement of a new, engaged attitude to the lower classes. Further, its influence can be shown to have been considerable, for the three other major encyclopedias published after Diderot's, but before the Revolution, plagiarized their distinguished predecessor shamelessly. The article "Peuple" of the *Grand vocabulaire françois* is an unlikely hybrid, consisting of a close copying of the definition of the dictionary of the Académie and the insertion into it of all of Jaucourt's article except the last two paragraphs. There is no attempt at integration or synthesis so that the description of the people as the "least considerable inhabitants" of a town or country is followed immediately by Jaucourt's idealization of the lower classes as the most useful and virtuous part of the state.[74] The *Dictionnaire universel* did somewhat better than the uncritical and unselective juxtaposition of old and new in the *Grand vocabulaire*. It reproduced the *Encyclopédie* article paragraph by paragraph, omitting only the last one, and then, taking "people" in the sense of "nation" or "state," ventured a number of pages of political theory of its own.[75] The article "Peuple" in the section of the *Encyclopédie méthodique* concerned with political economy briefly summarized Coyer's views on the people directly from the *Dissertation*, and then reproduced textually the two key paragraphs in the Jaucourt article condemning the "infamous policy" of keeping the laboring population in want, and presenting the people as obedient, respectful and patriotic. The rest of the article, which is the greater part of it, con-

---

this point. Neither Coyer nor Jaucourt asked for specific political rights for the people, but both men were concerned with the social and economic amelioration of their condition. This amelioration was to come from above, and was the desire of benevolent elitists, not democrats.

[74] P.J.J.G. Guyot, S.R.N. Chamfort et al., *Grand vocabulaire françois* (Paris, 30 vols., 1767-74), art. "Peuple." Henceforth GVF.

[75] J.B.R. Robinet, ed., *Dictionnaire universel des sciences morales, economiques, politiques et diplomatiques; ou Bibliothèque de l'homme d'état et du citoyen* (London, 30 vols., 1777-83), art. "Peuple." Henceforth DUS.

sists in a selective copying of Robinet's views on politics and population.[76]

It is remarkable that although Coyer's essay appeared first and had a wide influence, there is no evidence to suggest that Thomas, Baudeau, Jaubert or Berenger were indebted to him. Rather, they seem to represent the same current of opinion, but to do so independently.

Thomas wrote the *Epître au peuple* to compete for the poetry prize offered by the Académie Française for 1760. Though the piece was not crowned, this honor going to Marmontel for a poem on the utility of literature, it received the first mention, and a compliment from Duclos, the secretary of the Académie. With this encouragement, Thomas decided to offer his poem to the public.

The people, as described by Thomas, were the source of a nation's power and prosperity. They are styled "a respectable assembly of useful citizens," and in the author's view utility was no doubt their chief virtue. He apostrophized the people as follows:

C'est toi [peuple] qui des Etats soutenant la puissance,
Répands sur ces grands corps la gloire & l'abondance
. . . .
Tes bras, tes mouvemens, ta féconde industrie,
Multipliant partout les germes de la vie,
Par des travaux actifs animent l'univers.[77]

While the conqueror destroyed and ravaged the world, the people labored to preserve and make it fruitful. Thomas praised the peasantry for practicing "the first of arts," admired the industry of artisans, and pointed out that as soldiers the people were the defenders of their countries. To

[76] J. N. Démeunier, ed., *Encyclopédie méthodique: Economie politique et diplomatique* (Paris and Liège, 4 vols., 1784-88), art. "Peuple." Henceforth EM.

[77] A. L. Thomas, *Epître au peuple. Ouvrage présenté à l'Académie françoise en 1760* (n.p., 1761), pp. 7-8.

the people and their "noble industry" the author compared a proud but idle nobleman, "useless to the world" and concluded: "True honor consists in being useful to men."[78]

Like Coyer, Thomas emphasized the productive role of the lower classes, and like Jaucourt, he tended to idealize them. He did not deny that the people had faults, but he did endow them with a number of virtues that it is by no means certain they possessed: morality and health. The sources of these assumed virtues are moderate wealth and closeness to nature. Kings rule, the *grands* enjoy honors, and the rich the comforts that their wealth can buy them, but "le Peuple a des moeurs." Courtiers and other powerful men are a constant prey to ambition and unendingly pursue their own interests, but the peasant (*laboureur*), guided by "simple nature," is unselfish and generous. And while wealth leads to vice and unhappiness, the simple life is healthy and free from passion.[79]

Perhaps the boldest part of Thomas' idealization of the laboring population is his assertion:

> Peuple, tu ne sçais point, par de grands attentats,
> Epouvanter la terre & changer des Etats.[80]

Of course, this is precisely what the lexicographers of the first half of the century feared they would do. But for Thomas, the people, far from plotting against authority, were merely the "instrument and victim" of scheming and ambitious courtiers.[81] He approved the assumed passivity of the lower classes and warned them against taking matters into their own hands. Far better, he counseled, to accept their condition and look forward with confidence to the rewards that their virtues, both economic and moral, would undoubtedly meet with in another and better world.[82]

[78] Ibid., pp. 8-9.
[79] Ibid., pp. 6-12.
[80] Ibid., p. 10.
[81] Ibid., p. 11
[82] "Peuple, d'un oeil serein envisage ton sort.
    N'accuse point la vie, & méprise la mort.

No less than Coyer's satire, Thomas' poem contrasts sharply with earlier treatments of the people. It was, furthermore, the author's intention that it should do so, for he stated in the preface that "the goal of this epistle is to render the people respectable in the eyes of others, and to console it in itself."[83] As the great majority of the lower classes were illiterate, he could not have succeeded in achieving the second part of his dual purpose, and while it is difficult to say what success he had in achieving the first, the indications are that he was not without some. Both the *philosophe* Grimm and the conservative journalist Querlon acclaimed the poem, and asserted that the public preferred it to Marmontel's.[84] A number of other authors seem to have taken it as a model when they wrote poems of a similar sort.[85] We find, too, that a country curate had the *Epître* suitably expurgated, then printed for distribution to his parishioners,[86] and that it appears in its entirety, though without acknowledgment, as the preface to Berenger's *Le Peuple instruit par ses propres vertus*, in 1787.

Another strikingly sympathetic treatment of the lower classes is found in the *Idées d'un citoyen sur les besoins, les droits, et les devoirs des vrais pauvres*. The citizen with whose ideas we have to deal is the Abbé Baudeau, and though he was writing of "the poor," his work in fact treats the lower classes as a whole, for he was concerned not only with those actually below the poverty line, but also with those who were susceptible of being plunged below it by circumstances beyond their control.[87]

La vie est un éclair; la mort est un asile.

Ton sort est d'être heureux; ta glorie est d'être utile."

Ibid., p. 13.

[83] Ibid., p. 5.

[84] E. Guitton, "Populisme et poésie: de l' 'Epitre au peuple' (1760) au poème des 'Fastes' (1779)," in *Images du peuple*, p. 319.

[85] Ibid., p. 320.

[86] M. Michaud, ed., *Biographie universel* (Paris and Leipzig, 45 vols., 1854-65), vol. XVI, p. 402.

[87] Baudeau estimated the total population of France at eighteen mil-

Baudeau sought to impress on his reader the harshness of the lot of the people by putting into the mouth of a day laborer a speech describing and denouncing the conditions of his existence. Part of it reads as follows:

> Vivre pour nous, c'est-à-dire manger du pain noir, boire de l'eau, coucher sur la paille, être vêtu de toile en lambeaux; & voilà que le Collecteur venoit nous emporter notre bled, notre argent, notre chauderon & jusqu'à notre paillasse, pour payer les impôts. Il nous falloit donc becher la terre les trois quarts de l'année depuis le lever de l'Aurore jusqu'au coucher du Soleil, pour n'avoir pas même l'hiver du pain noir, de l'eau & de la paille. Que ceux qui nous ont fait dépouiller de tout & chasser de nos cabanes par les Collecteurs, travaillent eux-mêmes la terre à notre place: nous ne voulons plus être pis que les bêtes de somme; on les fait travailler moins que nous, & du moins on les loge & on les nourrit. . . .[88]

In the above passage the author was referring not to the disabled or infirm, but to ordinary agricultural laborers, and he showed himself particularly sympathetic to them. Like Coyer, Baudeau believed that the condition of the people was aggravated by social injustice, and perhaps even more than Coyer, he had an acute sense of the precariousness of the lives of the lower classes. Unskilled workers thought themselves lucky when, through their labor, they could assure their subsistence, but it took only an illness to make this impossible.[89] And even workers whose health was untroubled during youth and middle age were inevitably faced with indigence as they grew old.[90]

Baudeau also shared the respect of the writers just con-

---

lion, the number of potential "true poor" at three million, and the actual number of "true poor" at any one time at one hundred thousand (*Idées d'un citoyen sur les besoins, les droits, et les devoirs des vrais pauvres* [Amsterdam, 1765], p. 185).

[88] Ibid., p. 101. [89] Ibid., pp. 49-50. [90] Ibid., p. 26.

sidered for the laboring population as a whole. He referred to those engaged in some form of productive labor as "these citizens so little favored, and so worthy of being so," and asserted that on them depended "the sustenance, the support and the true worth of the state."[91] As Baudeau was a physiocrat, it is not surprising to find that he had special regard for the peasantry, calling it "the most useful class of the state."[92]

To this point the Abbé has been saying, though in a manner and with emphases of his own, what others who wrote on the people had said. The new element he introduced into the discussion was the assertion that by virtue of the services they rendered society, the people had certain definite rights, above all a right to subsistence. Having defined the "true poor" as those who, because of the effects of nature or misfortune, were unable to support themselves by their labor, Baudeau stated that "our fundamental axiom is that all the true poor have a real *right* to *demand* that their essential needs (*vrai nécessaire*) be fulfilled. . . ."[93] Nor was this a verbal lapse on the author's part. Baudeau spoke of the assistance to be tendered to the poor not in terms of charity but as an obligation that society owed them, and that they had a right to demand.[94] Assisting a worker who had been reduced to indigence was not an act of kindness, but one of justice: "It is a debt that we repay. . . ."[95] This idea, containing as it does the germ of socialism, was unusually generous for the time. Indeed, Baudeau alone of the writers consulted has the distinction of having set if forth.[96]

[91] Ibid., pp. 49-50.
[92] Ibid., p. 21. Baudeau also refers to the peasantry as "cette classe de Citoyens, les plus utiles à la Patrie" (ibid., p. 103).
[93] Ibid., pp. 9-10 and p. 169.
[94] Ibid., pp. 50, 141, 152, 155 and 177.
[95] Ibid., p. 89.
[96] Other writers refer to the "rights" of the people in a political or abstract sense, taking the "people" to mean nation or third estate, but do not ascribe any concrete or specific rights to the working population. See

Jaubert's *Eloge de la roture* appeared the year after Baudeau's book. The author pointedly dedicated his essay to all "virtuous commoners" and stated that it was his purpose to "reestablish the third estate in the place fitting to it, and to revive its rights which ambition, ingratitude, or ignorance have extinguished, but which nature has rendered imprescriptible."[97]

Jaubert did not restrict his selection of arguments and authorities to support his case. He used the Bible to prove the original equality of all men, and hence that the commonalty had precedence of antiquity over the other orders, and then went on to argue on the criterion of utility that the commonalty was the most considerable, most necessary, most useful and most deserving part of the state.[98] Twenty years before Sieyès, Jaubert asserted that the commonalty, defined as the third estate, was the state. He wrote:

> C'est la Roture qui fait les principales forces d'un Etat, c'est elle qui les entretient, qui les répare continuellement, & sans craindre d'être démenti, on peut assurer avec confiance; que sans elle aucun Etat n'existeroit, parce que si le Clergé & la Noblesse sont dans l'Etat, l'Etat n'est dans aucun de ces deux corps, au lieu que le peuple constitue essentiellement l'Etat.[99]

Although Jaubert opposed the commonalty to the clergy and nobility, it must not be inferred that he was arguing the case of the bourgeoisie against the privileged orders. For although it is true that one of his consistent themes was the superiority of merit to inherited nobility,[100] it is equally

---

below, chap. III, note 138, and A. Lichtenberger, *Le Socialisme au XVIIIe siècle* (Paris, 1895).

[97] Abbé P. Jaubert, *Eloge de la roture dédié aux roturiers* (London, 1766), pp. 9-10.

[98] Ibid., pp. 13-18 and 9-10. This is Jaubert's thesis, which he develops in his essay.

[99] Ibid., p. 42.   [100] Ibid., pp. 18, 26-27, and 43-44.

true that he more especially had the laboring population in mind. He referred to the peasantry as "the most numerous and most useful part of the nation"[101] and, comparing the lower classes to an idle (or supposedly idle) nobility, asserted:

Le peuple travailleur est plus utile à un Etat que ceux qui vivent dans l'oisiveté. C'est lui qui fait tous les ouvrages publics, & qui fournit des sujets à tous les métiers & à tous les arts. On trouve dans le laboureur le nourricier de la patrie, & dans le soldat son defenseur, c'est pourquoi on ne sçauroit avoir trop d'attention à leur conservation.[102]

For Jaubert the laboring population was, by virtue of its occupations, the mainstay of society and the state, and in the Abbé's view those who regarded these eminently useful men and their labors as base or vile were incapable of sound judgment.[103] In writing of the "peuple travailleur" and bringing to the fore the productive role of the lower classes, Jaubert departed from the definitions of the people offered by the dictionaries of the first half of the century, and followed the lead given by Coyer, Jaucourt, Thomas and Baudeau.

Berenger's pamphlet, *Les Quatre Etats de la France*, appeared in 1789, over twenty years after Jaubert's essay. It was written as an oration or letter to Louis XVI, and in it the author frequently apostrophized his monarch. Thus the literary genre of the piece is rhetoric, and in its figures of speech and classical allusions it is as polished and erudite as Thomas' poem or Coyer's satire. But at the same time it is more concrete and specific than either and recalls Baudeau's treatment of social problems. It also insists,

[101] Ibid., p. 63.
[102] Ibid., p. 77. A longer and even more emphatic passage praising the people for their productive role in society and pointing out the dependence of the upper classes on them is to be found in ibid., pp. 66-67.
[103] Ibid., p. 86.

perhaps more emphatically than any work so far considered, on the wrongs suffered by the people and on the means of redressing them. Yet in his recommendations for improving the lot of the laboring population Berenger illustrates the limits to which even those most sympathetic to the people might go.

Berenger retained the clergy and nobility as two of his four estates, but divided what was traditionally the third estate into two separate bodies, the magistrature and the people. Unlike most authors of the time, Berenger subordinated the clergy and nobility to the people, whom, he said, "must be counted first."[104] It is the productive role of the people, "born for agriculture and for industry" and described as "the arms and legs" of the body politic, that assures them this preeminence.[105] The people create wealth through trade and industry, and as the peasantry they are the mainstay of the nation. Berenger likened them to bees in their industry and to sheep in their fruitfulness and obedience.[106] In this, his pamphlet recalls the writing of those who had worked to recast the image of the people thirty years earlier. In his description of their condition and its causes, however, he goes somewhat further.

Coyer had described and purposely exaggerated the poverty of the lower classes. But his description, if nobly indignant and humanitarian in intent, was general and literary. Berenger, too, spoke in general and emotive terms of the "profound misery" of the people.[107] But he referred specifically to the destitute peasants of certain regions such as Champagne, Sologne, Limousin and Auvergne, and even described the conditions obtaining in the villages scattered along certain roads.[108] Nor was Berenger silent on the precise causes of this poverty. Though his analysis here is far from comprehensive, it does point to an issue which it was within the government's power to influence: taxation.

[104] L. P. Berenger, *Les Quatre Etats de la France* (n.p., 1789), p. 5.
[105] Ibid., pp. 5 and 9.   [106] Ibid., pp. 10 and 17.
[107] Ibid., p. 11.   [108] Ibid., p. 12.

The people suffered under "the burden of *misère* and taxes" and were crushed by "so many disastrous taxes."[109]

Observing that although the people created the wealth of the nation, they nevertheless lived in poverty, Berenger could scarcely avoid the conclusion that they were the victims of gross injustice.[110] Indeed, his intention in pointing out the wrongs to which the people were subject was to have them righted. Yet the form he wished to see these reforms take clearly reveals the limits of his social vision. In concluding his pamphlet Berenger addressed a brief "prayer" to each order. That for the people reads:

> La Philosophie a travaillé pour vous: ne la faites pas repentir. Gardez-vous de subvertir l'ordre ancien, ou d'intervertir l'ordre moderne. Ne troublez pas une révolution qui se fait d'elle-même, en la prématurant. L'épée & la violence ont forgé plus de fers qu'elles n'en ont brisé. Attendez tout de deux forces également victorieuses & pacifiques: la force des choses, & celle des lumieres. Enfin les fondemens de la Monarchie sont à découvert: il ne s'agit pas de nous ensevelir sous ses ruines, mais de la relever.[111]

Having offered the people respect and sympathy, Berenger then asked them, as Thomas had done, to keep their patience and to accept the assurance that wiser heads than theirs had their interests at heart.

Through the work of Coyer, Jaucourt, Thomas, and other writers and compilers, the image of the people current at the end of the seventeenth century and during the first half of the eighteenth had been radically recast. To be sure, not even during the High Enlightenment were the people deemed capable of independent thought or political choice. But after 1750 they were no longer regarded as "the least considerable part" of the community and were

[109] Ibid., pp. 9 and 18.　　[110] Ibid., pp. 11 and 17.
[111] Ibid., p. 52.

recognized as the majority. They were no longer portrayed as objects of mistrust and fear, but as worthy of sympathy and victims of injustice. And their economic role, which had previously been passed over in silence, was now emphasized, so that they were recognized as a necessary, and often the most useful, part of society.

This revaluation of the lower classes was not restricted to France;[112] but neither was it so thoroughgoing as the works so far discussed suggest. New ideas seldom achieve immediate and general acceptance. More often there is an overlapping of old and new, an illogical interweaving of tradition and innovation so that the same men or groups of men hold ideas that are hardly coherent or even compatible. A confused and messy business this, but one that more nearly reflects the realities of intellectual life in the eighteenth century, and probably in most other periods, than clearcut distinctions into friends of light and their foes.

In treating the *Encyclopédie*'s article on the people, Jean Fabre observes that the pendant to it, the article "Peuple romain," which is also by Jaucourt, reveals a mistrustful attitude toward the lower classes.[113] Nor is it the only piece in that huge compendium to do so. The brief article "Multitude," apparently by Diderot,[114] reverts back to the tone and spirit of the dictionaries of Furetière and Richelet, and

[112] For England, see A. W. Coats, "Changing Attitudes to Labour in the Mid-Eighteenth Century," in *Economic History Review*, 2nd series, XI (1958), and P. J. McNulty, "Adam Smith's Concept of Labor," in JHI, XXXIV (1973), and for Germany, Gagliardo, *From Pariah to Patriot*.

[113] This does not necessarily imply a contradiction. In treating the people sympathetically, Jaucourt followed the spirit of Coyer's essay; in treating them critically, he was true to the spirit of the classical sources he was following.

[114] Lough points out that Naigeon attributed this article to Diderot (*The Encyclopédie in Eighteenth-Century England*, p. 191), and Harry Payne has shown a close resemblance of part of this article to a passage from Diderot's correspondance (The *Philosophes and the People* [New Haven and London], p. 94, n. 3).

makes it impossible to speak of any one encyclopedist or Enlightenment attitude to the people. A multitude is defined as:

> . . . un grand nombre d'objets rassemblés, & se dit des choses & des personnes: une *multitude* d'animaux, une *multitude* d'hommes, une *multitude* de choses rares. Méfiez-vous du jugement de la *multitude*; dans les matières de raisonnement & de philosophie, sa voix alors est celle de la méchanceté, de la sottise, de l'inhumanité, de la déraison & du préjugé. Méfiez-vous-en encore dans les choses qui suppose ou beaucoup de connoissances, ou un goût exquis. La *multitude* est ignorante & hébétée. Méfiez-vous-en sur-tout dans le premier moment; elle juge mal, lorsqu'un certain nombre de personnes, d'après lesquelles elle réforme ses jugemens, ne lui ont pas encore donné le ton. Méfiez-vous-en dans la morale; elle n'est pas capable d'actions fortes & généreuses; elle en est plus étonnée qu'approbatrice; l'héroïsme est presque une folie à ses yeux. Méfiez-vous-en dans les choses de sentiment; la délicatesse de sentimens est-elle donc une qualité si commune qu'il faille l'accorder à la *multitude*? En quoi donc, & quand est-ce que la *multitude* a raison? En tout; mais au bout d'un très-long-tems, parce qu'alors c'est un écho qui répète le jugement d'un petit nombre d'hommes sensés qui forment d'avance celui de la postérité. Si vous avez pour vous le témoignage de votre conscience, & contre vous celui de la *multitude*, consolez-vous-en, & soyez sûr que le tems fait justice.[115]

Here the traditional picture of the people again emerges, but with a difference. It is above all the ignorance and stupidity of the multitude that are emphasized. The masses are regarded as incapable of judging in matters of reason, taste, morality or sentiment. The author of this article has adopted the Voltairean view that the masses are not only

---

[115] *Encyclopédie*, art. "Multitude."

given to "méchanceté" and stupidity but are also the seat of inhumanity, unreason and prejudice.[116] So conceived the "multitude," or people, are the polar opposites of the *philosophes*.

It is interesting that the author of this article asserted the *vox populi vox dei* proposition: ultimately the people are right on all matters. The reasoning by which this assertion is made to harmonize with the description of the people given above is curious. The multitude, the author says in effect, is right when it ceases to be itself, that is, when it finally sheds its unreason and prejudices (which are its essence) and adopts the views of "a small number of sensible men." Of course it is really the sensible few, the *philosophes*, who are right and not the multitude at all. The elitism of this view is obvious. Yet despite the mistrust of the masses which it so clearly expresses, this article also adds a new and important element to the discussion on the lower classes: the possibility of their slowly adopting the outlook of the "sensible few."

The ambivalence reflected in the two articles "People" and "Multitude" of the *Encyclopédie* is also found elsewhere in the literature of the period. In addition to the dictionaries and encyclopedias discussed so far, all of which were conceived as genuine reference works, there also appeared in the second half of the eighteenth century a large number of alphabetical compendiums whose object was more social comment than erudition. The best known, though not the earliest example, is Voltaire's *Dictionnaire philosophique*, and this title is not a bad name for the genre as a whole, despite the fact that works belonging to it are not in the strict sense philosophical, and have only incidentally adopted an alphabetical order.

The two earliest philosophical dictionaries, Neuville's *Dictionnaire philosophique ou Introduction à la connaissance de*

---

[116] For a judicious account of Voltaire's view of the people, see R. Mortier's article, "Voltaire et le peuple."

l'homme, the first edition of which dates from 1751, and Voltaire's, which appeared in 1764, do not have entries under "People," but four other works of this sort published between 1770 and 1789 do.[117] The *Dictionnaire social et patriotique* of Lefebvre de Beauvray does little, despite its promising title, to throw further light on contemporary attitudes to the lower classes. The author merely used the article "People" to illustrate one of his favorite theses—that the French are superior to the English—by showing that the people of London are quite as credulous and ignorant as those of Paris, and then went on to discuss "people" in a political rather than social sense.[118] Joly's *Dictionnaire de morale philosophique* is more revealing, but before discussing it a few words of explanation are in order.

Joseph Romain Joly (1715-1805) was a pious and learned Capuchin monk of Besançon. He was a member of the Académie des Arcades of Rome, and an extremely prolific, if not very popular, author. As a classical scholar, Joly was impressed with the high moral teachings of many of the ancient philosophers, and as a Christian, he wished to demonstrate that there existed a harmony between what was best in the philosophies of Greece and Rome and the teachings of scripture. His dictionary was conceived and written in this spirit, which seems more typical of the Renaissance than of the Enlightenment, and contains a fair account of the views of classical authors on various subjects, often with reference to the Bible. Joly insisted, however, that although his work was based on the classics, which he cited freely, it was not a mere compilation, for he used his

---

[117] None of these dictionaries have entries under "Nation." Two dictionaries of the same sort, Chantréau's *Dictionnaire national et anecdotique* (Politicopolis [*sic*], 1790) and the Anonymous *Dictionnaire raisonné de plusieurs mots qui sont dans la bouche de tout le monde, et ne présentent pas des idées bien nettes* (Paris, 1790), both do have entries under "Nation," while neither has articles for "Peuple."

[118] P. Lefebvre de Beauvray, *Dictionnaire social et patriotique, ou Précis raisonné des connoissances relatives à l'économie morale, civile & politique* (Amsterdam, 1770), art. "Peuple." Henceforth DSP.

discretion in lengthening and shortening passages and in commenting on them.[119]

Joly began his article on the people by citing the little-known rhetor and historian, Denis of Halicarnassus, to the effect that "the people is the body of a state, its strength and its arms. . . . It is charged with carrying out the orders of its leaders; but it is incapable of governing."[120] He then went on to quote Herodotus, Plato, the Bible, Cicero, Plutarch, Seneca, Virgil and Tacitus to illustrate and expand on the second half of Denis' statement without mentioning a syllable more about the first. Herodotus would rather be governed by a tyrant than the people; Plato calls the people ignorant, inconstant, ungrateful, fickle, envious, cruel, mettlesome (*fougueux*) and indocile; scripture describes them as unstable and treacherous as water. The greatest fault of the people is ignorance: they base their opinions on appearance rather than reality and follow their passions instead of reason. Inconstancy is their second great vice: they love novelty and are given to caprice; they are like children whose wishes are forever changing, or a field of wheat which is moved by any wind that blows.[121]

If these statements from classical authors seem strikingly similar to the articles on the people in the dictionaries of Richelet and Furetière, this is not without good reason. Down to quite recent times the classics formed the backbone of secondary and university curricula and were the common heritage of the educated classes. There could be nothing more natural for young men than to adopt the opinions and outlook of authors held up to them as paragons of virtue, wisdom and eloquence. But more than educational and cultural influences were at work here. Classical Greece and Rome were aristocracies, and the classical authors held and expressed not universalist, but aristo-

---

[119] J. R. Joly, *Dictionnaire de morale philosophique* (Paris, 2 vols., 1771), p. iv. Henceforth DMP.
[120] Ibid., art. "Peuple." [121] Ibid.

THE PROBLEM · 73

cratic, values. France during our period was of course also
an aristocracy, and the elites of the country were not only
nurtured on, but also for the most part shared, the disdain
for, and fear of, the lower classes universal among the
sages of antiquity.[122]

Against the consistently hostile classical attitude to the
people, one can place the more sympathetic Christian
point of view. Had Joly adduced Homer, Aristophanes and
Thucydides in addition to his other Greek authors he
could have cited more examples of disdain for the lower
classes without in any way altering the image of them he
presented. Had he, on the other hand, chosen to quote
more widely from the Bible, he could have presented a far
different view: from the Old Testament an emphasis on
social justice and the concept of a people greater than its
leaders, of a nation whose vocation it was to become in its
entirety a holy people; from the New Testament, the assertion of the sanctity of poverty and humility and hence of
the poor and humble. That Joly chose to subordinate the
scriptural to the classical view of the people and to neglect
the positive aspects of the scriptural view is significant, and
becomes the more so when one realizes that the same
choice was made, whether consciously or not, by the
lexicographers of the first half of the century.

Peter Gay has argued that the Enlightenment can be
looked upon as a synthesis resulting from a conflict between the classical and Christian traditions, and that the
classical tradition with its rationalism, naturalism and hu-
manism provided much of the groundwork on which the
philosophes built.[123] On the whole this thesis has much to be
said for it, but there are points on which it calls for qualification. Classical antiquity, even at its best, was not all

---

[122] An eminent literary critic and historian, Erich Auerbach, has argued
that classical authors were precluded by their ethicism from seeing the
lower classes either sympathetically or fairly (*Mimesis*, trans. by W. R.
Trask, [Princeton, 1973], pp. 131-33).

[123] Gay, *The Enlightenment*.

sweetness and light, and if the men of the Enlightenment were indebted to it for the framework of much of their world view, they also took over from it certain opinions which are, from a humanitarian and universalist perspective, retrograde. One such example is the antisemitism which Voltaire, Holbach and others took over from Cicero and certain minor writers of later antiquity.[124] Another case, I think it is clear, may be found in attitudes toward the lower classes. In this instance, too, the men of the Enlightenment had to overcome not only their Christian, but also their classical, heritage. Coyer, Jaucourt and certain others ignored the classical-Christain alternative of seeing the people as either dangerous or sanctified, as well as the aristocratic bias against manual labor, to emphasize the productive role of the lower classes. The novelty and significance of this departure should not be underestimated. But nor should one disregard the tenacity of the older attitudes toward the lower classes. We have seen that the two articles of the *Encyclopédie*, "Peuple" and "Multitude" are very different in spirit, and shall find a similar ambivalence in the two philosophical dictionaries still to be considered.

The relevant article in Bastide's *Dictionnaire des moeurs*, reads: "PEUPLE: Souverain dans ses opinions & dans ses habitudes, esclave dans ses devoirs & dans ses travaux."[125] Clément's article in the *Petit dictionnaire de la cour et de la ville* is scarcely longer and exhibits the same mixture of sympathy with disdain or mistrust as Bastide. It reads:

> Le fondement d'un état, c'est le peuple: si ce fondement n'est que de terre & de boue, l'édifice ne peut durer long-temps.

> Le peuple est souvent ingrat envers ceux qui l'ont bien servi: comme en temps de pluie & d'orage, on recourt à

[124] A. Hertzberg, *The French Enlightenment and the Jews: The Origins of Modern Anti-Semitism* (New York, 1970), pp. 299-306.

[125] J. F. Bastide, *Dictionnaire des moeurs* (Paris, 1773), art. "Peuple." Henceforth DM.

l'abri d'un arbre; & quand le beau temps est revenu, chacun en arrache une branche en passant.[126]

Bastide called attention to the blindness with which the
people adhere to their beliefs and prejudices, but also implied that their social position was an unjust one. They are
sovereign where they should be guided, but they are also
slaves where they should be masters. Clément, on the one
hand, regarded the people as the foundation of the state as
Coyer and Jaucourt had done, but on the other, conjured
up the image of their foolishness and ingratitude, vices
with which they were commonly taxed by classical authors
and others through the ages.

Clearly, then, mistrust and fear of the lower classes did
not disappear within a generation; but in the years after
1750 a new, more sympathetic attitude toward the people
seems to have gained general currency. How these attitudes were treated when confronted with another of the
key ideas of the period, education, is the main theme of
this study.

[126] J.M.B. Clément, *Petit dictionnaire de la cour et de la ville* (Paris, 1788),
art. "Peuple." Henceforth PDCV.

CHAPTER II

The Debate on Popular Education to 1769

To define a distinctively Enlightenment attitude to the education of the lower classes is not a simple matter. Such a definition cannot be conceived in terms of yes or no answers to the question "Should the people be educated?" and this for two reasons. First, both sides of the question had already been argued in the seventeenth century, Cardinal Richelieu inveighing against the evils of extending education too far down the social scale,[1] while a royal edict of December 1698 required that all children up to the age of fourteen attend schools and catechism classes.[2] Second, both sides of the question, as we shall see, were argued by members of the enlightened community in the eighteenth century. Further, whichever view was adopted, it was almost never expressed without qualification. The answers given to the question "Should the people be educated?" were generally "yes, but . . ." or "no, but. . . ." For these reasons it is best to speak not of the attitude of the Enlightenment to the education of the lower classes, but rather of Enlightenment attitudes on this question.

Opinion was not, however, evenly divided. A general consensus favoring the education of the lower classes emerged within the enlightened community, and while this view was never unanimous, it can be said to have predominated. What distinguishes the dominant Enlightenment view of the education of the people is less the assertion that the lower classes should be educated than the assumptions

[1] Richelieu, *Testament politique*, p. 204.
[2] Isambert, Jordan, Decrusy and Taillandier, eds., *Recueil des anciennes lois françaises* (Paris, 29 vols., 1822-33), vol. xx, p. 317.

and criteria upon which this assertion was based, and the
reservations with which it was qualified.

On close examination it will become apparent that the
reservations concerning the education of the people made
by many members of the enlightened community were far
more serious than has generally been supposed. It is no
doubt substantially correct to assert, as Peter Gay does, that
in the eyes of the *philosophes*, "men who wanted to keep
others in ignorance were enemies of humanity";[3] but to
deduce from this that the *philosophes* ultimately opted for
"universal enlightenment"[4] is to mistake the logic of the
Enlightenment for opinions actually held by members of
the enlightened community. It is unsound, for example, to
take the denunciation of ignorance, common in Enlightenment literature, to infer a demand for universal enlightenment.[5] Logically this should be so—but it is a pecu-
liarity of Enlightenment thought that this conclusion was
not always drawn, and that members of the enlightened
community were as concerned with enlightenment spreading too fast, or too far, as with the effects of ignorance. The
philosophes and other educated men of the time were aware
of the social utility of ignorance and illusion, and they were
less concerned with enlightening the lower classes than
with occupational training, economic utility and social control. The reasons for this emphasis must be sought in the
social conditions of the last decades of the old regime, as
well as in the thought of the period.

In the years following the expulsion of the Jesuits from
France, when the reorganization of the *collèges* was the
focus of attention, the issue of popular education was sel-

[3] Peter Gay, "The Unity of the Enlightenment," in *The Party of Humanity*
(New York, 1964), pp. 130-31.
[4] Gay, "The Party of Humanity," in ibid., p. 277.
[5] It would seem from his later work that Gay came to realize this. See
specifically his discussion of "social religion" in *The Enlightenment*, II, pp.
522-28. Even Voltaire approached the question of enlightening the
people with what Gay calls obvious caution (ibid., p. 528).

dom discussed. Not until the late 1770s and the decade of the 1780s did the people, as a result of worsening social and economic conditions, begin seriously to trouble the enlightened community. Education was seen as one solution to the problems raised by the lower classes. Yet while the men of the Enlightenment had developed a new concept of education, it is not clear that their social thought and more specifically their expectations concerning the role the people were to play in society had changed fundamentally.[6] Hence education was in danger of being regarded as a new tool with which to accomplish a traditional task.

THE *Examen* OF THE ABBÉ TERRISSE

To discuss the developments of the 1780's at this point is to anticipate. It is best to begin at the beginning, with the first comprehensive statement on popular education that may be regarded as characteristic of the Enlightenment. This is a memoir entiteld *Examen de la question s'il est utile ou préjudiciable au bien de l'Etat que les gens de la Campagne sachent lire et écrire*. It was read in the public session of 16 August 1746 of the Academy of Rouen by its author, the Abbé Terrisse, who was both a member of the academy and the dean of the cathedral chapter of Rouen.[7] Terrisse

[6] This question receives further treatment in chap. v.

[7] This memoir consists of twenty-one pages in-folio, and is conserved in the Bibliothèque Municipale of Rouen, *fonds de l'Académie* (uncoded). There are also three other documents (also uncoded) in the file containing the *Examen*. These are criticisms of Terrisse's memoir, written in 1763 by members of a committee appointed by the academy to edit a collection of works produced by its members. This collection does not seem to have been printed in the eighteenth century, but preparations for it have left records of the reactions of some of Terrisse's colleagues to his memoir. The criticism of the committee influenced considerably the final form that the *Examen* was to take. A shortened version of the *Examen* was published in the *Précis analytique des Travaux de l'Académie des Sciences, Belles-Lettres et Arts de Rouen, 1744-50* (Rouen, 1814), pp. 181-88. All references here are to the original manuscript.

chose to argue the affirmative side of the question. In emphasizing the evils of ignorance, the advantages to be derived from education, and the right of all to instruction, he
presents what many may wish to regard as the Enlightenment view of education at its purest.

Terrisse recalled how he had come to choose the utility
of literacy as the subject of his discourse. In a discussion of
how best to "make agriculture flourish and to keep the
peasant in the constant exercise of so necessary a profession," someone expressed the opinion that:

> . . . la science de la Lecture et de L'ecriture aujourdhui si
> commune chés les gens de la campagne estoit un abus
> qu'une sage politique devoit reprimer, et qu'il convenoit
> d'interdire absolument à Tous ceux qui exercent L'ag-
> riculture une faculté qui peut les detourner des Travaux
> penibles de leur estat, et leur procurer des moyens de
> parvenir à une condition plus douce.[8]

The Abbé adopted the contrary opinion and developed it
in his memoir, assuming that it would win the endorsement
of his audience, which consisted of members and guests of
the academy, "a society established to dissipate ignorance
and to help the taste for the sciences and arts flourish
throughout this province [Normandy]."[9]

Terrisse's arguments in favor of literacy for country
dwellers fall into two main categories, the first based on religious considerations, the second on social utility. He
treated the first category quite briefly and only "in so far as
religion itself is narrowly bound up with the good order of
civil society."[10] The function of religion in society, and the
importance of literacy in assuring its efficacy were described
by Terrisse as follows:

> . . . il n'est pas douteux que La Connoissance exacte de
> La religion ne Soit un grand frein pour retenir Le
> paysan dans le devoir; Les grandes verités qu'elle en-

---

[8] Terrisse, *Examen*, pp. 1-2.   [9] Ibid., p. 2.   [10] Loc. cit.

seigne Sur La morale, Les principes de Vertu qu'elle inspire, la crainte des chatimens que'elle fait envisager, le
retiennent plus que tout autre motif. La Lecture con-
tribuë beaucoup à faire mieux connoitre à L'habitant de
La Campagne les devoirs que la Religion lui impose; La
pratique de ces devoirs lui fait éviter tous ces crimes et
ces injustices qui troublent l'ordre de La Societé; il est
donc vrai *que La Lecture concourt* par cette raison au bien
de l'Etat.[11]

For an ecclesiastic, the Abbé showed a keen awareness of
the secular advantages of religion, but the contribution of
religion to the preservation of social order was not his
major concern. He was setting out to show that "independently of religion, the ability to read and write in country
folk is equally advantageous to the state and useful to civil
society."[12] It is this emphasis on the social utility of literacy
that is new and forward-looking in the *Examen*.

Terrisse observed that each adult male member of the
village community was expected to acquit himself of certain public offices such as tax collector, syndic, or treasurer.
How could he do so if he could neither read, nor write, nor
keep accounts? Further, the ability to read and write was
often valuable in making legal transactions. If, for example, the guardian (*tuteur*) of a minor was unable to sign his
name, he was obliged to have all acts passed before a notary, and this entailed considerable inconvenience and expense.[13] In such cases the value of literacy is obvious.

Terrisse then considered the country dweller's occupational need for education. To facilitate his analysis he distinguished three "orders," the first made up of comfortable
farmers (*laboureurs* and *fermiers*), the second of nonagricul-
tural occupations (*ouvriers* and *artisans*) and the third of day
laborers (*journaliers*). In the case of each "order," Terrisse
asserted, "reading and writing seem very useful," but con-

[11] Ibid., p. 3. [12] Loc. cit.
[13] Loc. cit.

tinued as if as an afterthought, "or at least cannot be regarded as dangerous."[14]

The arguments used to show the value of a basic education to the first two "orders" were again little more than
common sense. The *laboureur* had to know how to read,
write and calculate in order to do business at the local market, to pay his workers, and if he did not have his own land,
to understand his lease.[15] There was, however, another use
to which he could put his ability to read. Terrisse referred
to the "infinite number of writings" produced by his contemporaries on agriculture, and asked:

> Or pour qui sont composés ces Livres? Est-ce que pour
> quelques politiques oisifs qui ne sont peut-être jamais
> Sortis de paris, pour ces Lecteurs frivoles qui saississent
> avec avidité toutes les nouvelles idées, ou plutôt pour les
> Laboureurs qui sont Serieusement occupés de la culture
> de leurs terres?[16]

This, to be sure, is utility broadly conceived. The artisan,
too, is said to need to know how to read and write to be able
to work more efficiently; to read plans, for example, or to
make simple calculations.[17]

In the case of the day laborer, economic utility was dis-
carded for a far broader outlook. Terrisse admitted that
the day laborer had least practical need of literacy, but
asked, "why should he be refused during his youth the
means by which to improve his situation?"[18] The passages
in which the Abbé defended the right of the day
laborer—doubtless the most typical representative of the
people in eighteenth-century France—to an education are
the most interesting in the *Examen*, and among the most
radical that will be met with in this study. Terrisse asserted
in effect that all men have an inalienable right to an education. He wrote:

[14] Ibid., p. 4.
[15] Loc. cit.
[16] Ibid., p. 5.
[17] Ibid., pp. 5-6.
[18] Ibid., p. 6.

> . . . tous les hommes n'ont ils pas un Droit égal sur ce qui est du ressort de L'esprit et de la raison, et ne doivent ils pas jouir en commun des avantages de l'un et de l'autre, comme ils jouissent des avantages de L'air et de la Lumière? ne Seroit-ce pas exercer à l'egard des pauvres un Tirannie qui choque l'humanité, et n'auroient ils pas bien de Se plaindre des riches qui voudroient toujours les retenir dans la Servitude? nous Sommes hommes avant que d'etre riches, et la fortune ne doit pas nous autoriser à opprimer nos freres que des Talens developés pourroient peut étre elever un jour au dessus de nous. . . .[19]

The moral right of the day laborer, the most humble member of the society of the old regime, to an education is here predicated on the assumption, far from common at the time, that all men are fundamentally equal.

For Terrisse a degree of social mobility is not only just, but also expedient and even necessary. Society being in a constant state of flux, it was inevitable that the fortunes of some should decline and others rise to take their place. Interference with this order of things would be foolhardy:

> Le monde éprouve une vicisitude continuelle; des familles perissent, il s'en forme d'autres qui dans quelques siècles auront acquises ces caracteres d'ancienneté qui flattent la vanité des hommes: chaque famille a son commencement, ses progrés, son point brillant, sa decadence; une autre lui succede qui éprouvera à son tour la même revolution; Tel est l'ordre de La providence; ne mettons point d'obstacles à ses decrets, et ne fermons à aucun de nos fréres la voye de S'élever à une meilleur fortune si il La merite: y en a-t-il une plus Légitime que celle des talents, des arts, et des Sciences, dans laquelle l'art de Lire et d'écrire est le premier pas?[20]

To emphasize his point, Terrisse pointed out that even the *grands* had risen from what must once have been a "hard

[19] Ibid., pp. 6-7.   [20] Ibid., p. 8.

and laborious condition."[21] The implication is that it would be shabby of them to refuse to others the means by which they themselves had risen.

Finally, it was to the social utility of allowing the poor to improve their condition that Terrisse appealed to complete his case for the education of the day laborer. On the one hand, he argued, society would benefit from the services of the truly talented who, born poor and deprived of an education, could never have developed their abilities.[22] On the other hand, the very knowledge that the day laborer, provided he had the requisite ability, was not condemned to remain a day laborer all his life would foster hope and encourage industry:

> L'emulation est necessaire dans tous les êtats, elle anime les hommes, elle les porte au travail, elle les éleve au dessus d'eux mêmes, elle produit mille biens, et je pense qu'elle n'est pas moins avantageuse dans les conditions inferieures que dans les plus élevées."[23]

Hence, from whichever point of view he examined the question, Terrisse found that it was useful rather than harmful for the state that country folk acquire the skills of literacy.

He was aware, however, that certain of his politically minded contemporaries held that it was "useless, even dangerous" for the rural population to know how to read.[24] The Abbé therefore considered the objections that such *politiques* would raise, and refuted them. In doing so he revealed the premises upon which his opinion was based, and showed that he was perhaps not so far from his politically minded adversaries as might have been expected.

[21] Loc. cit.   [22] Loc. cit.

[23] Ibid., pp. 6-7.

[24] Ibid., p. 5. It is not easy to identify the "politiques" of the first half of the eighteenth century to whom Terrisse refers. But there is no justification for assuming that Terrisse is arguing against opinions that no one held. A friendly critic of the *Examen* wrote early in 1763:

The first objection to literacy among the rural population that Terrisse discussed concerned religion. Reading, it
was alleged, would raise doubts in peasants' minds, and
might "bring them to undertake an examination beyond
their capacities, or to intrigues which would trouble the
tranquility of the state."[25] To this the Abbé replied:

> . . . il ne paroit pas qu'il y ait rien à craindre; L'homme de
> La campagne qui Scait Lire et écrire, ne voit guerres [sic]
> Sur la religion que ses livres de prieres et quelques par-
> ties des offices de l'église; on ne doit pas apprehender
> qu'il se laisse aller à des doutes, ou qu'il forme de
> nouveaux Systemes. . . . L'experience nous fait connoitre
> que dans les paroisses ou il y a des Ecôles, la Religion est
> plus connüe, mieux pratiquée, et le bon ordre mieux ob-
> servé . . .[26]

Hence Terrisse does not defend the right of men to examine freely their religion, but rather asserts that the skills of
literacy do not encourage them to do so and are therefore
anodine.

A more serious objection to teaching country folk to read
and write, and one that Terrisse treated in far greater detail, was based on considerations of social utility. It was
claimed that if peasants were given the possibility of leaving agriculture and the continuous brutalizing labor that it
demanded, they would do so: the poorer members of the
rural community would develop a distaste for their condition, agriculture would be abandoned, and the countryside
depopulated, while peasants who remained on their farms

La question traitée dans ce Memoire est interessante. Quelques per-
sonnes persuadées de l'affirmative trouveront peut estre etonnant
qu'on la propose et qu'on la discute comme Susceptible de difficulté[.]
Cependant La negative a été soutenu par plusieurs auteurs et quelques uns d'eux qui ont écrit dans ces derniers temps Sur l'agriculture,
le gouvernement, et l'education l'ont encore agitée . . . (du Boullay,
"Criticism").

[25] Terrisse, *Examen*, p. 9.   [26] Loc. cit.

would become troublesome and litigious. According to the critics of Terrisse's thesis, the continued existence and proper functioning of the social order perforce demanded that:

> . . . il y ait toujour un grand nombre d'hommes qui restent dans les conditions inferieures, et qui Soient Uniquement occupés à des travaux corporels. parmi ces travaux il n'y en a point de plus necessaire, et de plus essentiel, que la culture des terres . . . or pour que ces travaux ne soient pas abandonnés, il ne faut pas que l'homme de la Campagne puisse S'élever à une condition plus douce; l'amour du bien étre regne dans tous les hommes, et la nature l'a gravé profondement dans leur coeur. Mais il est de bonne politique, d'en arrêter les funestes éffets, et de renfermer le pauvre dans des bornes qu'il ne puisse jamais franchir. La privation de la Lecture et de L'ecriture est un des moyens les plus éfficaces pour rétenir l'homme de la Campagne dans Son état; destitué de ces connoissances il sera forcé de rester dans l'état de Ses Peres, il s'y occupera tout entier.[27]

Though Terrisse admitted that this argument was repeated incessantly and that it had a great many partisans, he regarded it as mistaken and set about refuting it.

This argument's principal weakness, the Abbé asserted, was that it assumed too much. While it is true that all men wish to improve themselves, "it is not sufficient simply to wish to do so";[28] talent and ability are the necessary prerequisites of success. The vast majority of the people about whom he was writing, Terrisse believed, were simply incapable of improving their situation. The lack of natural ability and the conditions in which they lived precluded it. As for the great majority of country folk:

[27] Ibid., p. 11.
[28] Ibid., pp. 11-12.

> La Lecture et l'écriture ne leur serviront que pour les be-
> soins de cet état; quelques peines qu'ils Se donnent, ils ne
> vaincront pas la pauvreté qui les presse, et qui les con-
> damne à manger leur pain à la Sueur de leur front; Si
> dans une Suite de 20 ou de 30 années on voit un ou deux
> habitants d'une paroisse S'élever par leurs talents à une
> meilleure fortune, ou S'illustrer dans la république des
> Lettres, Le plus grand nombre Sera toujours retenû
> dans l'ancienne profession par le deffaut de talents
> naturels, par la pauvreté, par l'education et l'habitude
> plus forte encore chés les gens Simples que chès les au-
> tres, ou Si vous voulés encore par une certaine stupidité
> qui ne permet pas à plusieurs d'entre eux de considerer
> des objets plus elevés et plus flateurs. Ces differentes
> causes fourniront toujours assés d'hommes dans les con-
> ditions inferieures, et dans les travaux penïbles.[29]

Terrisse went on to argue that education had a beneficial
effect on agriculture and the peasantry. He contrasted the
flourishing state of agriculture in the countryside around
Rouen, where "almost all the country folk are educated," to
certain provinces of the interior where both husbandry

---

[29] Ibid., p. 12. Between the sentence that ends "à la Sueur de leur front"
and that which begins, "Si dans une suite . . ." one can, with a little effort,
read the following sentences which have been crossed out:

> ne craignons pas de voir sortir tout d'un coup du fond de nos cam-
> pagnes des Essaims de philosophes, d'orateurs, de juriconsultes et
> par là les terres devenir incultes. ce Seroit un phenonmene nouveau
> et bien singulier (ibid., p. 12).

Du Boullay cited these two sentences, then commented on them as follows:

> des essaims de philosophes d'orateurs de juriconsultes non; mais des
> Essaims de laquais et d'artisans de luxe [?] et c'est de cette maniere
> que l'objection seroit dans toute sa force et elle auroit autant contre
> les artisans des villes à qui la paresse fait abandonner souvent des
> metiers penibles pour une vie faineante et molle qu'ils esperoit
> trouver en devenant *laquais* ou *gens d'ecritoire* (du Boullay, "Criti-
> cism").

and education allegedly languished.[30] The neglect of agriculture was to be attributed not to education but to "the ingratitude of the foolish, laziness, the lack of consumption of goods, difficulty of transport."[31] Obviously it is specious to blame the ability to read and write for effects caused by other factors. Nor was it just to assume that literacy would result in more litigation and pettifoggery in the countryside, these being the result of a proclivity to injustice, not of education.[32] Good men will make good use of it, but "the vicious man abuses the best things."[33] To prevent the illiterate majority from being cheated by the literate few it was best to have all taught to read and write. The opposite course would result in the residents of the countryside being subjected to "the shameful yoke of a gross ignorance."[34]

Despite sharp differences of opinion on the anticipated effects of literacy on the rural population, it is clear that Terrisse shared some important suppositions with the *politiques* against whom he argued. He agreed that a sort of "people-condition" was necessary and inevitable. Men in this condition were "devoted exclusively to physical labor" which was recognized as harsh (*pénible*).[35] Both Terrisse and the adversary he gave himself agreed that the poor country dweller would escape from his condition to a better one if he could. The Abbé's radical statements on the

[30] Terrisse, *Examen*, p. 14. [31] Loc. cit.

[32] Ibid., p. 15. Another member of the committee preparing the academy's *Recueil* simply noted here: "On admettra difficilement l'indifference du laboureur pour les procès." (Ballière, "Criticism of the *Examen*.")

[33] Terrisse, *Examen*, p. 15. [34] Loc. cit.

[35] Though Terrisse tended to idealize the peasant, he also recognized that his condition was not a comfortable one. His labors are said to be in the same breath innocent and harsh (ibid., p. 16). The situation of the vast majority of the peasantry is characterized as an, ". . . état penible et Laborieux . . ." (ibid., p. 8). Again, the lot of "les conditions inferieures" is said to be "les travaux pénibles" (ibid., p. 12). The poor, finally, are frankly recognized to be living in *misère* (ibid., p. 6).

right of all to rise through education pale beside his assessment of an acceptable rate of upward mobility—one or
two members of a parish over a generation—and his insistence that the vast majority of farm laborers would never be
capable of improving their lot.[36] The real differences between Terrisse and his adversaries are small. The former
believed that the country dweller could not improve himself, the latter that he should not be allowed to do so. Finally, both Terrisse and those who would deny education
to the rural population base their arguments on social utility.

Terrisse differed fundamentally from the *politiques* in believing that the spread of education was compatible with,
and in fact advantageous to, the general well-being of society. The assumptions that a better educated peasant would
work more productively, and that a man with a chance of
improving himself would try to achieve the promised advancement through his industry, must be regarded as
characteristic of one Enlightenment attitude to the education of the people. This view, it would seem, is ultimately
grounded in an optimistic liberalism that will not admit
that goods of different orders, such as education and agriculture, could work other than in harmony, and that
things left to themselves would turn out favorably for all
concerned. Since all men naturally sought to rise in the
world, it was forcibly preventing the poor from getting an
education, and not, as the *politiques* argued, allowing them
to educate themselves, that was interference with the natural order of things.

Terrisse's outlook was conditioned above all by utilitarianism. If it could be proved, as his adversaries argued and
even some of his friends suspected,[37] that literacy did in

[36] Terrisse also asserted, and rightly so, that peasants really only desired
a limited and modest form of social mobility. "The ambition of the day
laborer is to be able to exploit some small plot of land that will furnish his
subsistence, that of the small farmer [*petit fermier*] to occupy a larger lease
[*ferme*]" (ibid., p. 13).

[37] See n. 29 of this chapter.

fact allow appreciably more than one or two residents of a parish to raise themselves above the condition of a day laborer, Terrisse would have found it difficult to defend the position he adopted in the *Examen*. Having given up the utility of education to agriculture, he would be left with the abstract right of all men, and of the country dweller in particular, to an education. It is unlikely that he would have cared to defend his position on this ground alone.

These reservations made, it can still be said that the Abbé Terrisse represents what one would expect to be the typical Enlightenment attitude to the education of the people. Proceeding from premises that are optimistic, liberal and utilitarian, and believing that no good can come from ignorance,[38] he argued the case for the instruction of the masses. Yet Terrisse's outlook, though it conforms with what may be regarded as the main thrust of Enlightenment thought, was not shared by all members of the enlightened community. For when the debate on the education of the lower classes began in the years following the expulsion of the Jesuits, it was the dangers and not the advantages of educating the people that were first emphasized.

THE DEBATE OPENS

The first short-lived debate on the education of the people arose incidentally from the publication in 1763 of the Breton magistrate La Chalotais' short *Essai d'éducation nationale*.[39] Just before publication of the *Essai*, La Chalotais achieved national fame for his part in the legal proceeding that led to the expulsion of the Jesuits from France, his reports on this subject selling some 12,000 copies.[40] The *Essai* seems to have achieved a lesser, but still

[38] "Ignorance of things useful in life can never procure any advantage, either for the state or for private individuals" (Terrisse, *Examen*, p. 21).

[39] L.R.C. de La Chalotais, *Essai d'éducation nationale ou Plan d'études pour la jeunesse* (Paris, 1763). The book is 153 pages in-12.

[40] J. Delvaille, *La Chalotais, éducateur* (Paris, 1911), p.14.

considerable, success.[41] The number of copies printed of this work is not known, but the fact that it was translated into Dutch (1767), Russian (1770) and German (1771) indicates something of its popularity.[42]

La Chalotais' *Essai* is principally concerned with providing a new curriculum for the *collèges*, and in setting forth the general principles upon which such a curriculum should rest.[43] As the *collèges* were chiefly the concern of the bourgeoisie and nobility, the people understandably count for little in the book. La Chalotais mentioned the lower classes only in passing, when he complained:

> Il n'y a jamais eu tant d'Etudians dans un Royaume où tout le monde se plaint de la dépopulation; le Peuple même veut étudier; des Laboureurs, des Artisans envoient leurs enfans dans les Collèges de petites Villes, où il en coûte peu pour vivre; & quand ils ont fait de mauvaises études qui ne leur ont appris qu'a dédaigner la profession de leurs pères, ils se jettent dans les Cloîtres, dans l'Etat Ecclésiastique; ils prennent des Offices de Justice, & deviennent souvent des Sujets nuisibles à la Société. *Multorum manibus egent res humanae, paucorum capita sufficiunt.*

[41] Grimm complained in September 1763 that "the work of M. de la Chalotais, full of wise and profound views, has had no success, because this illustrious magistrate showed himself in it more of a philosopher than a Jansenist" (Grimm, *Correspondance littéraire*, V, 391). Grimm's report does not, however, coincide with others. Voltaire, in a letter to La Chalotais, dated 22 June 1763, tells him that "Boxes of your book have just arrived at Geneva; it is read and admired" (Voltaire, *Oeuvres complètes*, Beuchot, ed. [Paris, 97 vols., 1828-34], vol. LXXXII, p. 348). Finally according to a Jansenist journal, the *Essai* enjoyed widespread popularity. It was asserted that ". . . all eyes are fixed on the *Essai d'Education nationale*, . . ." and that "Friends and enemies alike have read it" (*Nouvelles écclesiastiques ou Mémoires pour servir à l'histoire de la Constitution Unigenitus*, 31 October, 1763, p. 177).

[42] Delvaille, *La Chalotais*, p. 190.

[43] It was originally entitled, *Essai pour un plan d'études pour les collèges* (Voltaire, *Oeuvres*, LXXXII, 212).

Les Frères de la Doctrine Chrétienne, qu'on appelle *Ig-norantins*, sont survenus pour achever de tout perdre; ils apprennent à lire et à écrire à des gens qui n'eussent du apprendre qu'à dessiner et à manier le rabot & la lime, mais qui ne le veulent plus faire. Ce sont les rivaux ou les successeurs des Jésuites. Le bien de la Société demande que les connoissances du Peuple ne s'étendent pas plus loin que ses occupations. Tout homme que voit au-delà de son triste métier, ne s'en acquittera jamais avec courage & avec patience. Parmi les gens du Peuple il n'est presque nécessaire de sçavoir lire & écrire qu'à ceux qui vivent par ces arts, ou à ceux que ces arts aident à vivre.[44]

For reasons of economic utility the *procureur général* of the Parlement of Rennes would deny most peasants and artisans the right to learn to read and write. He argued, it seems, very much in the spirit of the *politiques* with whom the Abbé Terrisse had taken issue.

It is interesting to note that although La Chalotais regarded the effects of literacy among the people as pernicious, his *Essai* is as full as it possibly could have been of views characteristic of advanced eighteenth-century thought. La Chalotais showed himself a thorough-going empiricist, a partisan of sensationalist psychology and a utilitarian. He regarded nature as an infallible model and believed firmly in a universal moral code, "written in all hearts" and valid for all times and in all places.[45] Like Voltaire, he was an anticlerical,[46] but also a deist,[47] and regarded religious instruction as essential.[48] Finally, though

---

[44] La Chalotais, *Essai*, pp. 25-26.   [45] Ibid., p. 125.

[46] Though La Chalotais spoke of, "the vice of monasticism" (ibid., p. 13), and was violently anti-Jesuit and anti-ultramontanist, he treated the Oratorians, whom he regarded as Frenchmen before Catholics, respectfully (ibid., p. 16).

[47] ". . . the existence of God as Legislator is no less necessary to morality than is the existence of God as Creator to physics . . ." (ibid., pp. 124-25).

[48] ". . . of all subjects [*instructions*], religion is the most important . . ." (ibid., p. 15).

La Chalotais opposed having the laboring poor taught to read and write, he was a great enemy of ignorance[49] and an equally ardent spokesman for the *lumières*.[50] As a general principle he even seems to have held that all must receive some sort of education. He wrote near the beginning of the *Essai*:

> Les siècles les plus grossiers et les plus ignorans ont toujours été les plus vicieux & les plus corrompus. Laissez l'homme sans culture, ignorant & par conséquent insensible sur ses devoirs, il deviendra timide, superstitieux, peut-être cruel. Si on ne lui enseigne pas le bien, il se préoccupera necessairement du mal. L'esprit & le coeur ne peuvent rester vuides.[51]

Is there necessarily a contradiction between this statement and the one quoted earlier in which La Chalotais urged that the people ought not to be taught to read and write? It is difficult today to imagine an education that can dispense with literacy. During the eighteenth century, however, this was not so, especially in Catholic countries, where popular education consisted more in learning a catechism than in reading and writing.[52]

If La Chalotais' statement on the education of the lower classes strikes the modern reader as harsh, it does not seem to have troubled many of his contemporaries. The *Essai* was greeted enthusiastically, at least by the *philosophes*.

---

[49] "Ignorance is good for nothing, it harms everything" (ibid., p. 2).

[50] La Chalotais regarded enlightenment as an index of national well being. He wrote, " . . . the people that will be the most enlightened . . . will always have the advantage over those who will be less enlightened; it will surpass them by its industry, it will perhaps subjugate them with its arms" (ibid., p. 4). He also emphasized the moral value of enlightenment, asserting: "Enlightenment [*La lumière*] normally leads to virtue, darkness and ignorance lead to vice" (ibid., p. 123).

[51] Ibid., p. 3.

[52] H. Chisick, "School Attendance, Literacy and Acculturation: *Petites écoles* and Popular Education in Eighteenth-Century France," in *Europa* III (1980).

Bachaumont, a moderate journalist, but one unquestionably favorable to the *philosophe* cause, called La Chalotais
"this indefatigable magistrate" and strongly approved the
Essai, especially "the constant and reasoned war which M.
de la Chalotais never ceases to wage against the clergy (*la
gent monacle*)."[53] Grimm asserted that posterity would place
La Chalotais "among the foremost magistrates of France"
and called the *Essai* "worthy of immortality."[54] It would be
difficult, he wrote, to express in so little space "more wise,
profound and useful views, truly worthy of a magistrate, a
philosopher and a statesman."[55] In reviewing the *Essai*,
neither Bachaumont nor Grimm referred to the passage in
which La Chalotais complained that the people were being
educated. Apparently they did not feel strongly enough
about the issue one way or the other to mention it. Another
philosophe did regard the passage in question as worthy of
attention. This was Voltaire.

La Chalotais had sent the manuscript of his *Essai* to Ferney. Voltaire thanked him for it and flattered the magistrate by declaring, "You entitle the work: *Essay for a Plan of
Studies for the Collèges*; but I would entitle it: *Instruction of a
Statesman to Enlighten all Classes (conditions)*. I find all your
views useful."[56] Of the opinions expressed in the *Essai*, Voltaire chose to comment especially on only two. He agreed
with La Chalotais that married men were preferable to
bachelors as teachers, and he concurred, too, that it was

[53] Louis Petit de Bachaumont, *Mémoires secrets pour servir à l'histoire de la
république des lettres en France depuis MDCCLXII jusqu'à nos jours, on Journal
d'un observateur* (London, 36 vols., 1777-89), vol. I, p. 238 (13 May 1763).

[54] Grimm, *Correspondance littéraire*, v, 309.

[55] Ibid., v, 309. Grimm was not alone in gracing La Chalotais with the
epithet *philosophe*, or some derivative thereof. D'Alembert says of his *Compte rendu* against the Jesuits, "C'est le seul ouvrage philosophique qui ait
été fait jusqu'ici contre cette canaille" (Letter to Voltaire of 31 March
1762, in Voltaire's *Oeuvres*, LXXXI, p. 249). Voltaire wrote to La Chalotais
on 17 May 1762 calling the same *Compte rendu* ". . . le seul ouvrage
philosophique qui soit jamais sorti du barreau" (ibid., LXXXI, p. 283).

[56] Ibid., LXXXII, 212 (28 February 1763).

unnecessary to educate the people. On this second point he wrote effusively:

> Je vous remercie de proscrire l'étude chez les laboureurs. Moi, qui cultive la terre, je vous présente requête pour avoir des manoeuvres, et non des clercs tonsurés. Envoyez moi sur-tout des fréres ignorantins pour conduire mes charrues, ou pour les atteler.[57]

Voltaire could hardly have expressed more clearly his view that the laboring population had no need of education in order to fulfill its vocation.

Interestingly enough, a man who has been called "Voltaire's greatest enemy,"[58] and who is generally regarded as one of the most capable of the *antiphilosophes*, was expressing remarkably similar views at just this time. In reviewing a work on geography in his journal, the *Année littéraire*, Elie Fréron digressed to observe;

> . . . les Princes d'Allemagne ont fait trés-sagement de se réserver la connoissance des sublimes vérités de la Philosophie; il n'est pas avantageux à un Etat que le peuple s'en occupe; elles ne serviroient qu'à le détourner de son travail et à l'en dégoûter; son ignorance est toujours plus favorable à ceux qui gouvernent qu'une Philosophie trop généralement répandue parmi ceux qui ne sont nés que pour servir et pour obéir; et il y a lieu de croire qu'on ne les rendroit pas plus dociles et plus vertueux en les rendant plus habiles.[59]

Though Voltaire was speaking of primary education and Fréron of more advanced studies, both were agreed on the undesirable effects to be expected from instructing the masses. It may seem curious that one of the greatest spokesmen of the Enlightenment should concur with one

---

[57] Ibid., pp. 212-13.

[58] Fréron is so designated by F. C. Green in the title of a chapter of his book, *Eighteenth-Century France*.

[59] AL, 1763 v, 334-35.

of the harshest critics of the movement that it would not be a good thing to extend education too far down the social scale. But perhaps even more curious is the fact that criticism of this view came initially from a Jansenist. In his polemical essay entitled *Difficultés proposées à M. de Caradeuc de la Chalotais* . . . a certain J.B.L. Crévier questioned the magistrate's views on popular education and tried to show that they were incompatible with either sound political principles or the spirit of true religion.[60]

Jean Baptiste Louis Crévier was born to a Parisian worker in 1693. He attended the Collège de Beauvais in the capital, where he was fortunate enough to have the celebrated Rollin as his teacher and protector, and later taught in the same institution. Rollin, who was the principal of the *collège*, enjoyed a great reputation as a classicist for his *Histoire romaine*, and as a pedagogue for his often reprinted *Cours d'études*. But it was also well known that he was a Jansenist. He offered the fugitive Quesnel hospitality, even allowing him to officiate in the *collège* chapel, and conferred positions in the institution on priests forbidden because of their Jansenism to exercise priestly functions. In 1712 Rollin was forced by the government to resign his position in the *collège* because of his religious views; in 1734 his house was searched on suspicion of concealing the presses of the *Nouvelles ecclésiastiques*; and in 1739 he was among those excluded from the assembly of the University of Paris for protesting against the Bull Unigenitus. Under Rollin's influence the Collège de Beauvais came to be regarded as one of most ardent centers of Jansenism of the time.[61] After his death the illustrious and saintly educator was entered among the "defenders and friends of truth" in the *Nécrologe* of the Abbé Cerveau, the central document of French Jansenist hagiography.[62] Though Crévier never

---

[60] For the full reference to this work see n. 28 of chap. I.

[61] M. D. Chapotin, *Le Collège de Dormans-Beauvais et la Chapelle Saint Jean L'Evangeliste* (Paris, 1870), pp. 362-69.

[62] Abbé R. Cerveau, *Nécrologe des plus célèbres défenseurs et confesseurs de la vérité du dix-huitième siècle* (n.p., 2 vols., 1760), vol. I, pp. 443-44.

achieved this particular apotheosis, his obituary did appear in the *Nouvelles ecclésiastiques*.[63] He was also chosen to pronounce the eulogy over his master, and to continue his history of Rome. Indeed, Crévier enjoyed an international reputation as a classical scholar. When the young Gibbon wished a critical opinion of an emendation he proposed in the text of Livy, he wrote to Crévier, and in his own words received a "speedy and polite" as well as favorable reply.[64] In addition to carrying out his teaching and scholarly duties at the *collège*, Crévier also wrote several polemics against the antireligious strain of Enlightenment thought. The *Difficultés* is one of them.

The first difficulty Crévier raised against La Chalotais concerned the proposition that "The good of society requires that the knowledge of the people does not extend beyond their occupations."[65] La Chalotais had written what he intended as a plan of national education; yet, said Crévier, apostrophizing the magistrate:

> Vous ne voulez pas même que le peuple sçache lire et écrire. Toute l'institution du païsan sera de sçavoir se courber vers la terre, et parler aux animaux qu'il nourrit: celle du peuple, de sçavoir dessiner, manier le rabot et la lime; ou bien, selon les différentes plages, d'être condamné à servir dans un vaisseau, pour devenir matelot. L'institution nationale ne sera donc dirigée que vers un million d'hommes, et vingt millions y seront sans considération.[66]

A national education from which ninety-five percent of the nation is excluded—the contradiction is patent. But given that the vast majority of the population of the country were to remain without an education, Crévier continued:

[63] *Nouvelles ecclésiastiques*, 1766, p. 51.

[64] Edward Gibbon, *Autobiography*, D. A. Saunders, ed. (New York, 1961), p. 105.

[65] Crévier, *Difficultés*, p. 13. This sentence is of course cited from La Chalotais (see above, n. 44).

[66] Crévier, *Difficultés*, p. 13.

On demande, monsieur, si ces vingt millions d'hommes
auxquels vous refusez impitoyablement toute éducation,
n'ont pas de devoirs à remplir, et s'il n'est pas important
qu'ils les connoissent? Ces vingt millions d'hommes lais-
sés sans culture, ignorans, et par conséquent insensibles
sur les devoirs, ne deviendront-ils pas timides, super-
stitieux, peut-être cruels?[67]

The professor has convicted La Chalotais from out of his
own mouth, for these are precisely the effects that he at-
tributes to ignorance in the opening pages of the *Essai
d'éducation nationale*.[68]

It must be admitted that to deny men an education and
then to complain of the harmful effects of ignorance is to
fall into a conundrum of one's own making. But Crévier
did not pretend that this is the only way the two passages to
which he has drawn attention could be understood. He
recognized that "one might reply that the education necessary to these twenty million men is to know their religion
and to be skilled in their profession."[69] But even with the
logical contradiction overcome, Crévier regarded La
Chalotais' opinions as inadmissable. He replied that:

. . . regarder cette éducation comme suffisante pour
former l'homme, le chrétien, le citoyen, est presque nier
les suites du peché originel; que dans les villages ou il n'y
a pas d'école, les hommes ne paroissent différer des
brutes que par la figure; et que pour les moeurs, ils
vivent comme le cheval et le mulet, qui sont sans intelligence.[70]

Reading, Crévier insisted, was essential to adequate religious instruction, for "to deprive children of the means of
learning to read is to deprive them of the only means of

[67] Ibid., p. 14.
[68] Crévier has in fact quoted La Chalotais. The passage in question
from the *Essai* has been cited above, n. 51.
[69] Crévier, *Difficultés*, p. 15.
[70] Ibid., pp. 15-17.

learning to know God, to love Him and to serve Him."[71]
Literacy, for a Jansenist, is a right because to read the Bible
is a duty.[72] The radical corruption of human nature[73] demands sound religious instruction, and all the religious instruction possible. Education, for Crévier, was a lifeline to
salvation, and thus not only the right of every individual,
but an obligation for society.

Though Crévier was primarily concerned with religion,
he also met La Chalotais on his own ground, that of social
utility. He argued that literacy was a great help to the ordinary man in regulating his own affairs, and denied that
education drew workers from manual trades or tended to
depopulate the countryside.[74] Crévier's main concern was
to make the young into good Christians; but he insisted at
the same time that they be citizens as well. Criticizing La
Chalotais, he wrote: "Yes, sir, to refuse a man, whatever he
may be, some kind of education is to deprive the true God
of worshipers and the state of true citizens."[75] Crévier went
on to explain how he understood civic training for the
poor. To La Chalotais' fear that "overeducation" would result in social disjunction he opposed a concept of education
as social control. The poor were to be educated free of
charge, for:

> Ce n'est que dans une éducation gratuite, continue et
> lumineuse, à proportion de l'état et des dispositions des
> enfans, que l'on peut se flatter de faire naître aux

[71] Ibid., p. 17.

[72] "L'évangile, dit saint Bernard, n'est écrit que pour être lu. Comment
le lira celui à qui on aura defendu d'apprendre à lire? & quelle instruction
peut tenir lieu, ou dispenser de lire l'évangile?" (ibid., p. 17).

[73] Crévier asserted that, "dans l'état de la nature corrompue, l'homme
pécheur ne peut observer comme il faut la loi naturelle, & rendre à Dieu,
par cette observation, un culte qui lui soit agréable, sans la foi en Jésus-
Christ, & sans le secours de la grace de Jésus-Christ," and to strengthen
his argument quoted Nicole on, ". . . l'effroyable corruption du coeur de
l'homme, son injustice, sa vanité, sa stupidité, sa brutalité, sa misère . . . "
(ibid., p. 26).

[74] Ibid., pp. 17 and 33.   [75] Ibid., p. 18.

pauvres l'amour de leur état et de leurs devoirs, de leur faire connoître et aimer la religion dans laquelle nous avons le bonheur d'être nés, et de leur inspirer un éloignement absolu pour l'oisiveté, source et principe de tous les vices. . . .[76]

Though Crévier admitted the importance of forming the citizen together with the Christian, he and La Chalotais were fundamentally divided on the relative importance of the two categories. The magistrate rendered lip service to religion, but demanded that education be placed in the hands of the state:

Je prétends revendiquer pour la Nation une éducation qui ne dépende que de l'Etat, parce qu'elle lui appartient essentiellement; parce que toute Nation a un droit ina-liénable et imprescriptible d'instruire ses membres; parce qu'enfin les enfans de l'Etat doivent être élevés par des membres de l'Etat.[77]

Crévier, on the other hand, representing another and older point of view, asserted that "man belongs to God before belonging to the state. There is, one cannot deny it, even in relation to education, an order of duties independent of the laws and the constitutions of states."[78]

Despite the extent of his differences with La Chalotais, Crévier was always polite, even deferential in addressing him. Perhaps this was because La Chalotais, as the leader of the campaign against the Jesuits, was the enemy of his

---

[76] Ibid., p. 19. Crévier has here quoted and duly acknowledged a memoir of the administrators of the *hôpital des Enfermés* of Pontoise. This memoir was in turn quoted by Rolland d'Erceville in his *Compte rendu* on the state of the *collège* of Pontoise to the Parlement of Paris, 11 May 1763 (Rolland d'Erceville, De L'Averdy et Roussel de la Tour, *Compte Rendu aux Chambres Assemblées par M. le Président Rolland de ce qui a été fait par MM. les Commissaires, nommés par les Arrêts de 6 Août & 7 Septembre 1762* [Paris, 1763], p. 257).

[77] La Chalotais, *Essai*, p. 17.

[78] Crévier, *Difficultés*, p. 30.

enemy.[79] But it is possible, too, that Crévier had taken this tone from La Chalotais himself, for the Breton magistrate spoke with respect of an anonymous work entitled *De l'éducation publique*, of which Crévier was in all likelihood the principal author.[80]

De l'éducation publique has two parts. The first is a "methodical table of human knowledge," which in its empiricism and concern for applying science to practical uses seems encyclopedist in inspiration. The second part is a complete course of studies. Throughout the book the authorities and religion are scrupulously respected, while the "philosophic spirit," so predominant in La Chalotais' *Essai*, is all but absent. In substance *De l'éducation publique* is very much like the *Essai d'éducation nationale*, as the author of the

---

[79] The *Nouvelles ecclésiastiques* article of 31 October 1763 adopted a similar tone.

[80] The question of the authorship of *De l'éducation publique* is an agitated one. In the first edition of his *Dictionnaire des anonymes*, Barbier says of the work that "half appears written by a *philosophe*, the other half by a Jansenist" (quoted from the *Correspondance littéraire*, v, 259, n. 2). In the second edition of the *Dictionnaire*, Barbier identifies Crévier as the principal author. The *Journal encyclopédique*, 1763 IV-2, p. 33, asserts that "M. D." an "Auteur Philosophe," had written the work. Bachaumont says of it that "quoiqu'il ne soit plein que de vues saines & d'une philosophie sage et usuelle, on l'attribue à M. Diderot" (*Mémoires secrets*, I, 185; 21 January 1763). Grimm admits that ". . . il se peut que le philosophe ait vu ce manuscrit et qu'il y ait mis quelques phrases, . . ." but denies that the substance of the work could be his friend's (*Correspondance littéraire*, v, 259). A modern scholar has found from Diderot's correspondence that the encyclopedist did in fact retouch the work, and that he even had a hand in its publication (Roland Mortier, "The 'Philosophes' and Public Education," in *Yale French Studies*, no. 40, p. 67). Mortier goes on to suggest that the principal author of *De l'éducation publique* may be F. D. Rivard, an old teacher of Diderot's. This may be the case, but if so it changes little, for Rivard was a colleague of Crévier's at the Collège de Beauvais, and like him a Jansenist. It is more likely, however, that Rivard acted as an intermediary between his colleague and his old student, and that Barbier was right in suggesting Crévier to be the principal author of *De l'éducation publique*. At all events he was certainly correct in identifying the book as the product of the seemingly unlikely union of Jansenist and *philosophe*.

latter work himself noted.[81] There were only two points upon which La Chalotais differed fundamentally from the author of the work which had appeared just before his. First, Crévier preferred clerics to laymen as teachers, and second, he did not allow as many schools.[82]

Crévier did indeed want a large number of schools. He proposed a five-level system of education, beginning with *petites écoles* in the countryside and culminating with what amounted to *collèges de plein exercice* in major towns.[83] None, not even the most humble peasant, was to be without elementary instruction, for:

> Les Enfans les plus pauvres n'en sont pas moins les Enfans de la Patrie; c'est de-là qui viennent les Artisans, les Laboureurs et les Soldats sans lesquels il n'y a ni Etat ni patrie.[84]

The curriculum proposed for the schools of the first degree consisted of reading, writing, arithmetic, a catechism and a course in agriculture.[85] Crévier emphasized the utility of the subjects he wanted taught, and it was to utility

---

[81] La Chalotais, *Essai d'éducation nationale*, p. 150.

[82] Ibid., p. 150. These are precisely the two points on which Voltaire commends La Chalotais. See above pp. 93-94.

[83] The five levels of schools proposed by Crévier correspond to degrees of urbanization. The first is intended for villages, the second for *bourgs* (at least one thousand residents), the third for small towns (two to six thousand inhabitants), the fourth for middle-sized towns (up to fifteen thousand inhabitants), and the fifth for provincial capitals. Crévier, *De l'éducation publique* (Amsterdam, 1763), pp. 165-74.

[84] Ibid., p. 159. It will be noted that the reason given here to justify the education of the people is different from that given in the *Difficultés*. This should cause little surprise. First, this statement must be kept in perspective; the importance of religion is recognized throughout the work, so that there is no need to make a special plea on its behalf. Second, the nature of the two works of Crévier must be taken into account; the *Difficultés* is a polemic, *De l'éducation publique* an exposition. Third, in the later work, Crévier had a collaborator. Finally, it is not at all incongruous for a Jansenist to appeal his *patrie*. On a secular level Jansenist opposition to ultramontanism tends naturally to patriotism.

[85] Ibid., pp. 166-67.

that he had recourse to reply as if in advance to the sort of criticism that La Chalotais was to make of popular education:

> Il ne s'agit pas de les [peasants and workers] dégouter des travaux auxquels ils se trouvent comme naturellement destinés; mais de les en rendre plus capables. Il convient d'augmenter les cultivateurs plutôt que d'en diminuer le nombre; mais il faut aussi les former à ce qu'ils doivent être, et s'il en est qui announcent quelque talent supérieur, il faut des ressources pour les seconder.[86]

It will be seen that Crévier's efforts to parry likely objections to popular education in no way prevented them being made.

The response in *philosophe* circles to these two works by Crévier varied. We have already seen La Chalotais' reaction to *De l'éducation publique*. Bachaumont reported that the book had been generally well received and himself approved it.[87] When discussing La Chalotais' *Essai* later in the year he compared it with the work of Crévier and his collaborator, observing that the principles of the two books were similar, but that they differed in methodology.[88] Grimm evaluated the two works rather differently. He admitted that they had much in common, but asserted that Crévier's book was vastly inferior to La Chalotais', and that "there is a great difference between a philosopher who proposes a reasoned plan and a professor who pedantically arranges the distribution of classes."[89] Mentioning the *Essai* in a letter to La Chalotais, Voltaire wrote, "I am in no way surprised, sir, that the *pedantic, heavy, grimy* [*crasseux*] and *vain* [i.e. Crévier] should be angry that a man who has not the honor to be a pedant of the university should teach him

---

[86] Ibid., p. 161.

[87] Bachaumont, *Mémoires secrets*, i, 185 (21 January, 1763).

[88] Ibid., i, 238 (13 May, 1763).

[89] Grimm, *Correspondance littéraire*, v, 309.

his business."[90] Grimm was no kinder, styling the author of the *Difficultés* "a sad and flat pedant."[91] When Crévier died in 1765 at the age of 73, Grimm disparagingly noted that he had continued Rollin's *History*, written a history of the University of Paris and other works, "which are full of all the dullness and pedantry of a good Jansenist that one would believe was a thousand leagues from the center of light, or several centuries behind the one in which we live."[92]

Reading the *philosophe* criticisms of Crévier, one cannot help but be taken aback by the arguments used. Name-calling is not a very elevated form of argumentation, and all the more so when the names are unmerited. Crévier showed himself more than a narrow-minded cleric in *De l'éducation publique*, and much more than a pedant in the *Difficultés*. He was not at all the benighted fanatic he was described to be. But there is, after all, some truth in the allegation that he was far from the "center of light."

For while Crévier could write (or at least collaborate in) a work whose treatment of the sciences was encyclopedist in inspiration, in matters of religion and moral philosophy he was far indeed from the world of the *lumières*. When engaged in polemics, as against La Chalotais, the elderly Jansenist scholar was restrained, reasonable and moderate. But the views he expressed with reason and moderation were predicated upon the supposition that man and the

---

[90] Voltaire, letter to La Chalotais, 9 June, 1763, in Voltaire's *Oeuvres*, LXXXII, 331. Voltaire has underscored the epithets, *"pedant, lourd, crasseux et vain"* to bring attention to the fact that he is quoting from himself. He had previously written in a satirical poem entitled, "Les Chevaux et les Anes ou Etrennes aux sots" (1762):

> Le lourd Crévier, pedant, crasseux et vain,
> Prend hardiment la place de Rollin,
> Comme un valet prend l'habit de son maître.
>
> (*Oeuvres*, XVI, 180)

[91] Grimm, *Correspondance littéraire*, V, 391.
[92] Ibid., VI, 449.

world are corrupt; that without divine grace man is incapable of good; that salvation is the *summum bonum*; and that
the ephemeral interests of this world must everywhere be
subordinated to the ultimate good of the world to come. It
was for reasons of this order that Crévier pleaded the cause
of the people for an education. It is true that he denied
that the education he was advocating would result in the
abandonment of agriculture or in social upheaval, but he
did so because he was aware of the objections that his pro-
posals would raise among certain of his contemporaries.
For him the argument from social utility was subordinate
and auxiliary to other considerations. What was important
to the elderly Jansenist was not that a peasant who had
learned to read and write might become a lackey or clerk
or author in a town, but that he might, with the aid of devo-
tional books, be helped toward his salvation. If there was a
risk to be taken here, Crévier would take it gladly, for the
stakes more than justified it. For Voltaire and La Chalotais,
on the other hand, there was no wager, only the danger of
disrupting society for the sake of an illusion.

THE DANGERS OF EDUCATION AND THE JANSENIST IMPERATIVE

Certain other works that appeared shortly after the expulsion of the Jesuits from France, while for the most part
devoted to the *collèges*, also raised the question of the education of the people. The dangers of education reaching too
far down the social scale were discussed in particular by
Guyton de Morveau, Jean Henri Samuel Formey and the
legal officer Granet. Morveau, who served in the Parlement of Dijon, was also a distinguished chemist and a
member of the Dijon Academy. After 1789 he played an
active part in the Revolutionary assemblies, where, among
other things, he sat on the committee of public instruction
and was instrumental in the founding of the *Ecole*

Polytechnique.[93] Formey's career was no less impressive. He was secretary of the Berlin Academy, privy counselor to Frederick II, and a collaborator in the *Encyclopédie*. Indeed, he was more an encyclopedist than most. Formey intended to publish a philosophical dictionary of his own, and was only dissuaded from doing so by the publishers of Diderot's *Encyclopédie*, who bought the manuscript of his projected book. He then collaborated on the work directed by Diderot and d'Alembert, contributaing no less than eighty articles.[94] Formey was also a Protestant pastor, a professional educator, and an active defender of Christianity.[95] The more humble Granet was a legal official of the *sénéchaussée* of Toulon. The opinions of these men, very much in harmony with those of La Chalotais, will serve to amplify the position of those members of the enlightened community who saw more harm than good in popular education. The opposing view on the instruction of the lower classes was championed by the pedagogue F. D. Rivard, Crévier's colleague at the Collège de Beauvais, and like him, a Jansenist.

In his *Mémoire sur l'éducation publique*, Guyton de Morveau, like a true son of the Enlightenment, proclaimed the utility of letters to be unquestionable.[96] Using rhetoric typical of the period, he condemned ignorance and its effects, asserting that:

> ... l'gnorance n'a jamais fait que du mal, qu'elle entraîne toujours après elle la barbarie, & que si elle est un bou-

[93] For a fuller sketch of Morveau's career see Barnard, *The French Revolution and the Schools*, p. 138.

[94] Jacques Proust, *L'Encyclopédie* (Paris, 1965), p. 82.

[95] Formey was a professor of eloquence and later held the chair of philosophy in the *collège français* of Berlin. Among his publications are the *Philosophe chrétien* (1749), *Pensées raisonnables opposées aux pensées philosophiques* (1749), and an *Anti Emile*, with the subtitle *tais-toi Jean-Jacques* (1763).

[96] Guyton de Morveau, *Mémoire sur l'éducation publique avec la prospectus d'un collège, Suivant les Principes de cet Ouvrage* (n.p., 1764), p. 35.

clier impénétrable contre le Pyrrhonisme, elle est aussi le principe de l'acharnement de l'erreur & des fureurs de la superstition, mille fois plus à craindre: qu'il est au contraire de l'essence des Lettres d'éclairer l'esprit, d'élever l'ame, d'adoucir les moeurs, de préparer à la vertu.[97]

Yet Morveau, like La Chalotais, who held similar views on the worth of the *lumières*, did not regard learning as an unqualified good. But he was rather more clear than the Breton magistrate in explaining the principles on which education was to be extended or restrained. Morveau quoted a "Philosophe moderne" to the effect that:

... tous les talens ne doivent pas être developpés, parce qu'il faudroit pour cela que le nombre de ceux qui les possedent, fut exactement proportionné aux besoins de la société; & que si on enlevoit au travail de la terre tous ceux qui sont plus propres à un autre talent, il n'en resteroit pas assez pour la cultiver & nous faire vivre.[98]

The principle of economic utility to which Morveau appealed demanded that only after essential professions were filled (those of farmer, merchant, artisan and soldier) could the class of men of letters grow without prejudice to the state. In the France of his time, Morveau held, education at the secondary (*collège*) level was too readily available and too widespread, so that, "a remedy should be sought for the excessive progress of Letters."[99] Guyton did not share La Chalotais' fear of the working population learning to read and write,[100] but he was concerned about *collèges* spoiling potential members of the labor force.

---

[97] Ibid., p. 36.

[98] Ibid., p. 43. The quotation is from Rousseau's *Nouvelle Héloïse*, book v, letter 2.

[99] Guyton, *Mémoire*, p. 45.

[100] Morveau was convinced that among the "rough men" who made up the population of rural France, "the torch of philosophy will always remain extinguished ..." (ibid., p. 15). "Philosophy" is of course not to be confused with literacy.

Views similar to those of Guyton were expressed by a German Protestant replying to an essay contest set by a Dutch academy. The question proposed by the *Société des sciences* of Harlem for 1762 was, "how should one govern the mind and heart of a child in order to render him happy and useful?" The German whose essay won the prize offered by the academy was J.H.S. Formey.

Formey, too, believed that, "it is not fitting that all men be instructed," and added that he did not regard this opinion as excessively bold.[101] It must not be assumed, however, that when he used the term "instructed," Formey had all forms of education in mind. He insisted that all must be taught the general principles of morality and religion and was convinced that the teaching of these principles presupposed the ability to read and write. Though he did not think it expedient that the education of the lower classes be any broader than this, Formey seems not to have shared La Chalotais' antipathy to *petites écoles* and charity schools.[102] He would, on the other hand, have agreed with Morveau that the generalization of secondary education was to be feared.

The new element introduced by Formey into the discussion was to consider not only the economic, but also the social, utility and inconveniences of educating the people. The lower rungs of the social scale, Formey observed, are never very comfortable for those who occupy them. Should the laboring poor come to understand their situation, and what it might (or ought to) have been, they would fall into restiveness or despair. Now neither of these frames of mind are conducive to satisfactory fulfillment by the lower classes of their vocation, which is to perform the most un-

---

[101] J.H.S. Formey, *Traité d'éducation morale Qui a remporté le prix de la Société des Sciences de Harlem, l'an 1762, sur cette Question: "Comment on doit gouverner l'esprit & le coeur d'un Enfant; pour le rendre heureux & utile"* (Liège, 1773), p. 21. Future references will be given with the author's name and the designation *Traité*.

[102] Ibid., pp. 21-22.

pleasant and least rewarding tasks in society. But Formey is
far too eloquent on this point not to be allowed to speak for
himself. He writes:

> Pour que les hommes demeurent tranquilles dans des
> conditions & dans des occupations qui les rabaissent,
> presque au niveau des Bêtes de somme, il est à propos
> qu'ils n'élevent & ne fortifient pas leur âme de manière à
> s'appercevoir trop clairement de sa noblesse & de son
> excellence, à sentir trop vivement cette égalité naturelle
> & primitive à laquelle la forme des Sociétés porte de si
> rudes attentes. Alors ils tomberoient aisément dans le
> découragement & dans le murmure; ils feroient comme
> ces Négres, que, tantôt désolés de leur captivité, sçavent
> la terminer en se suffoquant eux-mêmes par un art sin-
> gulier qu'ils ont de replier la langue & de la retirer dans
> le gosier; ou tantôt, furieux des mauvais traitements
> dont ils sont excédés, se révoltent & causent de funestes
> ravages, dont on a des exemples. Si ces Négres avoient
> plus de lumières encore, plus de connoissances tant ré-
> fléchies qu'expérimentales, ils porteroient leur joug avec
> bien plus d'impatience, ils seroient bien plus habiles à le
> secouer. L'application est aisée.[103]

Formey's application of this principle was to advise governments to "preside over the dissemination of knowledge
(*lumières*) so that there should be enough but not too
much."[104] To illustrate his point that the *lumières* may
spread too far or too fast the permanent secretary of the
Berlin Academy observed:

> C'est plutôt un malheur qu'un bonheur pour une Na-
> tion, lorsqu'un certain goût de lecture & d'étude s'y ré-
> pand trop, & gagne jusqu'aux plus bas étages de la
> Société. Au lieu que cela fasse des gens instruits, sensés, &
> solides, cela fait des discoureurs & des raisonneurs, qui
> veulent juger de tout, dont la tête s'embarrasse et

---

[103] Ibid., p. 23. [104] Ibid., p. 24.

s'échauffe mal-à-propos sur des sujets qui ne sont ni ne peuvent devenir de leur ressort, & qui perdent par-là cette docilité qui est le pivot du Gouvernement.[105]

Ignorance, it appears, has its value, learning its dangers. The balance between them is precarious.

Even more sensitive than Formey to the dangers of educating the laboring poor was Granet, the lieutenant general of the *sénéchaussée* of Toulon in the years following the expulsion of the Jesuits from France. In a long memoir written during 1764 on the state of education in the area around Toulon, Granet repeatedly warned of the dangers of the people receiving anything more than religious instruction. He quoted Mandeville to the effect that "in order to render society happy it is necessary that a great number of its members be ignorant as well as poor,"[106] and endorsed the English writer's opinion that "each hour that poor children spend on books is that much time lost to society."[107] Still following Mandeville, Granet asserted that the ability to read, write and do sums was necessary for those for whom these skills were professional requirements, but that "this knowledge is highly pernicious for poor folk."[108]

It is little wonder, in the light of the opinions just cited, that Granet admired La Chalotais' book, which he referred to as "a work which contains the principles and the base of national education," and quoted in full the passage in which the author complained of the poor attending schools.[109] Granet further picked up La Chalotais' hint about the *Frères des écoles chrétiennes* being the successors of the Jesuits. He emphasized the similarities between the two orders, implying that the fate of the one was deserved by the other. Graneţ's own suggestion for an educational pol-

---

[105] Loc. cit.

[106] Granet, *Mémoire sur l'éducation publique dans le ressort de la sénéchaussée de Toulon*, A Mun. Toulon, GG 54, p. 100. Henceforth *Mémoire*.

[107] Ibid., p. 111.

[108] Loc. cit.   [109] Ibid., pp. 122-23.

icy for the poor was to shut down primary schools ("Les Ecoles élémentaires," i.e., *petites écoles*) and to close the *collèges* to "every son of a worker (*ouvrier*) or peasant . . . unless there should be a deserving exception."[110]

Views opposed to those of Morveau, Formey and Granet came initially from men who would not always be recognized as belonging to the enlightened community. In the mind of F. D. Rivard, Crévier's colleague at the Collège de Beauvais, there was no balance to be maintained between learning and ignorance. The former he regarded as good, the latter as evil, and evil was to have no place in the world Rivard hoped to see emerge.

Rivard was not only a professor of philosophy, but also the author of numerous texts on the natural sciences, mathematics, geography and French grammar. He is credited by one of his students—Diderot—with having introduced the teaching of mathematics into the University of Paris.[111] He was, too, a Latinist of consummate ability, for he published an edition of the vulgate without a single error. But above all, Rivard was a sincere and devoted Catholic. He practiced good works, among them the establishment of charity schools for the urban poor, and retired from his distinguished career as a teacher to end his life in penance and prayer. His Catholicism was not, however, altogether orthodox. Rivard was sufficiently devoted to the Jansenist cause to oppose the University's acceptance of Unigenitus in 1739, and as a result was excluded from that institution's assembly. Like Rollin he was ranked among the friends and defenders of truth, and like Crévier, his obituary appeared in the *Nouvelles ecclésiastiques*.[112]

Rivard had little in common with those who sought a "remedy for the excessive progress of Letters" or wished to

---

[110] Ibid., pp. 148-49.   [111] Diderot, *Oeuvres*, III, 452.

[112] Chapotin, *Le Collège de Dormans-Beauvais*, p. 369; Abbé R. Cerveau, *Suite du Nécrologe des plus célébres defenseurs de la vérité du dix-huitième siécle, depuis 1767 jusqu'à 1778* (n.p., 1778), pp. 225-28; *Nouvelles ecclésiastiques*, 1778, p. 99.

close the schools to the lower classes. On the contrary, he proposed that *petits collèges* to teach the 7e to 3e classes[113] be opened in the faubourg St. Antoine for the convenience of its residents who could not afford the cost of a *pension*.[114] It was the opinion of this professor of philosophy that all children, even those "with mediocre or very limited ability" should have an education equivalent to the lower classes of the *collèges*.[115] He viewed with equanimity the prospect of a child either adopting a trade or continuing his education after the 3e class.[116] Rivard did not in fact expect the majority of students to continue beyond the 3e, but he did favor providing the capable poor with necessary aid so that they could continue their studies.[117]

It is largely by his conception of man without education that Rivard's insistence on treating the poor with all possible consideration and providing basic instruction for all is to be explained. The uneducated are said to pass their

[113] The *collège* of the old regime provided an almost exclusively literary and classical education that was of no immediate professional value (Morveau, *Mémoire*, p. 78). The first class was usually the *sixième*, and was followed by the *cinquième*, *quatrième*, and *troisième* classes. The *deuxième* was usually referred to as the humanities class and the *première* as the rhetoric class. After rhetoric came a philosophy course, which was generally two years long, the first year being devoted to logic, the second to "physique." A *collège de plein exercice* had all classes up to and including philosophy, but it was common, especially in the case of provincial *collèges*, to have classes only up to humanities or rhetoric.

[114] F.D. Rivard, *Recueil de Mémoires touchant l'Éducation de la Jeunesse, Surtout par rapport aux Études* (Paris, 1763), p. 74. The proposed *collèges* are also to provide teaching experience for the students of a training school for teachers that Rivard was proposing.

[115] Ibid., p. 79.

[116] A child would normally enter the 7e class of a *collège* at the age of about eight, and by the time he would have reached the 3e would be 12 or 13 (ibid., p. 242).

[117] Ibid., p. 340. Though Rivard favored social mobility through education when a poor child's talent unquestionably justified his advancement, he normally wanted the poor, "raised well according to their condition [état]" (ibid., p. 240). On the other hand, he also cautioned against advancing the rich who lack the necessary ability or talent (ibid., pp. 340-41).

whole lives in a state of "ignorance and stupidity" which is likened to "a kind of childhood."[118] If they remain without proper instruction, men are trapped in the state of sinfulness and corruption in which all are inevitably, though through no fault of their own, born. In Rivard's eyes, the ignorance in which the greater part of France's population lived was pernicious. But more than this it was also manifestly contrary to the intentions of providence, for he deduced from the fact that man was endowed with intelligence the proof that men were meant to develop and use their minds.[119]

The first and greatest task of education for the author of the *Recueil* was to bring man to the recognition of his Creator.[120] It seems that implicit in Rivard's outlook is the proposition that if man was born part of corrupted nature, he must work to raise himself toward the state of grace. Education was one way of doing this. Rivard regarded catechisms and sermons as important educational tools, though inadequate in themselves. He also felt that the Christian had to be fluently literate so that he could profitably read "books of piety and instruction so that they can better learn the things they have been taught."[121] Rivard even wished to see "almost all children" taught Latin so that they could read works of piety written in that language and understand the church service.[122]

Rivard was not content, however, to have men learn their religion from books alone. Like many of his contemporaries—Voltaire among them—he believed that

[118] Ibid., pp. 328-29.

[119] "Si Dieu a donnè aux hommes un fonds de bon sens & d'intelligence, c'est sans doute afin quils s'en servent. Or pour être en état d'en faire usage, il faut que ce fonds soit cultivé: autrement c'est comme une terre en friche qui ne produit que des ronces & des épines" (ibid., p. 324).

[120] The three principal benefits to be derived from education are listed in order of declining importance as follows: "(1) to know God (2) to acquit themselves of their different duties with respect to all men (3) to procure for themselves the necessities of life . . ." (ibid., p. 326).

[121] Ibid., p. 323.   [122] Ibid., pp. 323-24.

the works of the Creator are everywhere written in nature, and could be read by those who had the requisite understanding of natural science.[123] Just as the Jansenist pedagogue found proof of a divine presence in nature, so too did he find that "it is by natural knowledge that one proves the truth of religion. . . ."[124] Though Rivard deplored the spread of incredulity and the doctrines of certain "so-called philosophers," he had the confidence to argue that the young were best armed against incredulity not by ignorance, but by a critical exposure to the doctrines of unbelievers, and by study of the "true" philosophy.[125]

Education was not for Rivard, and for those who thought like him, merely a matter of training the mind. Its principal goal was a moral one, and the most important "science" that of overcoming the passions.[126] This moral education, although more important, was more difficult, by reason of the "corruption that man derives from his origin, and of which everyone has sad experience."[127]

This avowal of the Augustinian concept of man as radically corrupt and incapable of achieving his salvation without grace brings out an underlying paradox in the writings of the two scholarly Jansenists whose views are under consideration. While admitting the inefficacy of works—of which education is one—without grace, Crévier and Rivard placed great emphasis on the task of educating the young. It is as if they held that man does do his part to achieve salvation, although the strict Augustinian doctrine is that grace is given gratuitously, and man is powerless to change this.[128] Nor do either Crévier or Rivard draw the perfectly

---

[123] Ibid., pp. 329 and 336-37.   [124] Ibid., p. 29.

[125] Ibid., pp. 30, 48 and 347-48.   [126] Ibid., p. 384.

[127] Ibid., p. 84. Rivard remarked elsewhere that, "we all bear in ourselves a fund of corruption always ready to bear bad fruit . . ." (ibid., p. 218).

[128] Rivard recognized this explicitly in stating that "men only have the power and even the will to do good in that they receive it from His omnipotence . . ." (ibid., p. 390).

logical conclusion that since man is corrupt by nature he will pervert the morally neutral skills acquired through education. They do not fear, for example, that a peasant, who like all men has a natural penchant to evil, will turn to books containing unorthodox doctrines or simply to good lusty novels, rather than books of piety after having learned to read. Yet nothing could be more logical. The Jansenist outlook—or perhaps simply the outlook of these two Jansenists[129]—does not appear altogether consistent. Whether explained by compassion for one's fellows and equals (for all souls are equal) or by the belief that although all human effort is vain one is nevertheless obliged to make this effort, the inconsistencies in this view do credit to those who held and expounded it.

Yet these inconsistencies do not, perhaps, defy explanation. Jansenism is characterized not only by a theological premise, but also by a certain "psychological orientation," which an outstanding scholar of the subject asserts has two main aspects. On the one hand there is the conception of a "profoundly demanding form of Christianity, which wishes to be lived without compromises or concessions,"[130]

---

[129] One may say, paraphrasing La Bruyère, that he who says Jansenism says more than one thing. There is the theological side of the movement, inspired by a rigorist Augustinianism, but there is also its political aspect, Gallican and oppositionist, which supported the king against the pope and the parlements against the crown. Nor should one neglect the transformation the movement underwent after its official condemnation in the eighteenth century. In a recent article bringing attention to the need to study the relation of Jansenism to the Enlightenment, Robert Shackleton points out that "the Jansenist political outlook changed from the divine-right ideas of Jansenius and Quesnel to maxims of resistance and fundamental law after the bull *Unigenitus* of 1713" (VS, LVIII, 1967, p. 1,390). Jansenism of course had its mystics and millenarians too. But it would be foolish to seek to identify serious intellectuals such as Crévier and Rivard with the convulsionaries of St. Medard. The warning of Orcibal that it is more accurate to speak of kinds of Jansenism rather than "Jansenism" is germane (J. Orcibal, "Qu'est-ce que le jansénisme?" in *Cahiers de l'association internationale des Etudes françaises*, no. 3, July 1954, p. 52).

[130] L. Cognet, *Le Jansénisme* (Paris, 1968), p. 124. Orcibal likewise asserts

and which resulted in the cases of Crévier and Rivard in a certain humility and an unquestionable sincerity. On the other hand there is what M. Cognet calls "an intense consciousness of the rights of the individual and especially of personal thought in opposition to the absolutisms of authority."[131] It is this aspect of the Jansenism of the two men that is in evidence when they demand that the people not only have religious instruction, but also that they be sufficiently instructed to understand what they are taught, and be made capable of continuing to study by themselves.

The religious function of education in Rivard's *Recueil* has been emphasized because it is fundamental. It must, however, be kept in perspective, for Rivard also treated education from the point of view of La Chalotais, Morveau and Formey. He justified educating the people not only on the grounds of religious obligation, but also on those of utility and social order. Though he sought to form good Christians, he insisted that he was at the same time training good citizens for the state.[132] He pointed out that lack of education resulted in loss of human resources to both church and state and that ordinary men if uneducated would more often prove a liability to society.[133] Like Terrisse, Rivard argued that an educated peasantry would contribute to the improvement of agriculture, which, he noted, was an overriding concern of contemporaries.[134] But realizing that this view of things was not widely held, he added a long note to the *Recueil* just before publication

that "one of the rare traits common to the Port Royalists was a passionate attachment to primitive Christianity, whose purity and saintliness they wished to revive" ("Qu'est-ce que le jansénisme?" p. 46).

[131] Cognet, *Le Jansénisme*, p. 124. R. Tavenaux sees the individualism fostered by Jansenism as the key to its appeal to those groups, especially of royal officers and magistrates, which were not fully integrated into feudal or royal structures ("Jansénisme et vie sociale en France au XVIIe siècle," in the *Revue d'histoire de l'église de France*, no. 152 [January-June 1968], pp. 33 and 46).

[132] Rivard, *Recueil*, p. 386.

[133] Ibid., pp. 79 and 228.   [134] Ibid., p. 326.

denying what so many then believed, namely, that educating country dwellers would bring them to conceive "a distaste for their labors which are harsh [*pénibles*] and regarded as scarcely honorable."[135] In contrast to Formey, Rivard regarded education as a support of the social order. For the Jansenist it was ignorance, not an excess of learning that was dangerous. In his opinion:

> . . . la tranquillité de l'Etat est intéressée à ce que les sujets soient instruits: une populace qui croupit dans l'ignorance est facile à émouvoir, une imagination échauffée est capable de la porter aux dernieres extrémités, parce qu'elle n'est arrêtée par aucun principe qui la retienne dans le devoir: il n'en est pas de même des peuples qui sont instruits; ils sçavent ce qu'ils doivent à l'Etat et au Souverain, et d'ailleurs ils sentent mieux les dangers qu'ils courroient en lui manquant de soumission et de fidélité. Tout cela fait voir la nécessité de prendre les moyens convenables pour instruire les Peuples de la Religion et de leurs devoirs, tant par rapport à Dieu que par rapport aux hommes.[136]

So conceived, education poses no threat to social order. Rather it assures that religion be respected and the temporal authorities obeyed, and becomes, in fact, a form of social control.

Rivard's arguments here met those of the magistrates and *philosophes* on their own ground. The Jansenist seems half a *philosophe* himself—and no doubt he is. Peter Gay has rightly criticized the popular view of the Enlightenment for taking over many nineteenth-century misrepresentations of the movement.[137] It is my opinion that certain eighteenth-century misrepresentations have survived also, and that the most notable of these concerns the church and Christianity.

---

[135] Ibid., p. xl.
[136] Ibid., p. 325.
[137] Gay, "The Party of Humanity," p. 265.

The Catholic church was not the great monolith of darkness that many *philosophes* believed or pretended it was, nor were all devout Christians fanatics or obscurantists. This has often been assumed to be so, however, and for this reason the ability of the church, or perhaps better, of Christianity, to adapt to the Enlightenment has been seriously underestimated. It is of course true that on certain fundamental issues, such as the authority of the church, the gulf remained unbridgeable; but there were other areas where the gap was diminished, and even ceased to exist. In fact there was a vast middle ground on which Christianity and even its rigorist Jansenist variant and the Enlightenment could come to terms. If this has too often been overlooked, it is because the relation of the church to the Enlightenment, at least in France, has for the most part been seen through the polemics of churchmen and *philosophes* (especially *philosophes*), and polemics tend to maximize differences. While Voltaire was declaiming against *l'infâme*, the Jesuits were adopting the science of the Enlightenment,[138] and certain Jansenists, as we have just seen, were couching their arguments in terms of economic and social utility. To accept the concepts of the new science and the language of utility was at least in part to accept the new mentality.

It is worth emphasizing the partial acceptance of the Enlightenment attitude of mind by Rivard and Crévier for it underscores the fact that enlightenment values spread gradually and unevenly. Conversely, it should be noted that certain *philosophes* retained important elements of the Christian world view. Formey is a case in point.

In writing his essay on how education might render men

---

[138] F. de Dainville, "L'enseignement scientifique dans les collèges des jésuites," in *Enseignement et diffusion des sciences en France au XVIIIe siècle*, R. Taton, ed. (Paris, 1964). It should be noted, too, that the Jesuit *Journal de Trévoux* at first received the *Encyclopédie* well, and came to criticize it harshly more on account of plagiarism than of unorthodoxy (Palmer, *Catholics and Unbelievers*, pp. 18-19).

both useful and happy, the Berlin academician stated that it was his intention to produce not only a "worthy member of temporal society" but also a "presumptive member of eternal society."[139] Though Formey's outlook was for the most part formed by the science and philosophy of his day, he could assert that "the wellspring of happiness is in heaven and all that we possess of it on earth should be regarded as a stream flowing from that source."[140] He could also refer casually to the existence of an elect few, and though in places he evidenced a Rousseauist faith in the goodness of human nature, the pastor-encyclopedist also affirmed that "without God and without religion man is the most vile and the most unhappy of all creatures."[141] At this point significant differences in the outlooks of Formey and Rivard or Crévier seem to vanish. Since the three men shared the same basic set of ideas, is it justifiable to regard the first (his activities as an encyclopedist aside) primarily as a *philosophe*, and the other two primarily as Jansenists? I submit that it is, for although all three men do share the same basic set of ideas, they structure them differently, and this is the crucial point. In Rivard's system of values, as in Crévier's, utility will be subordinated to religious considerations, in Formey's utility predominates. Thus it is correct to regard Formey as a *philosophe* and Crévier and Rivard as Jansenists; but one misses the point if he fails to see how much of the *philosophe* there is in the Jansenists, and in this case, how much of the Christian in the *philosophe*.

THE EMERGENCE OF THE DOMINANT ENLIGHTENMENT VIEW OF POPULAR INSTRUCTION: A "FITTING" EDUCATION

The dominant Enlightenment attitude toward the education of the people originates in the resolution of a fundamental contradiction in the writings of La Chalotais,

---

[139] Formey, *Traité*, p. 6.
[140] Ibid., p. 239.
[141] Ibid., pp. 235, 51 and 122.

Morveau and Formey. On the one hand, all three of these men condemned ignorance and praised enlightenment; on the other, they all, in varying degrees, opposed the spread of education among the lower classes. If such a position is inconsistent, it is at least readily explicable. La Chalotais and the other two like-minded authors were caught in a dilemma, on the one horn of which were the dangers contingent upon the ignorance of the laboring population, and on the other, those that followed upon its education. So conceived, the education of the people indeed poses an insoluble conundrum. But then it is precisely the refusal to accept this conundrum that characterizes the dominant Enlightenment view of popular education.

Other writers searched for a middle way between ignorance and overeducation. They found it in the concept of an education fitting to one's place in society, and in some cases an education designed to induce the lower classes to accept their place in the constituted social order. This concept of popular education was most notably set forth and elaborated at this time in a report presented by a *président à mortier* to the Parlement of Paris in 1768, in an extended article which appeared in a physiocrat journal during 1765-66, and in a discourse pronounced before a provincial academy in 1769.

Rolland d'Erceville's report to the Parlement of Paris in May 1768 contained a plan of education which is of special interest in that it expresses the views not primarily of a theoretician, but of a man actively engaged in implementing educational reforms. Rolland was one of the commissioners appointed by the parlement to handle the reorganization of the former Jesuit *collèges* within its jurisdiction, and played a central part in the administration of the great Parisian *collège*, Louis-le-Grand. His 1768 report is consciously eclectic, presenting a plan of studies which, the parlementaire asserted, "is not my work, but the result, or rather an extract, of all that has appeared, or all that has been brought to my attention concerning

Education. . . ."[142] In its ambiguities and contradictions as well as in its fundamental assumptions it reflects the attitudes of many of his contemporaries to education.

Characteristically, Rolland evoked the dangers of both ignorance and learning. He pointed out that "the more ignorant the people is the more ready it is to be subjugated, either by its own prejudices or by the charlatans of all kinds that beseige it."[143] Conversely, "a kingdom is never more flourishing than when reason is most generally cultivated."[144] But the cultivation of reason is not without drawbacks. A bad or incomplete education may produce "de fruits grossiers, ou peut être même dangereux"; superficial learning and bad taste may be "more harmful to a people than ignorance and barbarity."[145]

In commenting on a memoir of the University of Paris, Rolland was similarly ambivalent. He noted what he considered the justified apprehension of the university that "too great a number of students depopulate the countryside and harm the trades [Arts] and agriculture"; yet he ascribed to the University the view that "education cannot be too widespread."[146] Rolland accepted both these statements, and explained them as follows:

> . . . je suis persuadé que le principe, *qu'il est nécessaire et convenable de procurer de l'Education à tous les Sujets du Roi*, doit avoir ses bornes, & je suis bien éloigné de penser que ce principe autorise la multiplicité des Colléges . . . car il est vrai tout à la fois, & que l'éducation ne peut être trop

[142] Rolland d'Erceville, *Compte Rendu aux Chambres assemblées, Par M. Rolland, des différens Mémoires envoyés par les Universités sises dans le Ressort de la Cour, en exécution de l'Arrêt des Chambres assemblées, du 3 Septembre 1762, relativement au plan d'Etudes à suivre dans les Collèges non dépendans des Universités, & à la correspondance à établir entre les Collèges & les Universités* (Paris, 1768), p. 3.

[143] Ibid., p. 20.   [144] Ibid., p. 18.   [145] Ibid., p. 10.

[146] Ibid., p. 18. Rolland has in fact reversed the sense of the University's memoir, which in observing that there was a danger of education draining the productive professions was implying precisely that education could be too widespread.

générale, & que les Colléges de plein exercice sont trop multipliés; l'on ne doit jamais perdre de vue ce principe, *que chacun doit être à portée de recevoir l'éducation qui lui est propre*; or chaque terre n'est pas susceptible du même soin & du même produit, chaque esprit ne demande pas le même degré de culture; tous les hommes n'ont ni les mêmes besoins, ni les mêmes talens, & c'est en proportion de ces talens & de ces besoins que doit être reglée l'éducation publique.[147]

In Rolland's view all should receive an education, but this education should be limited both by socioeconomic need and by ability.[148]

The emphasis on the proper limits within which education was to be contained is essential, for knowledge was seen as a force that was never neutral. If practiced poorly, education threatened to produce unsatisfactory results, so that it may be regarded as dangerous; if not properly limited, it was thought, learning would siphon off necessary labor from the trades and agriculture. On the other hand, if education were properly directed, national well-being would be fostered, and "both religion and the state would gain faithful servants."[149] Members of the enlightened community saw clearly both the dangers and advantages of education. They chose in increasing numbers to risk the dangers for the sake of the advantages, and at the same time sought to minimize the dangers by keeping instruction within boundaries set by social and economic utility.

The concept of an education suited to one's place in society, expressed so forcefully by Rolland in 1768, had already been suggested at the very beginning of the debate

[147] Ibid., pp. 18-20.

[148] Rolland reasoned that: "There is no one in the state who should not have religion, morals and knowledge relative to the occupation he exercises; the knowledge of reading and writing, which is the key to all other kinds of knowledge, should therefore be universally widespread . . ." (ibid., p. 20).

[149] Ibid., p. 20.

on the education of the people. It has been noted that Crévier did not want the people to conceive a distaste for their
condition, and that Rivard desired to see the poor educated according to their social standing (*état*).[150] This idea
was also developed in a number of plans which proposed
different sorts of schools for different socioeconomic
groups. One case in point is *De l'éducation publique*, in which
a five-level system of education suited to the needs of five
broadly defined social categories is set forth.[151] Another
example is a *Plan d'éducation*, written in 1763 and submitted to the Parlement of Bourgogne, which outlines a four-
level system of education for both sexes.[152] A third such
plan is contained in an extended article entitled "De l'éducation nationale," which appeared anonymously in the
physiocrat journal, the *Ephémérides du citoyen*, in 1765 and
1766. Though anonymous, this article was the product of
the pen of the Abbé Baudeau, a leading physiocrat and
editor of the *Ephémérides*.[153]

As a great deal had been written on education in the
years following 1762, Baudeau observed that there was a

[150] See above, nn. 86 and 117.   [151] See above, n. 83.

[152] The four classes of schools proposed for boys are first, for those engaged in agriculture, secondly, for artisans, thirdly, a preparatory school
for the well-off and young gentlemen and fourthly, a *collège* which is to
teach both French and Latin Humanities. The corresponding structure
for girls is as follows. First, schools for the country where rural economy is
to be taught. Secondly, schools for the urban poor, where housekeeping
and domestic work are to be taught. Thirdly, urban schools for those who
are neither indigent nor affluent, and finally, schools in the cities for "des
Démoiselles & Filles de qualité." Cited from Rolland, *Compte rendu* of 13
May 1768, pp. 19-20.

[153] The *Ephémérides* journalist identifies himself as the author of an
anonymous work. *Idées d'un citoyen sur les besoins, les droits, et les devoirs des
vrais pauvres* which appeared in 1765 (*Ephémérides du Citoyen ou Chronique
de l'Esprit National*, vol. II [1766], 76). Barbier identifies the author of this
work as Baudeau. The *Ephémérides* journalist also asserts that he was one
of the first to give a thorough criticism of contemporary educational practice in 1762 (ibid., I [1765], 59). The book to which he refers is the *Idées
d'un citoyen sur l'éducation* which also appeared anonymously, but whose
author is again identified by Barbier as Baudeau.

need for a synthesis on the subject, and he modestly suggested that he might fill this gap with what he called "a complete system of truly national education."[154] Now such a system, it was clear, would have to make provision for the entire population. But, Baudeau asked, could the whole of society be encompassed in one scheme? Was it fitting that the foremost citizens of the state (the *grands*) be obliged to attend public schools? And should those born on the lowest rung of the social scale (the "Enfans du peuple") be allowed to attend them?[155] Baudeau decided all these questions in the affirmative, but regarding the education of the people as a highly controversial issue, he postponed detailed discussion of it for a later installment of the article.

To facilitate the task of outlining a system of education for the whole country, Baudeau divided French society into five main groups. First come the royal family and the *grands*; then the rest of the nobility and the high magistrature; third, the "Bourgeoisie de premier étage"; then what we would call the "petite bourgeoisie" and artisans ("Le Commerce de détail, les Offices inférieures et les Arts"); and finally, and without any differentiation, the peasantry, called simply "the inhabitants of our countryside."[156] Baudeau continued:

> Après avoir distingué la Nation en cinq Ordres ou Classes différentes, suivant les états et la naissance, nous croyons qu'il faut établir des Ecoles publiques de cinq espèces correspondantes, et que tous les enfans du Peuple François, y doivent être formés: c'est notre idée fondamentale qu'il s'agit de développer.[157]

All should receive instruction, but it should vary with the status of each and the function each is expected to fulfill in society.

The *grands* were to be trained to key positions in government, administration and diplomacy; the nobility and

---

[154] *Ephémérides*, 1765 I, 98.
[155] Ibid., p. 103.
[156] Ibid., p. 105.
[157] Ibid., 1766 II, p. 66.

high magistrature to top positions in the church, army and parlements; the "bourgeoisie de premier étage" to the liberal professions, the fine arts, and subordinate positions in the church and sovereign courts. Schools for the petite bourgeoisie and artisans were to teach reading, writing, "L'arithmétique vulgaire" (i.e., weights and measures and conversion of currencies), the elements of practical geometry and the principles of "dessin."[158] For the fifth order in Baudeau's classification, the peasantry, "it will be necessary to have *petites écoles* in each rural parish" but the Abbé added immediately, "and we will be obliged to prove their necessity."[159]

In fact the *Ephémérides* journalist addressed himself much less to demonstrating the necessity of education in the countryside than to proving that the peasantry had a right to an education. He asked: "Are the inhabitants of our villages, who graze our flocks, and who gather the harvests, who cultivate the vineyards, citizens like us? that is the preliminary question."[160] Baudeau asserted that formerly the peasantry of France had been subjected to servitude, "precisely like the negroes of our colonies."[161] Thus, under feudalism France was a country of "a million true citizens, and twenty million true slaves," in which the nobility "reigned as real tyrants over the unhappy people."[162] It was not only in the interests of the feudal nobility that their serfs remain ignorant, but essential that they be kept thus, for:

Quand on veut qu'une grande & forte multitude reste dans la dépendance absolue d'un petit nombre de despotes, il faut qu'elle soit ignorante: vouloir assujettir au pouvoir arbitraire & tyranique, un Peuple qui sait & qui raisonne, c'est la plus absurde des chimeres.[163]

[158] Ibid., pp. 66-80.

[159] Ibid., p. 80.

[160] Ibid., 1766 III, p. 19.

[161] Loc. cit.

[162] Ibid., pp. 19-20.

[163] Ibid., p. 21. Baudeau here seems to have taken his inspiration from Montesquieu. See *L'Esprit des lois*, book IV, chap. v.

But the status of the people, whom Baudeau styled with Coyer, "the most numerous and most useful part of the nation" had changed.[164] At the time of writing, the Abbé maintained "our simplest peasants seem to have by virtue of our laws civil standing, honor, property, or a least the ability to acquire them. . . ."[165] The "preliminary question" raised by Baudeau is resolved. If the rural population have civil status and may own property, they are decidedly citizens. And as the administration of one's property and the understanding of one's civil rights depend upon the ability to read and to write, it is clear that all citizens have the right to a minimal education.[166] The attempt to deprive the peasant of the skills of literacy is termed a "violence" against both, "the law of property" and "the first articles of the Social Contract."[167] There can be no justification for depriving the inhabitants of the countryside of the "simple and easy instruction which is fitting for them."[168]

The third statement on the education of the lower classes we will consider here is a discourse read in the closing session of the *Société Royale* of Metz for the year 1769, by the director of that body, the Baron de Tschudy.[169] Like Baudeau and Rolland, Tschudy did not set out to treat the education of the lower classes, but was brought to a consideration of it in discussing a related subject.

Tschudy chose as the theme of his discourse "the ideas

[164] *Ephémérides*, 1766 III, pp. 20-21.   [165] Ibid., p. 22.
[166] Ibid., pp. 22-23. This minimal education would consist in reading, writing and arithmetic (ibid., 1766 v, 147).
[167] Ibid., 1766 III, 26.
[168] Ibid., p. 32. It is noteworthy that Baudeau, unlike most others who argued for the education of the lower classes, readily admitted that a peasant who learned to read and write often abandoned his plow. But far from concluding that if all peasants were literate they would all leave the countryside, he reasoned that none would, for the ability to read and write by having become general would have lost its commercial value (ibid., pp. 28-32).
[169] The full text of Tschudy's discourse has been lost, and is now known only from a seven page *procès-verbal* in the "Etat de la Société royale des sciences et des arts de Metz, au mois d'août 1769," Bibliothèque Munici-

best suited to encouraging patriotism."[170] It was in education, or "la communication des lumières," as he had it, that
he found the most efficacious of these means. Unlike Rolland, Tschudy saw no danger in education, only in the lack
of it;[171] and unlike Baudeau, he emphasized not the right
of the people to an education, but the utility of education
to the state and society. Tschudy is the first author encountered in this study to treat education primarily as a means
of social engineering.

Education was not understood by the director of the
Société Royale of Metz as speculative philosophy or learning
for its own sake. On the contrary, education was seen to
have a social and political function, which was to support
and invigorate society by producing social harmony and
encouraging patriotism. It was Tschudy's thesis that:

> ... l'instruction de toutes les classes de l'Etat feroit mieux
> connoître à chacune d'elles ses relations diverses, lui
> montreroit les avantages de sa situation & lui rendroit
> chers ses devoirs qu'elle verroit clairement liés à son
> bonheur. . . . [*sic*] . . . Les lumières répandues dans les
> diverses classes des différens corps politiques con-
> tribueront à les affermir & à les faire prospérer.[172]

The Baron illustrated his thesis with a speculative history
of society which in many places recalls Rousseau's two *Discourses*, and an analysis, following Montesquieu, of the usefulness of education in various kinds of governments. He
found it valuable even in a despotism, where morality,
conditioned by education, had the power to moderate the

---

pale of Metz, mss. 1342. The *procès-verbal* contains quotations from the
original discourse, as well as a resumé of the rest. The letters p.v. will be
used to indicate where the resumé, and not quotations from the original,
have been cited.

[170] Tschudy, *Discours*, p. 10 (p.v.).

[171] The evils attributed to ignorance include superstition, regicide and
rebellion (ibid., p. 16).

[172] Ibid., pp. 10-11.

actions of an absolute ruler. It is, however, in moderate forms of government that education acts most beneficially:

> La propagation des lumières est sur-tout utile dans les Gouvernemens tempérés, préférables aux Aristocraties électives et aux Démocraties pures. En France, par exemple, le Peuple plus éclairé seroit, s'il est possible, encore plus soumis; ou sa soumission réfléchie seroit du moins plus sûre. . . .[173]

The aspect of education that appealed especially to Tschudy was its potential for harmonizing relations among conflicting classes, for rendering the people "still more submissive," and for welding society into a unified whole. The Baron and academician was not alone in his appreciation of this. If other members of the enlightened community did not draw the conclusions that Tschudy did about the potential effects of education among the lower classes quite so quickly and completely as he, his discourse nevertheless represents the general trend of enlightened opinion in the twenty years preceding the Revolution.

It appears, then, that the opinions expressed on popular education once the issue began to be debated did not follow the lead given by the Abbé Terrisse. The most vigorous spokesmen for popular education during the 1760s were two Jansenists, while men who valued the *lumières* were reluctant to educate the lower classes. This position, which contradicted the imperatives of enlightenment thought, was progressively abandoned for a middle way that sought a mean between too much and too little education. As the debate on popular education heightened in the two following decades, this middle way or concept of a fitting education for the people became the focal point of the discussion.

[173] Ibid., p. 14 (p.v.).

CHAPTER III

The Debate: 1770-1789

INTRODUCING an Italian work on public instruction in 1773, the *Journal encyclopédique* observed:

> Il a déjà paru chez toutes les nations éclairées plusieurs ouvrages sur l'éducation publique; mais la plûpart de ces écrits, uniquement consacrés aux moyens de réformer les études, n'offrent aucune instruction à la classe la plus nombreuse de citoyens, à celle qu'on puisse regarder comme le soutien de toutes les autres.[1]

The essay in question was not, however, devoted primarily to popular education, but rather presented another multitiered plan of instruction similar to those of Crévier and Baudeau. But it did not take long before the instruction of the people began to be treated in its own right, and again the initiative seems to have come from Italy. The Academy of Mantua announced as the subject of one of its essay contests for 1775, "A philosophical dissertation on the education of children, specifically: which plan would best suit the children of the lower classes [*enfans du bas peuple*], and how could it be directed to the public good?"[2] The French were not slow in taking up the lead given by their neighbor.

In 1778 the Count de Thélis, a liberal noble from the Forez, published a *Plan d'éducation en faveur des pauvres enfans de la campagne*. In 1779 the Academy of Châlons-sur-Marne proposed as the subject of its annual essay contest the question, "Quel seroit le meilleur plan pour l'éducation du peuple?" The following year Father Gourdin, a Benedictine monk, submitted to the Academy of Lyon a memoir entitled "De l'éducation physique et morale con-

[1] JE, 1773 VIII, 270.   [2] JE, 1774 II, 535.

siderée relativement à la place que doivent occuper les Enfans dans l'ordre de la Société." Philipon de la Madeleine's
Vues patriotiques sur l'éducation du peuple was published in
1783, and in the same year Jacques Sellier, the founder
and director of the *école des arts* of Amiens, wrote his
"Lettre sur l'instruction des enfants du peuple," which has
remained in manuscript. In 1786 J. A. Perreau, a *litterateur*
and educator, published a work entitled *Instruction du
peuple,* while the following year there appeared *Le Peuple
instruit par ses propres vertus* of L. P. Berenger, an ex-
Oratorian, former *professeur de collège*, writer and royal censor. Thus, after having been treated parenthetically in discussions on education for almost twenty years, a whole
spate of works devoted specifically to the instruction of the
lower classes appeared, marking the emergence of popular
education as a subject in its own right. This shift of interest
did not go unremarked.

In announcing the essay contest proposed by the
Academy of Châlons-sur-Marne for 1779, the *Journal
d'éducation* underscored the novelty of the subject, observing that "the education of the nobility and of the comfortable part of the nation has always been much discussed; but
the instruction of the people has only ever received superficial attention."[3] The academy, too, was well aware that it
was focusing attention on a relatively new issue. The official announcement stating that none of the entries submitted for 1779 were considered worthy of the prize observed
that all manner of educational treatises and plans had been
written for the well-off, "but that authors have until now
disdained treating the education of the people."[4] Gourdin
noted that most educational theorists had treated domestic
education, and that those authors who wrote on public
education did not distinguish between different social
groups. In this case, even if an author's principles were

[3] *Journal d'éducation*, Jan. 1778, p. 53.
[4] "Prix proposés par l'Académie des Sciences, Arts & Belles Lettres de
Châlons-sur-Marne dans son Assemblée publique de 25 Août [1779]."

sound, "applied indifferently to all classes of citizens, to the child of the poor as to that of the rich, to the son of the artisan as to that of the noble, these principles necessarily become false, and perhaps dangerous."[5] Clearly, it had now come to be felt that a definite and distinct program of popular education was needed.

Why this need should have been felt late in the 1770s rather than concurrently with the sharp growth of interest in education generally after 1762 is not immediately apparent. One possibility is that the expulsion of the Jesuits from France and the publication of *Emile*, which together sparked the debate on education in 1762, focused attention upon the reform of the *collèges* and on educational theory. Whereas this explanation may account for the failure of educational thought to take up the instruction of the lower classes in a systematic way before the end of the 1770s, it does not explain why it should have done so then. The answers, however, are not far to seek.

It is probably true that propertyless laborers pose a problem, actual or potential, in any preindustrial society subject to subsistence crises. Certainly France, before the nineteenth century, was such a society. Between 1730 and 1770, however, good harvests and relative prosperity made for a degree of social peace, and the lower classes of France posed only a potential threat to their social superiors. After 1770, however, a period of serious economic disjuncture began.[6] As a result, large numbers of day laborers and others who had managed to make ends meet in better years were reduced to poverty (or perhaps more correctly, to a more intense degree of poverty), then to mendicancy, vagrancy and brigandage.[7] The problem was actualized.

Together with the socioeconomic conditions prevailing

[5] Gourdin, *De l'éducation*, fol. 94r.

[6] A. Soboul, *La Civilisation et la Révolution française: I. La crise de l'ancien régime* (Paris, 1970), p. 468.

[7] G. Lefebvre, *The French Revolution from its Origins to 1793*, trans. E. M. Evanson (New York, 1967), pp. 52-53, and Hufton, *The Poor*, p. 24.

after 1770, certain ideological factors also helped focus attention on popular education. There was, first, a strong, even unreasonable belief in the effectiveness of education as an agent of reform and social control. Second, during the eighteenth century and especially after 1762, the consciousness that France was a nation grew, and with it the realization that the lower classes were part of that nation.

The belief in the power of education and the growth of nationalism before the Revolution are issues that call for and will receive further discussion below.[8] In this chapter I intend to follow the development of the debate on popular education down to 1789 and to inquire what purpose members of the enlightened community expected the instruction of the lower classes to serve, and what they thought this instruction should consist in.

THE PEOPLE AND THE PURPOSE OF THEIR EDUCATION

How writers in the eighteenth century defined the people and how they saw the social and economic role of the lower classes naturally determined how they regarded popular education, and as their premises differed, so too did the kind and scope of education they intended for their social inferiors. If, for example, the people were taken as all those who did not belong to the privileged orders, a broad plan of education became necessary, whereas if the people were defined as day laborers and the poor, a narrower plan would suffice. In fact, most authors do not trouble to qualify the term "people" when they use it, so one is left to take their meaning from the context. Here, as elsewhere, Goyon and Philipon make explicit what other writers usually assume.

Goyon first referred to the people as "this multitude of citizens who in a private capacity truly make up the body of the nation."[9] Narrowing his definition by analogy he con-

[8] See chap. IV.   [9] Goyon d'Arzac, *Essais de Laopédie*, p. 1.

tinued, "That which arms, hands and legs are to the physical and rational individual, the people is to the state [*Corps Politique et Social*]."[10] It was the function of the people to supply the needs of the state in the areas of provisioning (*subsistance*), upkeep (*entretien*) and defense.

Having defined the people, Goyon then divided them into five main categories. These are first, the self-sufficient peasantry, and second, comfortable artisans. The third category is reserved for merchants. In the fourth group we find more familiar figures: *manoeuvres, journaliers* and *gens de peine* who work for the first three groups, while the fifth category is reserved for the indigent and foundlings.[11]

Philipon's definition of the people corresponds roughly to the last two categories of Goyon's classification, and to what I have so far understood by "lower classes." The people, as Philipon saw them, were "the last rank of citizens, the class of those men upon whom necessity imposes the need [*loi*] to devote themselves to mercenary, manual and servile labor in order to live."[12] The lives of the people were said to be "a tribute to labor," and should some of them succeed in raising themselves above this condition, they would, for Philipon, cease to be *peuple*.[13] "The people is obliged in order to live to devote itself to physical labor; it is that which characterizes it essentially."[14]

Philipon saw in the laboring masses the potential for both great good and great ill. On the one hand, as peasants they fed the state, as soldiers they protected it, and as artisans (*ouvriers*) enriched it. On the other hand, it was from the same class that brigands, vagabonds, murderers and other disturbers of the peace came. It was precisely because "the people can equally well render great services or do great harm" that its education was so important.[15]

Whether defining the people broadly, as Goyon did, or

[10] Ibid., p. 2. [11] Ibid., pp. 2-3.
[12] Philipon, *Vues patriotiques*, pp. 5-6.
[13] Ibid., pp. 79 and 6.
[14] Ibid., p. 14. [15] Ibid., p. 7.

narrowly, in Philipon's fashion, writers concerned with popular education seldom deviated from the view that the dual purpose of their instruction was to encourage economic utility and to assure social order. The emphasis varied with the interests and outlook of each writer, but those positing a fundamentally different goal for popular education, such as Rivard and Crévier, are in a very small minority indeed. Almost all adhered to some version of the theme of a "fitting" education for the people, and virtually all accepted either Goyon's or Philipon's definitions of them.

The fundamental principle upon which Goyon's prize-winning essay rests is that the education a child receives should correspond to his social position.[16] Though he believed that men were equal by nature, he knew that the functions they performed in society had to be as different as their relative social and occupational standings. The educator had therefore to "proportion his help to the condition, duties and needs of his students."[17] Philipon set out to devise a plan of education that would render the people both useful and harmless. He regarded it as vital that the lower classes be trained to industriousness and that they learn to shun mendicity. The people was further to learn:

> . . . à se conformer à son état, à en diminuer les peines par son travail, à les adoucir par sa resignation, à sortir même de cette misère où l'a jeté le hasard de la naissance. . . .[18]

When Philipon came to summarize the purpose of popular education, however, he did so in the following terms: "To make it love its lot, that is the true goal of the education of the people. . . ."[19] Philipon, it seems clear, regarded education primarily as an instrument of social control.

When treating the nature of the education fitting for the

---

[16] Goyon d'Arzac, *Essais de Laopédie*, p. 2. [17] Loc. cit.

[18] Philipon, *Vues patriotiques*, pp. 9-10. [19] Ibid., p. 24.

lower classes, Philipon provides another example of the now familiar combination of the condemnation of ignorance and praise of enlightenment together with the refusal to enlighten the great majority of mankind. As he had already denounced the proposition of Rousseau that the poor had no need of education, the reader is prepared for the spirited denunciation of ignorance that follows.[20] Only tyrants and imposters, Philipon thundered, would find any advantage in bending the common man "under the yoke of ignorance."[21] We are, however, less prepared for the endorsement of La Chalotais' opinion, quoted at length, that the people ought not be allowed to study, and the recommendation that *petites écoles* be closed on the ground that they drain workers from essential occupations.[22] Philipon saw no contradiction here. The people were to be educated, but they were to receive a "fitting" education. For Philipon such an education for the lower classes consisted in physical and moral training, and instruction in handling their own affairs: "In this ignorance is good for nothing and error is dangerous."[23] Literary education was quite another matter. Here ignorance was considered preferable. "I know of no weapon more dangerous," Philipon asserted, "than knowledge in the hands of the people."[24] He would forbid outright the study of either philosophy or theology to the lower classes.[25] In Philipon's view the only fitting subjects for the people were those of immediate occupational or domestic utility.[26]

To judge from the frequency with which the argument that education must be geared to socioeconomic standing was heard in these years, it must have been, so to speak, in the air. In 1774 the *Journal encyclopédique* magisterially delivered itself of the following opinion:

[20] Ibid., p. 8.   [21] Ibid., p. 13.
[22] Ibid., pp. 15 and 19.
[23] Ibid., p. 13.
[24] Ibid., pp. 13-14. Philipon has taken Montaigne as his authority here.
[25] Ibid., p. 36.   [26] Ibid., p. 133.

Le but général de tout plan d'éducation est que ceux
qu'on y assujettit devient, en le suivant, aussi utiles qu'ils
peuvent l'être dans le rang & dans la situation où la providence les a placés. Tous les accessoires qui font perdre
de vue ce but, doivent être rejettés comme chimériques
& pernicieux.[27]

Similarly, for the Abbé Jacques Pernetti, an assiduous
member of the Academy of Lyon and a prolific author, the
purpose of education was to "render men capable of serving each other in whatever condition [*état*] they are
placed."[28] He advised members of the lower classes (*classe
inférieure*) that they should not attempt to learn Latin, but
take up an occupation more fitting to their fortune and
condition.[29]

For the author of a memoir read before the Academy of
Lyon and entitled simply "Pensées sur l'éducation," one of
the most important functions of instruction was to maintain social harmony. The anonymous author took as his
starting point the assumption that society must necessarily
be composed of men of different occupations and conditions. He then observed:

> . . . dans Les dernieres classes de la Société Composées
> d'agriculteurs et d'artisans, asservis à un travail grossier
> et assidû, il est inutile, il seroit dangereux de trop savoir;
> plus instruits Cette espece d'hommes, n'en remplisoit pas
> mieux Son état; elle Seroit exposée a S'en dègouter.
>
> Or Ces Classes d'hommes sont nécessaires dans la
> Sociéte. Il ne Convient donc pas d'instruire tous Les
> hommes dans toutes sortes de Connoissances.[30]

[27] JE, 1774 III, 90.

[28] J. Pernetti, "Réponse aux questions d'un père sur l'éducation"
(1775) A Ac. Lyon, mss. 147, fols. 2-3.

[29] Ibid., fol. 17r.

[30] Anonymous, "Pensées sur l'éducation," A Ac. Lyon, mss. 147, fol.
49r.

Similarly, in his *Inquiries Concerning the Poor*, the English author Farlan stated that the class (*classe*) into which a child was born had to be considered when educating him, and that for the poor a liberal education would prove more harmful than beneficial.[31] Gourdin, too, believed that it was inappropriate to give the same education to peasants and artisans as to nobles and the wealthy, and laid it down as a general principle that "education should be absolutely relative to the place which the child occupies or should occupy in the great family of the state."[32]

The view that education should be suited to social standing and not spread as far and fast as possible in order to enlighten the masses was espoused not only by Benedictine monks and timid gentlemen in provincial academies. Lezay-Marnesia, a liberal noble, reforming seigneur, member of three academies and friend of Saint Lambert and Chamfort, believed that the people should be educated, but almost exactly echoed Gourdin in asserting that they should receive "instruction exactly suited to their social standing [*condition*]."[33] No less radical a thinker than Holbach also shared this belief. He observed that "The common people is made in order to keep busy,"[34] and that education has fundamentally different objectives in different classes of society.

> L'éducation devroit apprendre aux Princes à regner, aux Grands à se distinguer par leur mérite & leurs vertus, aux Riches à faire un bon usage de leurs richesses, au Pauvre à subsister par une honnête industrie.[35]

It seems clear that if it was generally agreed that the lower classes should be instructed, it was just as widely believed

[31] JE, 1783 v, 59.   [32] Gourdin, *De l'éducation*, fol. 94r.
[33] C.F.A. de Lezay-Marnesia, *Le Bonheur dans les campagnes* (Neufchatel, 1785), p. 112.
[34] P.H.D. d'Holbach, *Systême social, ou Principes naturels de la morale et de la politique avec un examen de l'influence du gouvernement sur les moeurs* (London, 3 vols., 1773), vol. iii, p. 84.
[35] Ibid., iii, 117.

that their instruction should be carefully limited. What those limits were we shall now examine.

THE SKILLS OF LITERACY

Goyon, having defined the people broadly, was obliged to develop an equally broad system of education. This he did by proposing three distinct sorts of schools. *Grandes écoles*, intended for the children of wealthy artisans, merchants and peasants (*riches colons et fermiers*), were to offer a course of studies lasting nine years. The first three were to be devoted to learning to read in both French and Latin, and to the study of moral and religious catechisms; the second three to writing, arithmetic and the reading of manuscript business documents, such as contracts and leases; and the last three to *dessin*, the use of weights and measures, and the elements of rural economy. In his final year in the school each student had also to specialize in either agriculture, mechanics or commerce.[36] Though the length of this course of studies was comparable to that of *collèges*, its content could hardly be more different. Goyon would have replaced the literary education which merchants and comfortable farmers generally sought to procure for their sons with an education geared to their immediate occupational needs. There can be little doubt that nothing could have pleased the social groups in question less.[37]

The course of studies for the *moyennes écoles* was more

[36] Goyon d'Arzac, *Essais de Laopédie*, pp. 10-13. The *grandes écoles* were to have three teachers.

[37] "Les enfans de la classe des Bourgeois sont les plus difficils à instruire, en naissant on en veut faire des Marquis; on les met dans des petites pensions pour leur apprendre a lire et ecrire, on les envoye dans les colleges pour des humanités; Ils rentrent dans la maison a seize ou dix huit ans, on les mets dans le magasin ou dans l'etude, on leur donne un maitre a ecrire, des maitres de danse, d'armes, et de musique, voila leur education ils ne savent ni le calcul n'y le commerce n'y les Lois [sic]" (Jacques Sellier, Letter to the Intendant of Amiens, 6 December 1783). AD Somme, C 1547[6], pp. 1-2.

limited. Lasting six years, the program encompassed the subjects taught in the first two stages of the *grandes écoles*.[38] The curriculum of Goyon's *petites écoles*—not to be confused with the schools that generally bore that name—was to be taught in three years. It was not, however, to include the skills of literacy. Goyon believed that "the needs of the children of the people do not demand, and the faculties of their parents do not permit, other than a very modest [*modique*], education."[39] This education, he felt, could suitably be reduced to "three very brief catechisms of religion, morality and economy."[40] These catechisms were to be learned in the traditional manner, which is to say orally. Beyond the material contained in them, Goyon was convinced, no further education should be provided. He even asserted that in matters extending beyond the contents of his suggested curriculum, "ignorance is for them a real good," and explained: "better educated they would feel the rigor of their condition more keenly without being any more able to improve it."[41]

Literacy, Goyon argued, was of no real use to the *bas peuple*. Their ability to read and write contributed nothing to society. To emphasize his point Goyon asked rhetorically:

De quelle utilité Est-il pour un Laboureur, un Vigneron, un Pecheur, un Boucheron, un manouvrier, d'apprendre à lire et à écrire? ils sauront; il est vrai, anonner leurs prières dans une langue qu'ils n'entendent pas; ils feront, si l'on veut à même de defigurer, au pupitre de leur Paroisse, quelques mots de pleinchant, de dechifrer quelque livres de contes ridicules, ou de plates chansons; ou bien ils se jetteront dans le grimoire de la chicane pour plaider, ou engager les autres à plaider leur famille, leur voisins, leur Curé, leur seigneur; Mais la terre, qui la travaillera? les Troupeux, qui les gardera?

[38] Goyon d'Arzac, *Essais de Laopédie*, p. 14.
[39] Ibid., p. 27.　　　[40] Loc. cit.　　　[41] Ibid., p. 9.

Les differens détails rustiques et pénibles, qui s'en chargera?[42]

The answer, of course, is that no one will. Like La Chalotais, Goyon was convinced that men of humble origins who had learned the skills of literacy would with difficulty, if at all, be persuaded to return to their plows and workshops. Accordingly, he suggested that it would be well to "suppress in the countryside and in small towns [*Bourgades*] so many useless teachers [*Magisters et Regents*]."[43]

At this point, however, the voice of the academy in the person of its commissioner, Meunier, made itself heard. The paragraph of Goyon's manuscript from which the last two references come has been boxed off and crossed out, and beside it, in a tiny, almost illegible hand, Meunier wrote:

> il est necessaire pour le bien de l'humanité [à] apprendre à lire Et à Ecrire aux enfans les plus pauvres. C'est le moyen de leur apprendre plus facilement leurs devoirs Essentiels dans l'ordre de la religion Et de la société! Un patre peut devenir un homme interessant, mais il faut retrancher les connoissances inutiles à leur Etat.[44]

One feels that in this fragment of marginalia an authentic voice of the enlightened community has spoken. The view that the people ought not be initiated into the skills of literacy—neither La Chalotais, Granet nor any other critic of popular eduation denied that they should receive some form of instruction—is branded as retrograde.

In fact, the distance between the views of Meunier and those of Goyon is not great. The similarities in their outlooks are evident in Meunier's emphasis on teaching the lower classes their duties, while avoiding any "connoissances inutiles," and in a key passage in Goyon's essay in which he wrote:

[42] Ibid., p. 8. [43] Loc. cit. [44] Loc. cit.

L'Enseignement du Peuple est une chose délicate: il marche entre deux écueils egalement dangereux, entre deux extrémités qu'il faut egalement éviter, Le trop et le trop peu. L'ignorance est pour cette Classe de l'humanité, ainsi que pour toutes les autres, La source de quantité de vices et de maux, quand elle porte sur les objets essentiels à sa perfection et à son bonheur . . . L'ignorance pour lors est une porte ouverte à l'oisiveté, à la fainéantise, au libertinage, à la misère, ou à la mendacité [*sic*] cette lépre honteuse qui ronge l'Etat. . . . Combien d'un autre Coté, Les inconvéniens du savoir sont ils à craindre pour les hommes en général, et particulierement pour Le Peuple, quand ce savoir passe les bornes convenables, quand il s'étend à des choses dangereuses, ou même inutiles? Toute connoissance etrangère à leur devoirs, à leur profession leur devient nuisible; tout Talent deplacé devient presque un defaut.[45]

Like Rolland, Goyon believed the dangers of learning to be as great as those resulting from ignorance. And like the president of the Parlement of Paris, he believed it possible to find a mean between the two extremes.

Unlike Goyon, Philipon readily admitted that the poor should be taught to read and write; but like the Bordeaux *parlementaire* he had reservations about putting the skills of literacy into the hands of the people and sought to limit them by impracticable stipulations. Philipon recognized the importance of being able to read a contract or lease, and as documents of this sort were always handwritten, he considered it necessary for the lower classes to be able to read script. But books were another matter: "To facilitate the reading of books for the people is in all futility to develop this taste in them, to arouse their desires, to cause them privations, and to distract them from their work."[46] Philipon would especially forbid the laboring poor to read fables, fairy tales or the *bibliothèque bleue*. If they were to

[45] Loc. cit.

[46] Philipon, *Vues patriotiques*, p. 140.

read at all, he would provide them with such books as Franklin's *La Science du bonhomme Richard*, and the *Manuel du cultivateur*.[47]

Writing received even shorter shift at Philipon's hands than reading. A man of the people should know how to sign his name so that he can pass an act before a notary; that is all. Should members of the lower classes learn to write fluently, "they will either become criminals, falsifying documents; or they will neglect their work."[48] No such evils were expected from arithmetic, which was regarded as both useful and harmless. Accordingly, it was recommended as a substitute for writing. Practical geometry and drawing were also considered suitable for the people.[49] In all these subjects instruction was to be by example and through practice. The students were not to learn the theory or fine points of any of them for fear that "they distract them from their occupations."[50]

Goyon's refusal to teach the lower classes to read and write and Philipon's hesitations on this score are reflected in other works on popular education that appeared at about the same time. C.A.J.L. de Montlinot, a cleric and doctor who also directed a poorhouse, did not even think of the education of the indigent in terms of literacy. In an essay which won the contest proposed by the Royal Agricultural Society of Soissons for 1779, Montlinot observed that "in general too little care is taken of the education of the people in Europe."[51] He suggested that workshops be opened in the larger cities where the poor could receive free instructions in the trades, but beyond this he would not go.[52]

[47] Ibid., pp. 137-38.
[49] Ibid., pp. 146-51.
[48] Ibid., p. 145.
[50] Ibid., p. 157.
[51] C.A.J.L. de Montlinot, *Discours qui a remporté le prix à la Société Royale d'Agriculture de Soissons en l'année 1779; Sur cette question proposée par la même Société: Quels sont les moyens de détruire la Mendicité, de rendre les Pauvres valides utiles, & de les secourir dans la ville de Soissons* (Lille, 1779), p. 89. I am indebted to M. Daniel Roche for bringing this essay to my attention.
[52] Ibid., p. 90.

In considering Jacques Necker's *De l'importance des opinions religieuses*, we move from the views of an erudite poor warden to those of the chief financial officer of the French state during the critical year 1789. Necker maintained that "any sort of education which demands time and thought can in no way suit the most numerous class of men."[53] The people, the Swiss financier argued, ought not to be initiated into the skills of literacy. Indeed, Necker believed the only proper and necessary education for the lower classes to be religious instruction.[54] This, too, was the view of the author of the "Pensées sur l'éducation," who having observed that peasants and artisans might well conceive a distaste for their rather harsh lot if educated, concluded that "religion and morality are all that it is useful to teach this immense portion of humanity."[55]

An unlikely figure to find in this company of enlightened obscurantists is the *philosophe-abbé* Coyer. Yet here he must be placed. Despite the sympathy he had shown for the lower classes in his *Dissertation sur la nature du peuple* of 1755, in his *Plan d'éducation publique* of 1770, Coyer offered the opinion that the rural poor were already receiving too much schooling. He expressed the wish that "all should receive a fitting education."[56] But it was his belief that *petites écoles*, because they taught the skills of literacy and sometimes even Latin, did not provide a suitable education for the rural poor and should therefore be closed. What education was fitting for the agricultural laborer? None. Coyer explained:

> L'ignorance, qui serait un mal dans les villes, est un bien au village. La vie y est ordinairement assez dure. L'ignorance la plus grossière est nécessaire pour tout souffrir.[57]

[53] J. Necker, *De l'importance des opinions religieuses* (London, 1788), p. 52.

[54] Ibid., pp. 55 and 60.

[55] "Pensées sur l'éducation," fol. 49r.

[56] F. G. Coyer, *Plan d'éducation publique*, in *Oeuvres*, III, 359.

[57] Ibid., p. 360.

Only the more comfortable peasant (*fermier*) needed to know anything more than how to work the land. Following La Chalotais—though he did not acknowledge that he was doing so—Coyer stated: "Le bien publique demande que les connaissances du peuple ne s'étendent pas plus loin que ses occupations."[58] The public good, for simple folk, was a harsh master.

An unusual suggestion on how to preserve the people from the dangers of literacy while allowing them to enjoy its advantages appeared in the *Affiches de Picardie* of 1771. Under the title "Lettre sur l'éducation Physico-morale des Enfans de la Campagne," the anonymous author described an experiment in popular education carried out by an unnamed ex-intendant on one of of his estates.

> Il y a établi des Ecoles où on exerce les garçons à toutes sortes de travaux manuels, à la portée de leur age, suivant leurs talens & leurs dispositions: cependant on ne leur montre ni à lire ni à écrire; ce qui est uniquement reservé pour l'Ecole des filles.[59]

This arrangement pleased the anonymous author immensely, and he suggested that it be adopted throughout France. He expected it to frustrate the efforts of the laboring poor to escape "the harsh laborious state" to which they were subject and to arrest the depopulation of the countryside. He further believed that by making the husband dependent on his wife, this system would tighten family bonds among the poor.[60]

A reply to this proposal was written by a country curate of the region. In a concise but devastating article that appeared shortly after in the same journal, the priest pointed out that the suggested plan was impractical, that it was incompatible with the needs and requirements of religion,

[58] Ibid., p. 372. Where La Chalotais has "Le bien de la société," Coyer has "Le bien public." Otherwise the two sentences are identical. Compare above, chap. II, n. 44.

[59] *Affiches de Picardie*, 1771, p. 166.

[60] Ibid., p. 167.

and that it would result in no good for civil society.[61] It is not necessary to follow the curate's reasoning step by step, but there can be little doubt that he, and with him the partisans of popular literacy, emerged the victors from this encounter.

Just over a decade later, another controversy on the nature of the education suitable for the lower classes was sparked by the appearance of a "Projet en faveur des petites Ecoles de la campagne" in the *Journal de Troyes*.[62] In response to this article, which was basically a plan for the establishment of a training college for rural schoolmasters, a local noble, who signed himself the Chevalier de B., pointed out that the author of the project was putting the cart before the horse in proposing to found a training school for teachers while "it is still not determined whether it is more useful to instruct the peoples of the countryside, or to leave them in ignorance."[63] The Chevalier did not take it upon himself to resolve so important a question, but let it be understood by the difficulties he found in educating the people that it was probably better not to do so.

In a subsequent contribution to this discussion, a bourgeois of Mezières informed the journal that he had discussed the question raised by the Chevalier de B. with his cousin, who had not the least difficulty in resolving it. The bourgeois, quoting his cousin the curate, whom he said spoke "like a miniature,"[64] wrote:

> Moi, Monsieur, qui ne suis qu'un païsan, je vous résous cela sans berguiner: je dis qu'un villageois qui ne sait que lire, écrire, sa religion & un peu calculer pour le faciliter

[61] Ibid., pp. 194-95.

[62] *Journal de la Ville de Troyes & de la Champagne Meridionale*, 1784, pp. 41-42.

[63] Ibid., p. 54.

[64] Ibid., p. 152. I have not been able to discover just what a "miniature" in this sense is, but I suspect that it might be a form of folk art, specifically, decorative painting. If this is so, it would account for the curate's colorful speech. See Soboul, *La Crise de l'ancien régime*, pl. 59.

dans son petit commerce, n'est sûrement point un Savant. Je conviens qu'il ne faut pas qu'il aille plus loin; mais si vous lui montrez la *Jographie*, la *Jométrie*; si vous vous entremettrez de lui faire comprendre les effets de la *délectricité* & de la machine *plématique*; si vous voulez lui persuader que le soleil, qu'il ne croit pas plus large que la gueule de son four, est un million de fois plus gros que la terre. Mon Cousin dit qu'avec toutes ces choses, vous renversez la tête de votre païsan, vous en faites un homme dangereux, vous le jettez au delà de la portion de son entendement; il confondra tout & sera un ignorant d'autant plus insupportable, qu'il se croira un Savant du premier ordre. Il méprisera ses égaux & même son Curé; il négligera son labour & tous ses travaux.[65]

That the laboring poor were to be taught their four r's and little else was a view widely held in the enlightened community, though seldom was it expressed in such colorful language.

In his three-volume treatise on education, Guillaume Grivel, a lawyer, author, academician and contributor to both Diderot's *Encyclopédie* and Panckoucke's *Encyclopédie méthodique*, asserted that reading, writing and arithmetic, as well as basic notions of agriculture and botany, were a minimal requirement for any child, "of whatever social standing [*condition*] he may be."[66] He made it clear, however, that he considered a literary education inappropriate for families of artisans, and of course those any lower in the social scale.[67] Gourdin similarly believed that peasants and even day laborers should be taught the skills of literacy but prevented from exercising them too widely; and Perreau thought it necessary that "from their childhood the lower classes [*les gens du peuple*] be instructed in their religious

[65] *Journal de Troyes*, 1784, p. 152.
[66] G. Grivel, *Théorie de l'éducation, ouvrage utile aux pères de famille et aux instituteurs* (Paris, 3 vols., 1775), vol. I, p. 382.
[67] Ibid., p. 363.

duties and that they learn to read, write [and] to count sufficiently to manage their affairs. . . ."[68]

Thélis was in basic agreement with these views,[69] and so too was Sellier. Though the director of the *école des arts* of Amiens criticized the effects of the education given by La Salle's order and by *écoles de dessin*, he regarded ignorance as pernicious, and wanted all to receive a measure of instruction.[70] "Men without education," Sellier said, "do not differ from animals."[71] He did not, however, approve of spending the entire day at reading and writing, but believed that "it is good that everyone should know how to read and write a little, and that they should know their religion well."[72] Beyond this, some arithmetic, "practical geometry" and perhaps, if the child were particularly talented, drawing or drafting, were all that was required. Extending the studies of the poor any further was unnecessary: "it would be better to teach them to work from an early age."[73] But for the idea of purposely keeping the poor in ignorance of the skills of literacy, which, curiously enough, Sellier called "a system invented and supported by the newly enriched,"[74] he had nothing but disdain. "The ignorance of peasants," he stated flatly, "is good for nothing."[75]

Sellier's views in this matter were shared and vigorously expressed by certain other, better-known members of the enlightened community. Helvétius praised the ancients for their belief that ignorance could never be of any use, and asserted that its results were inevitably fanaticism, crime

---

[68] Gourdin, *De l'éducation*, fol. 98r; Perreau, *Instruction du peuple*, p. 60.

[69] Thélis, *Mémoire* VI, p. 20.

[70] Sellier, "Lettre sur l'instruction des enfants du peuple," pp. 5-6.

[71] Sellier, "Discours sur l'instruction des pauvres," AD Somme, D 152.

[72] Sellier, "Lettre sur l'instruction des enfants du peuple," p. 7.

[73] Ibid., pp. 7-8.

[74] Sellier, "Lettre sur l'éducation des habitants de la campagne," AD Somme, C 2074⁶, p. 1.

[75] Ibid., p. 4.

and indocility.[76] Having raised the issue of whether it was desirable to educate the people, he asked ingenuously: "And why indeed should instruction prove harmful?"[77] Only those who sought to oppress or mislead the people would oppose their being educated.[78] Similarly, Holbach believed that "the truth seems dangerous only to those who falsely believe it to be in their interest to mislead mankind."[79] To the proposition that harmful truths at least should be kept from the people, he replied simply that it is impossible for truth to result in harm.[80]

Like Helvétius and Holbach, Diderot too regarded ignorance as the root of a good many evils, and accused those who sought to deny the people an education of wishing to exploit and mislead them. But the editor of the *Encyclopédie* was more specific about popular education than his two collaborators. He favored a system of education for "the people in general" and would have them taught the four r's. Though Diderot insisted on the right of the lower classes to learn the skills of literacy, he was not willing to go much further. Secondary education was to be reserved for the nobility, and for "comfortable citizens of the third estate."[81]

In apparent contradiction to this position is Diderot's assertion that universities should be open to students of all classes.[82] This highly theoretical claim was based on the

[76] Helvétius, "Letter to Lefebvre-Laroche," in *Oeuvres*, XIV, 100-01.

[77] Ibid., p. 99. Elsewhere, however, Helvétius expressed the opinion that the people would never be able to receive an education worthy of the name. See *De l'esprit*, book II, chap. 4.

[78] Helvétius, "Letter to Lefebve-Laroche," in *Oeuvres*, XIV, 107-08.

[79] Holbach, *Système social*, I, 19. The question of whether it is "useful" to mislead the people was chosen by the Academy of Berlin as the subject of its essay contest for 1780. A selection of the French responses has been published by Werner Krauss, ed., *Est-il utile de tromper le peuple?* (Berlin, 1966).

[80] Holbach, *Système social*, III, 156-57.

[81] Diderot, "Essai sur les études en Russie," in *Oeuvres*, III, 416-19.

[82] Diderot, "Plan d'une université pour le gouvernement de Russie," in *Oeuvres*, III, 433.

conviction that no one with great talent should be prevented from studying for lack of means.[83] It did not imply the opening of institutions of higher learning to the lower classes, for this would have deprived society of the artisans and peasants upon which it depended. Diderot believed that "nothing is more disastrous for society than this disdain of fathers for their occupation and these senseless emigrations from one condition [*état*] to another."[84] The encyclopedist, though himself the son of a modest provincial artisan, did not care to facilitate such "emigrations" by encouraging the lower classes to study. Nor, indeed, would most educated Frenchmen, who would have shared Diderot's view. But perhaps the grudging and limited acceptance of the advisability of teaching the people the skills of literacy was best summed up by the Abbé Durosoy, an ex-Jesuit, professor of theology and litterateur when he wrote, "The greater part of mankind scarcely needs to read except in order to learn to live well; and in order to learn to live well, it is not necessary to read much."[85]

POPULAR LITERACY: LIMITS AND RESERVATIONS

If a significant minority in the enlightened community questioned the suitability of initiating the lower classes into the skills of literacy, there was near unanimity for the view that the people should not proceed beyond a rudimentary primary education, and that the *collèges* remain closed to them. Sufficient familiarity with the alphabet and the basic rules of arithmetic to manage their own affairs together with a certain amount of occupational and moral training was on the whole regarded as acceptable for the lower classes; Latin and the humanities were not.

One of those who objected to the laboring population at-

---

[83] Ibid., p. 525. To this effect Diderot supported the idea of scholarships for poor but able students ("Essai," pp. 421-22).

[84] Diderot, "Plan," p. 527.

[85] Durosoy, *Philosophie sociale*, 59.

tending *collèges* was François Mauduit, himself a professor of humanities at the Collège d'Harcourt in Paris. Mauduit made his views known in a Latin discourse delivered at the opening ceremonies of the *collège* for 1773.[86] The discourse aroused some controversy at the time, and was variously interpreted by different critics.

According to the *Année littéraire*, Mauduit argued not that the lower classes should be systematically excluded from *collèges*, but that they should be admitted only after a thorough examination and clear proof of outstanding ability.[87] If this evaluation is correct, Mauduit's primary concern was the ability and intelligence of his students and not their social background. In support of this view Fréron quoted the professor to the effect that the poor should receive a primary education, and that those who were sufficiently intelligent and hard working should receive "all kinds of help" in continuing their studies.[88] However, Mauduit saw no difficulty in retaining rich students in his class even if they were of less than average ability (*incapables*). Their wealth, he reasoned, gave them an advantage in their studies, and even if they were to derive no benefit from them, their livelihoods were assured and society would not suffer on their account.[89] Furthermore, throughout his discourse the professor emphasized the dangers and inconveniences of allowing the laboring population (*vulgaire profane; infaustos pueros*) into *collèges*. Generally failing to gain entry into the liberal professions, "they become the burden of the state, because they have lost their time and the means of learning to earn their livings;" and should they take holy orders, they will only become "the shame and opprobium of religion."[90] Fréron found these opinions eminently reasonable, and commended the author for his "patriotic zeal."[91]

[86] F. Mauduit, *Utrum vulgo Plebeiorum liberos humanioribus litteris excole oporteat* (Paris, 1773).
[87] AL, 1773 VIII, 198-207.   [88] Ibid., p. 203.
[89] Ibid., p. 202.   [90] Ibid., p. 205.   [91] Ibid., p. 206.

The critic of the *Journal encyclopédique*, on the other hand, understood Mauduit to be arguing that the people should be excluded from the *collèges* on principle, and the extremism of this view, together with some rather emotive language the professor used, led him to argue the case for their admission. To the assertion that the republic of letters is weakened as it is extended, the journalist replied that the Middle Ages, in which learning had been most narrowly restricted, was most ignorant, while the eighteenth century, in which learning was broader than it had ever been before, was generally regarded as an enlightened age.[92] He did not, however, directly respond to Mauduit's condemnation of contemporary thought, and specifically the critical, secular and allegedly socially disruptive elements of this thought, which the orator attributed to "the liberty that everyone without distinction dares to take to participate in our learned exercises."[93] Rather, he pointed out that the *collèges* had originally been endowed in favor of the poor, and that the university did not as a body share Mauduit's opinions.[94] The journalist also studiously avoided any reference to the social implications of allowing the poor to attend *collèges*. But then he was no doubt aware that free tuition at *collèges* by no means provided unrestricted entry to these institutions for lower-class children, for they could never in the normal course of things afford the primary instruction that was a necessary prerequisite to secondary studies. Philipon irately asked in this respect, "Is it not absurd that in order to procure a free education for his son, a citizen is obliged to send him at great expense to a master in order to learn the elements of reading, writing and Latin?"[95]

Other writers who, during the last decades of the old regime, touched on the suitability of allowing the laboring

[92] JE, 1774 II, 102-03.   [93] Ibid., p. 105.
[94] Ibid., pp. 105-06.
[95] Philipon, *De l'éducation des collèges* (London, 1784), p. 122.

population to attend *collèges* tended to follow the lead given by Mauduit and Fréron. In a well-written and insightful collection of observations, musings and social criticism, Cerfvol returned to the theme of the social dangers involved in permitting the people to seek a secondary education. He noted that artisans insist on sending their sons to *collèges*, that the classics make poor training for cabinetmakers, and that in the end a young artisan who has learned Latin is generally unable to enter the liberal professions and unwilling to work at a manual trade. Thus, "Because he could not be a cabinetmaker, he is nothing; because he was once socially displaced, entry into all conditions [*états*], into all occupations, is forbidden him."[96] As the result of his unfortunate education the young déclassé can expect at best to be reduced to poverty, at worst to crime.

Bertrand Verlac, a teacher of mathematics in the royal military school of Vanves, shared Cerfvol's feelings on this matter. He complained that education had become too general, calling it a "disordered luxury" when it extended too far down the social scale, and likening it to a sickness in the body politic.[97] But what Verlac complained of was the stubbornness with which the humble persisted in sending their sons to *collèges*, not to *petites écoles*. He wrote:

> On ne sauroit le dire assez clairement, l'habitude de faire apprendre le latin à tous les enfans, a dégénéré en manie. Fils d'artisans, de journaliers, de domestiques, cuistres de Couvens, tout apprend le latin, & tout aspire à la soutane.[98]

If, in Verlac's opinion, secondary education was too widespead, primary education was not. He asked whether the

---

[96] Cerfvol, *Le Radoteur ou Nouveaux mélanges de philosophie, d'anecdotes curieuses [et] d'aventures particulières* (Paris, 2 vols., 1777), vol. I, p. 104.

[97] B. Verlac, *Nouveau plan d'éducation pour toutes les classes de citoyens* (Paris and Vannes, 1789), pp. 4 and 15.

[98] Ibid., p. 16.

curriculum of the *petite école* was adequate, and concluded that it should be extended to include moral and civil instruction beyond the catechism and basic notions of agriculture.[99]

The views of L. S. Mercier, a close observer of Parisian life during the 1780s, paralleled those of Verlac. On the one hand, Mercier believed that "it is absolutely necessary that each individual know how to read, write and count."[100] On the other, he too decried the presence of the sons of artisans and shopkeepers in *collèges* and complained:

> Aujourd'hui le petit bourgeois (qui ne sait pas lire) veut faire absolument de son fils un *latiniste*. Il dit, d'un air capable, à tous ses voisins auxquels il communique son sot projet: *oh! le latin conduit a tout; mon fils saura le latin.*
>
> C'est un très-grand mal. L'enfant va au collège, où il n'apprend rien: sorti du collège c'est un fainéant qui dédaigne tout travail manuel, qui se croit plus savant que toute sa famille, & méprise l'état de son père.[101]

In order to put an end to this situation, Mercier called upon the government to close many of the *collèges*.[102] He also stated, so as to emphasize the importance of the views he has just put forth, that he had written no more important chapter in the *Tableau*. The chapter "Latiniste" from which these statements have been taken is number 415.

Like Cerfvol, Verlac and Mercier, the Benedictine Gourdin regarded the skills of literacy as necessary for the lower classes, and like them he devoted a long and eloquent passage to describing the evils wrought by peasants and artisans attending *collèges*. The student, having followed his classes for a number of years, loses his taste for

---

[99] Ibid., pp. 102-05.

[100] L. S. Mercier, *Tableau de Paris* (Amsterdam, 12 vols., 1783-88), chap. 119. References to this work will be given to chapters rather than volume and page numbers.

[101] Ibid., chap. 415.   [102] Ibid., chap. 415.

his father's trade without having attained a competence in another and is thus declassed. At the same time he comes to feel scorn for his father who by his humble efforts has paid for his education.[103] The implied moral is that for artisans and shopkeepers to give their children a secondary education not only saps the foundations of society, but also courts domestic tragedy. Returning to the public inconveniences of this practice, Gourdin added:

> ... il n'est que trop demontré par une funeste expérience que l'homme du peuple qu'on applique au latin, et toujours dans le dessein d'en faire un prêtre devient infailliblement, Si faute de talent ou d'application &c. il ne parvient point au but, un poid affligeant et Souvent dangereux pour l'Etat, et Si, Sans autre vocation que la haine du travail, ou la honte de partager la misere de ses peres, il entre dans l'état Ecclesiastique, il en devient l'opprobre et le Scandale.[104]

Perreau, who thought it necessary that the lower classes be taught the three r's, also believed that it was "very dangerous" for a good artisan to give his son a secondary education.[105] His reason: the boy will end as a déclassé without a profession.[106] Pernetti's objections to allowing the laboring population to attend *collèges* are identical with those so far considered. If sent to *collèges*, children of peasants and artisans will live "obscure, ignorant, unoccupied [*oisifs*] and often dangerous lives for lack of having been initiated into some useful occupation."[107]

The uniformity of the objections to the people sending their children to *collèges* reveals an unusual degree of agreement among members of the enlightened community. Further, the fact that three authors explicitly referred

---

[103] Gourdin, *De l'éducation*, fol. 97.
[104] Ibid., fol. 102r.
[105] Perreau, *Instruction du peuple*, p. 66.
[106] Ibid., pp. 66-70.
[107] Pernetti, "Réponse," fol. 17v.

to this practice as "dangerous" while others held its likely results to be the break-up of families and the creation of social misfits indicates something of the seriousness with which it was viewed. Only the Jansenists Crévier and Rivard suggested that members of the laboring population should as a matter of course attend *collèges* for at least a few years, or fully believed that scholarships should be established for their benefit. As we have seen, the fundamental premises of the Jansenists were very different from those of most writers on popular education.

While most members of the enlightened community were reluctant to see the people develop a taste for learning, they sought to render popular education more economically and socially useful. To this end they suggested lessons in agriculture, botany, trades and morality, both civic and general. It is curious that while members of the enlightened community wished to teach new subjects, they generally sought to do so in a traditional manner. In many cases they proposed that the new lessons be taught by means of a catechism.

In suggesting that the laboring poor not be taught to read and write, but only three catechisms of religion, morality and rural economy, Goyon is the most clearcut example of this tendency. But he is not the only one. Gourdin, too, called for the composition of a "farmer's catechism,"[108] and many other writers shared this predilection for the catechism as an educational tool, especially for the teaching of morality.

Helvétius suggested that a "catechism of probity" should be written to show the true nature of virtue, and Diderot regarded the composition of a moral and political catechism as desirable.[109] Le Mercier de la Rivière asked that a text be produced that could serve as a "civil and political

[108] Gourdin, *De l'éducation*, fol. 98r.
[109] Helvétius, *De l'esprit*, II, 17; Diderot, "Essai," pp. 417-18.

catechism, which sets forth clearly and simply the natural and fundamental principles of social order and universal morality."[110] Brissot de Warville lamented the fact that France had no "social, civil and criminal catechism for the people," and Vauréal, too, believed that a short, simple moral catechism would be useful.[111] The *Journal encyclopédique* endorsed this opinion in reviewing Vauréal's book, and observed, "It would be necessary that in the catechism of a beneficent government one could learn to be humane, sociable and patriotic."[112]

In his *Tableau de Paris*, L. S. Mercier described a cleric catechizing a group of girls. The questions and answers were fluent but spoken without the least understanding on the part of the little girls, who the author suspected were "thinking of other quite different things. . . ." Meditating upon this spectacle, Mercier exclaimed, "But who will provide us with a catechism of morality?"[113] Obligingly, Verlac concluded his plan of education with a short pamphlet entitled "De la nature de la liberté en général, de la liberté civile et des principes du gouvernement," which he suggested "can serve as a national catechism."[114] Both Grimm and Saint Lambert tried their hands at writing catechisms of this sort,[115] and so did Tschudy.[116] In 1778 Necker

---

[110] Le Mercier de la Rivière, *De l'instruction publique ou Considérations morales et politiques sur la nécessité, la nature et la source de cette instruction, Ouvrage demandé pour le ROI DE SUEDE* (Stockholm, 1775), p. 111.

[111] Brissot de Warville, *Bibliothèque philosophique du législateur*, quoted in JE, 1783 IV, 381; Vauréal, *Plan ou Essai d'Éducation générale et nationale, ou La Meilleure Éducation à donner aux hommes de toutes les nations* (Bouillon, 1783), p. 183.

[112] JE, 1783 VI, 403-04.

[113] Mercier, *Tableau de Paris*, chap. 378.

[114] This is printed at the end of the *Plan*.

[115] P. Hazard, *European Thought in the Eighteenth Century* (New York, 1963), pp. 168-69.

[116] Tschudy, "Catéchisme de morale fait pour des enfans agés de 8 à 9 ans où se trouvent les grandes principes sur la justice, le courage, la bienfaisance [et] la formation des sociétés" (B Mun. Metz. mss. 1467³).

complained of the demand for a moral catechism that would have no recourse to religious principles.[117] But this demand was hardly to be met, even during the Revolution. Most catechisms produced even then retained deism as a moral base.[118]

The distinctive feature of the catechism as a pedagogical tool is that it does not call for a mastery of the skills of literacy.[119] As such it was admirably suited to the needs of an illiterate population and was astutely adopted by the church as its favored means of instruction in earlier, less lettered times. Why this teaching method should have appealed to many men inbued with the values of the Enlightenment, and among them some, such as Diderot, Mercier and Verlac, who regarded the teaching of reading and writing at all levels of society as necessary, calls for explanation.

It is of course possible that the significance of the retention of the term "catechism" is semantic rather than real; that is to say, that it was retained by habit, and that no special meaning was attached to it. Although this is possible, it is not likely. The terms "lesson" or "course" were current at the time. Why do they not appear as often as "catechism" in discussions of popular education? The reason, I suggest, is that many members of the enlightened community hesitated to tie the education of the poor too closely to the skills of literacy. If the people could not read they could not abandon their plows and planes for the *collèges*, and the possibility of knowledge spreading too far or too fast was much reduced. Besides, the knowledge really essential to the poor could be acquired without knowing how to read and write.

[117] Necker, *Opinions religieuses*, p. 24.

[118] J. A. Leith, "French Republican Pedagogy in the Year II," in the *Canadian Journal of History*, III (1968), pp. 57-59.

[119] J. R. Armogathe, "Les catéchismes et l'enseignement populaire en France au dix-huitième siècle," in *Images du peuple*, p. 114.

MORAL AND RELIGIOUS EDUCATION

From the expulsion of the Jesuits from France in 1762 to the outbreak of the Revolution in 1789, the concepts of economic utility and social control dominated writings on popular education. During the decade of the 1760s, however, the issue of social control was in most cases subordinate to that of utility, whereas in the twenty years that followed, the reverse was generally true.

With the shift of emphasis to education as social control, discussion of this issue broadened considerably. To be sure, restriction of education, or keeping the people in a state of relative ignorance, continued to be recognized as one means of controlling them. But on the whole some form of instruction came to be regarded as a more efficacious means to the same end. Against the potential dangers of educating the lower classes, certain authors argued that only by educating the people could social peace be assured. Thus Robinet, writing in one of the great reference works produced in the second half of the eighteenth century, asserted:

> Il faut des lumières pour se laisser gouverner. L'expérience prouve que plus le peuple est abruti plus il est capricieux & obstiné: la difficulté est bien plus grand de vaincre son opiniâtreté, que de persuader des choses justes à un peuple assez policé pour entendre raison.[120]

There was also at this time a growing conviction that the people were more than an inert and passive mass. They came to be regarded as citizens of the state, rather than merely as subjects, and it was argued that in order to fulfill their obligations and duties to the state, nation or *patrie*, they must receive a civic education. Religious instruction for the lower classes was deemed essential by all writers consulted for this study, even those who may have had

---

[120] DUS, art. "Science," XXVIII, 158.

doubts about the truth of religion, or who were outright atheists.[121] But at the same time it came to be suggested more and more often that religious instruction be supplemented by a secular, and usually civic, education. Certain of the writers who held this view came to look upon education not only as a means of maintaining social stability, but also as a way of achieving social reform, and in some cases, the regeneration of society. If Sellier, Perrache, Coyer and Montlinot continued to emphasize the utilitarian aspect of popular education after 1770, most other authors writing at the same time followed the Baron de Tschudy in looking upon education as a means of social engineering.

For Goyon, one of the chief advantages to be derived from instructing the lower classes was social peace. He would have the children of the poor taught "the general principles of universal morality . . . relative to the place which they occupy in society . . . ," and the application of these principles to the ordinary circumstances of their lives.[122] More specifically, the moral education of the poor should be aimed at instilling in them "virtue, the love of order and of duty."[123] If it succeeded in doing so, Goyon believed, criminality would be all but destroyed,[124] and the

[121] Elegantly expressing an idea that can at best be described as shabby, an anonymous contributor to the *Mémoires sur les écoles nationales* wrote: "If I had the honor of being a minister of state and the misfortune of being an atheist, I should still wish to be one of its [Catholicism's] most zealous protectors" (*Mémoire*, XIV, 3). Philipon was of a similar opinion. He asserted that, "if a few men could, absolutely speaking, live without religion, this would not be the people" (*Vues patriotiques*, p. 231). Diderot, who was an atheist, believed that "Atheism might be the doctrine of a small school, but never that of a large number of citizens." Accordingly, he would retain a church and priests, "not as the teachers of sensible folk, but as the guardians of madmen, and their churches, I would allow them to remain as the asylums or the retreat [*petites-maisons*] of a certain kind of fool that could become dangerous if they were neglected entirely" ("Plan," p. 517).

[122] Goyon d'Arzac, *Essais de Laopédie*, p. 5.

[123] Loc. cit.

[124] Ibid., p. 21.

rich could expect to find "greater security in the morals and probity of the lower classes [*des Petits et des Pauvres*]."[125]

Though he emphasized the importance of secular moral training, Goyon by no means neglected religious instruction. His concept of the religion fitting for the lower classes was not, however, a very elevated one. He insisted that:

> . . . ce n'est pas au gens du Peuple qu'il s'agit de prouver le Christianisme. Qu'ils soient instruits des dogmes et des Precepts essentials de cette Religion Divine qui apelle par préference les enfans et les simples; cela suffit.[126]

The concept of the Deity that was to be taught to lower class children was neither that of the Lamb, nor that of a beneficent Father, but rather one resembling a Big Brother or omniscient Policeman.[127] Obedience to the laws was to be encouraged by a double sanction. First, exposure to the temporal consequences of breaking them: "the apparatus of torture, the image of long and frightful sufferings"; and second, by instilling a belief in "eternal torments with which divine justice punishes that which escapes the justice of man."[128]

For Philipon, even more than for Goyon, social control was an overriding concern. He observed:

> La route qui s'ouvre devant l'enfant du peuple, n'est qu'une vaste carrière de misères & de peines. Dès qu'il existe un moyen de les lui adoucir, ce seroit cruauté de ne pas le lui faire connaître.[129]

---

[125] Ibid., p. 29.   [126] Ibid., p. 5.

[127] "La pensée qu'on aura soin de leur incplquer [sic] fortement d'un Dieu temoin continuel de leurs actions, juge eclairé de leurs sentiments les plus secrets et rémunérateur aussi magnifique de la Vertu que Vengeur implacable du Crime, Cette Pensée, sans cesse présente à leur esprit sera de tous les freins le plus puissant contre la fougue des passions qui par la suite, entraineroient leur Coeur" (ibid., p. 7).

[128] Ibid., p. 22.

[129] Philipon, *Vues patriotiques*, pp. 159-60.

Somewhat surprisingly, Philipon found in singing one such means. He regarded it as a distraction capable of turning the attention of the people from its wretched circumstances, and, together with dancing, as a means of creating among the lower classes a frame of mind which he designated "gaiety." It was vital that the people develop this frame of mind for,

> . . . si la gaiété ne détourne habituellement son attention des misères qui affligent son état, il le prend en haine, & finit souvent par jeter là le fardeau de la vie, ou par imprimer de violentes secousses à l'administration.[130]

"Gaiety" hardly seems an adequate guarantor of social peace. But it was not just to expedients such as these that Philipon looked to reconcile the people to their lot.

Generosity and beneficence are virtues of the rich, abstaining from doing harm that of the poor.[131] It was the task of moral education to direct the poor away from drunkenness, theft and idleness, and toward their opposites.[132] Ultimately, it was the goal of this instruction to teach the people its true rights in order to "prevent it from forming imaginary ones."[133] But it was less in the teaching of rights, real or imagined, than in the practice of religion

---

[130] Ibid., p. 125.

[131] Ibid., p. 214.

[132] Ibid., pp. 203, 206-07 and 211.

[133] Ibid., p. 230. The rights of the laboring poor, for Philipon, consisted in enjoyment of the fruit of their labor: "as soon as he is paid for his work, every citizen is quit toward him [the worker] . . ." (ibid., p. 219). Le Mercier de la Rivière held a similar view. He asserted that the idea of, "an equal right to the means of existence [moyens d'exister] and of rendering ourselves happy" was untenable, and that the only right the people could claim was that to personal property, which is to say, to their persons. As society, in Le Mercier's view, was founded on the right of property, it guaranteed the right to "personal property, that which makes you [the poor] your own masters in disposing of your persons according to your wishes, provided, however, that you do not use these rights to infringe upon [blesser] the property of others: that is all you can demand of society" (De l'instruction publique, pp. 49 and 51-52).

that Philipon conceived the moral edification of the laboring poor.

The religion of the people was to consist in a "firm and
blind adherence to the truths of the gospel."[134] To attempt
a reasoned explanation of the basis of religion to the
people would be wasted effort: "it has neither the time nor
sufficient intelligence to think [*raisonner*]."[135] Yet while
Philipon would have had the poor adhere to religion
blindly, he wished them to avoid superstition, and especially fanaticism. Accordingly, he would have allowed the
lower classes to attend mass only once a week. This would
also prevent the people from wasting time praying when
they might be working.[136]

The function Philipon ascribed to religion was nothing if
not worldly. Like Goyon, he saw in religion, "a bit that re-
strains it [the people] on the slope of crime," and counseled
that since the people could never comprehend the principles of the rights of property, religion might well serve as
the "safeguard of the property of others."[137] Another
function of religion was to offer the poor consolation in
time of distress.[138] And this indeed was the ultimate task of
the moral and religious instruction destined for the lower
classes: to make them content with an admittedly harsh lot.
The people were to be taught that their suffering and
obedience were in accordance with the Divine Will, the
proof being that:

> . . . la providence ayant devoué le peuple au travail, l'ap-
> plication qu'il y donne, & la soumission aux peines de
> son état, deviennent le meilleur hommage qu'il puisse
> offrir à la providence.[139]

The poor were also to be taught that an omniscient and
omnipotent being, remarkably like Goyon's Big Brother

---

[134] Philipon, *Vues patriotiques*, p. 240.
[135] Ibid., p. 241.
[136] Ibid., pp. 238-39.   [137] Ibid., pp. 231 and 233.
[138] Ibid., p. 232.   [139] Ibid., p. 239.

deity, would not fail to reward and punish them: "They will tremble then in fear of losing in the other life the fruit of the affliction to which they are subjected [*devoués*] in this one."[140] One would have to look far to find a cruder or more explicit case of religion being proferred as an opiate for the masses. Indeed, Philipon deliberately sought to keep from the laboring population the true causes of its poverty and wretchedness, for he expressed the wish that the effect of the moral and religious instruction of the people might be to "confuse [*étourdir*] it about the evils that beset it on all sides."[141] Summarizing his thought on this matter in a metaphor of striking force and clarity, Philipon wrote:

> Si les moderateurs des nations ne veulent pas que le peuple soulève contr'eux les chaînes dont il est chargé, ils ne sauroient les couvrir trop de fleurs.[142]

Given that the author of the *Vues patriotiques* did not believe it possible significantly to improve the condition of the lower classes, it is perhaps not surprising that these poorly camouflaged chains are the distinctive feature of his book.

Necker was, if possible, even more concerned than Philipon with the potential power of education as a means of social control. Fully aware of the wretchedness of the people, the Swiss banker believed that society as it was then constituted precluded any improvement in their condition. A privileged few who lived in luxury, the masses reduced to poverty: "such are the inevitable [*inséparable*] effects of the laws of property."[143] Rather than calling these laws into question, Necker sought a means of inducing the poor to accept their condition. This he found in a combination of religion and ignorance.

Religion, Necker argued, would occupy the thought of the common people, keep up their courage, and offer

[140] Ibid., p. 242.   [141] Ibid., pp. 160-61.
[142] Ibid., p. 164.
[143] Necker, *Opinions religieuses*, p. 35.

them consolation and hope.[144] The hope offered was not, however, of improved living conditions, but of eternal beatitude after death, and of course the one was to compensate for the other.[145] Like Philipon, Necker expected religion to distract the people from their condition and from its causes, but unlike him, he did not fear that too much time spent in religious observances would lead the lower classes into superstition, or reduce their productivity. On the contrary, the worse the condition of the people became the more they needed the hope and consolation of religion. In what he called an "important observation," Necker laid it down as a principle that "the more the weight of taxation keeps the people in despair [*abattement*] and in wretchedness, the more indispensable it is that they be given a religious education."[146] Though the place of religion in Necker's book is relatively small, its function, which was to create among the poor an attitude of mind the keynotes of which were resignation and hope, was vital.

Less pessimistic about the possibilities of social reform and eventually improving the lot of the lower classes, Lezay-Marnesia was nevertheless convinced that it was necessary to maintain and strengthen the religious faith of the members of the laboring population, for without such faith, he believed, they would scarcely have the courage to face life. He characteristically wished the lower classes to be taught piety and to accept a divine sanction for morality, but to avoid superstition. But above all, he wanted the people to find consolation for the ills they suffered in this life in the anticipation of a beatific afterlife. He asserted:

Il faut leur apprendre à connoître, à aimer, à craindre un Dieu juste, puissant & bon. Il faut éloigner d'eux la superstition absurde; mais les pénétrer de l'esprit d'une religion dont les menaces sont si terribles pour les riches pervers, & qui fait des promesses si magnifiques aux pauvres résignés & patiens. Dans la peine, dans la souf-

[144] Ibid., pp 11-12.   [145] Ibid., p. 50.   [146] Ibid., p. 58.

france, dans l'abandon, ils se souviendront qu'ils ont leur Dieu pour père; ils leveront leurs yeux au ciel, & le courage & la consolation ranimeront leurs coeurs.[147]

If these opinions, expressed by little-known representatives of the Enlightenment, seem atypical of a movement which has generally been described as fundamentally secular and democratic in character, they in fact are not. The great figures of the Enlightment, such as Voltaire, Diderot and Rousseau, all proved equally forceful advocates of social religion.[148]

While there was general agreement that religion was an indispensable element of popular education, the belief that it was also important to teach a morality based on secular criteria tended to become more widespread. Perreau, for example, believed it possible to demonstrate to the poor that "their interest, even in this life, is narrowly bound up with the fulfillment of their duties."[149] Holbach lamented the fact that the people were taught a morality that centered on an afterlife and called for the teaching of "a human morality, which proves to men of all social standings [états] that it is in their interest in this life to be just, good, honest, temperate, etc."[150] Though members of the enlightened community emphasized religious or secular

[147] Lezay-Marnesia, *Le Bonheur dans les campagnes*, pp. 112-13.

[148] On this issue see Payne, *The Philosophes and the People*, chap. v. Boss ("The Development of Social Religion," p. 577) observes that:

> Some of the philosophes who most vehemently attacked the evils of organized religion as the inevitable consequence of ignorance and superstition found it necessary at the same time to defend the social utility of belief. They proposed, in effect, a new kind of organized religion, a *social* religion—that is, one which would promote social harmony and tolerance while satisfying the conservative desire to strengthen the bonds of moral obligation within society and provide a sound foundation for social stability.

[149] Perreau, *Instruction du peuple*, p. 2.

[150] Holbach, *Ethnocratie, ou Le gouvernement fondé sur la morale* (Amsterdam, 1776), pp. 195-96.

principles in accordance with their particular outlooks, they rarely if ever called for one to the exclusion of the other. Gourdin, for example, was in favor of priests acting as teachers and suggested that on holidays they hold classes calculated to produce "the honest man and the good citizen."[151] Thélis believed that "if the inhabitants of the countryside are afflicted with wretchedness [misère], religion alone consoles them in their unhappiness."[152] He made religious instruction an integral part of the curriculum of the écoles nationales, but he also placed patriotism among the foremost values that the schools sought to inculcate.[153]

This relatively new emphasis on civic training is prominent in the works of two physiocrats, Turgot and Le Mercier de la Rivière. In a memoir submitted to Louis XVI in 1775[154] Turgot complained that there were schools for the training of all manner of professionals, but none "to form citizens."[155] Emphasizing the duties rather than rights of citizenship, the philosophe and minister pointed out that one means of maintaining the social order, endearing the king to his subjects and stimulating industry, was to:

> ... faire donner à tous une instruction qui leur manifeste bien les obligations qu'ils ont à la société et à votre pouvoir qui la protège, les devoirs que ces obligations leur imposent, l'intérêt qu'ils ont à remplir ces devoirs pour le bien public et pour leur propre.[156]

The effect of such an education would be to render children having received it "loving of their country, submissive to authority through reason, not through fear."[157] Like

---

[151] Gourdin, De l'éducation, fol. 100r.

[152] Thélis, Mémoire XIII, 18.

[153] See H. Chisick, "Institutional Innovation in Popular Education in Eighteenth-Century France: Two Examples," FHS, x (1977).

[154] Turgot, "Mémoire sur les municipalités" in Oeuvres de Turgot, G. Schelle, ed. (Paris, 5 vols., 1913-23), vol. IV, pp. 574-621. The editor points out that this memoir was written by DuPont de Nemours at the request of Turgot.

[155] Ibid., p. 579.   [156] Ibid., p. 580.   [157] Ibid., p. 581.

Tschudy, Turgot emphasized the rights of the nation rather than those of the individual.

In the same year that Turgot submitted his "Memoir on the Municipalities" to Louis XVI, Le Mercier de la Rivière wrote a brief treatise on education for the King of Sweden. The thesis of Le Mercier's book is that "a government should be the principal educator of its subjects."[158] It follows, then, that politics is intimately bound up with education, and that a government may be looked upon as "a public school."[159]

Like Turgot, Le Mercier did not set forth a curriculum of studies but simply laid down the principles on which a good educational system should be based. He suggested that two sorts of schools be established, the one to teach subjects that are agreeable but superfluous, the other for those that are essential for all. The purpose of these second schools was not to produce scientists and litterateurs, "but only citizens."[160] The subjects to be taught, Le Mercier suggested, could be condensed into a civil and political catechism. This would suffice to "instruct men in their essential and reciprocal duties [and] in the mutual obligations that they should impose on themselves and in their own interest."[161] Le Mercier too, it seems, conceived civic education from the point of view of the duties rather than the rights of citizens.

Thélis and the physiocrats were not alone in looking to moral instruction as a means of fostering social coherence and patriotism. Diderot insisted that schools teach the "duties of citizens," and indeed "all the subjects [connaissances] necessary to a citizen."[162] Frederick the Great concluded a brief essay on education with the observation that good instruction was of prime importance because "it con-

[158] Le Mercier, *De l'instruction publique*, p. 13.
[159] Ibid., p. 14.
[160] Ibid., p. 111.
[161] Loc. cit.
[162] Diderot, "Essai," pp. 418 and 421.

stitutes the ornament and glory of the nation [*patrie*]."[163]
The Count de Vauréal, who like Thélis was an army
officer, looked upon education as the basis of what he
called the "national spirit," and ascribed to it the task of
producing "true and useful patriots."[164] Vauréal was convinced that social strife and the ruin of empires were the
results of too little attention being paid to education:

> . . . le peu de soin de l'éducation des hommes, le peu d'at-
> tention à la tournure de leurs idées & à leur donner de
> bonne heure des opinions vraies sur leur devoir & leur
> dépendance raisonnable. . . .[165]

This is a view to which Verlac would have subscribed. The
teacher turned author himself wished the morality of the
people to be such as to induce the lower classes to find
happiness "in the observance of its duties and in the practice of the moral and social virtues."[166]

Vauréal believed that just as neglect of education could
result in great ills, education properly directed could produce correspondingly great advantages. Ultimately he
looked to education as a source of moral regeneration.[167]
Similarly, Grivel expected that education, if directed to
drawing all classes in society closer together, could ultimately turn the state into "an immense family which would
henceforth have only one will and one interest."[168]

OCCUPATIONAL INSTRUCTION

At the outset of the debate on popular education La
Chalotais had argued that any poor peasant or artisan who

---

[163] Frederick Hohenzollern II, *Lettre sur l'éducation* (Berlin, 1770),
pp. 31-32.
[164] Vauréal, *Plan*, pp. 57 and 101.
[165] Ibid., p. 59.
[166] Verlac, *Plan*, p. 110.
[167] Vauréal, *Plan*, p. 59.
[168] Grivel, *Théorie de l'éducation*, I, 212.

saw beyond his sad occupation (*son triste métier*) would never acquit himself of that occupation satisfactorily. This argument was widely accepted and used by those opposed to educating the lower classes down to the Revolution and beyond. Yet a very similar argument was used by partisans of popular education to favor their cause. They argued, in essence, that the more a man knew of his occupation the better would he exercise it. The difficult and delicate question was to know whether an artisan would use the knowledge he had acquired in preparation for his trade in order to "see beyond it."

Terrisse, Crévier and Rivard, all, it will be recalled, pointed to the proliferation of literature concerned with agriculture and asserted that works on agronomy would remain without practical effect until the men who tilled the soil were capable of reading and understanding them. They maintained simply that agricultural improvement and the economic advantages to be derived from it depended on a better educated peasantry. This argument was extended by other members of the enlightened community to the trades and commerce, and on the whole formed the most widely accepted positive argument in favor of educating the people. It was widely believed, the issues of morality and religion aside, that the education of the lower classes should extend as far as their occupational needs required, but no further. Montlinot, we have seen, wanted the poor given free lessons in the trades though little else, and Formey, if he feared the effects of too widespread a literary education, favored occupational training for the people. Grivel wanted the working classes taught both the skills of literacy and the basic notions of agriculture and botany, while Lezay-Marnesia called for the creation of agricultural schools and for the composition of texts on rural economics.[169]

[169] See above, n. 66. Lezay-Marnesia, *Le Bonheur dans les campagnes*, pp. 114-15.

In the matter of occupational instruction, as in many others, Goyon provides one of the best and fullest examples. We have seen that he proposed three kinds of schools with different curricula for the various groups he distinguished within the "people." Whereas the content of the curricula varied greatly, the nine-year course including Latin, arithmetic and commerce, and the three-year course neglecting even the skills of literacy, the principle on which they were based remained constant. Goyon sought to provide each group with the education suited to its occupational needs and to facilitating its domestic chores. Believing that merchants, artisans and well-off farmers needed an extended course of studies, Goyon proposed for them the ambitious curriculum of his *grandes écoles*. But since those engaged in manual labor had no comparable need, he deemed such instruction for them superfluous and suggested a catechism of rural economy would suffice. It was all a matter of keeping things in proportion and suiting instruction to need.[170]

Philipon, in treating the education of those who must live by "mercenary, manual and servile labor," was obviously not concerned with the instruction of merchants or skilled artisans. Children attending the schools Philipon envisioned were expected to become casual laborers, and as such were not to be prepared for any particular occupation. Rather, they were to be "fit for all."[171] Since manual laborers are by definition dependent on their bodies for their livelihood, physical training counted for a good deal in Philipon's book, as we shall see below. But Philipon must not be taken too much at his word when he says he seeks to develop only the physical capacities of the people.[172] He also suggested that his schools have a teacher for medicine and animal care,[173] and was concerned that the laboring

[170] Goyon d'Arzac, *Essais de Laopédie*, pp. 13-14.
[171] Philipon, *Vues patriotiques*, p. 132.
[172] See below, n. 199.
[173] Philipon, *Vues patriotiques*, p. 79.

poor develop a mentality conducive to their carrying out their simple but necessary tasks with the least hindrance possible.

Philipon believed, no doubt with complete justification, that the lower classes had a tendency toward superstition and fear of the unknown.[174] These qualities he regarded as liabilities in poor peasants and laborers, and suggested that they be taught a modicum of natural science as a corrective. By being shown the true cause of thunder and lightning, for example, they would lose their fear of these phenomena.[175] Or again, it might be demonstrated that certain fears are ungrounded by bringing children into contact with the objects of those fears. One might, Philipon blithely suggested, take students from his schools to play in graveyards at night so that they could learn for themselves that there was no reason to fear either the dark or the dead.[176] It is striking that Philipon wanted his students taught the natural sciences not in order that they might better understand the world, but simply that they might not be hindered in their hewing of wood and drawing of water. Daniel Mornet's characterization of Diderot's views on the purpose of popular education can with equal justice be applied to Philipon, and for that matter, Goyon and a good many others: they all sought to "make more useful men, not more thoughtful ones."[177]

The discussion on occupational education for the lower classes was not without practical results. A large number of schools for the working population were formed in the second half of the eighteenth century, and especially after 1770. On the whole these schools fall into two categories, the first comprised of work schools, which were primarily a form of poor relief, and the second, of *écoles de dessin* and *écoles des arts*, which were intended to train skilled artisans.

[174] Ibid., p. 191. [175] Ibid., pp. 159-60.
[176] Ibid., p. 194.
[177] Mornet, *Origines intellectuelles*, p. 421.

As I have described these schools elsewhere,[178] I will only touch on their more general features here.

Work schools for girls generally taught some aspect of textile manufacture and often paid the students a fee for their work. Whether the skills of literacy or even religion were taught, and how serious the attempt to teach them was, varied from one institution to the other. Boys' schools usually combined some form of military training with instruction in agriculture and the trades, and in them closer attention was paid to the skills of literacy than seems to have been the case in girls' schools. The Duke de La Rochefoucauld-Liancourt established work and trades schools for both boys and girls on his estates, while similar schools were founded by a self-styled Count de Pawlet in Paris and by Thélis in Burgundy and the capital. Despite differences in emphasis and organization, the work schools seem to have shared a common origin as attempts at poor relief or experiments in enlightened beneficence.

The *écoles de dessin* and *écoles des arts* which began to proliferate after mid-century were inspired by economic rather than social considerations. These schools were based on the assumption that science could profitably be applied to the everyday problems of business, commerce and the trades, and that a more competent workforce would contribute greatly to national prosperity. They offered occupational training for artisans, clerks and often even ordinary workers (*ouvriers*), but were on the whole geared to the needs of the most highly skilled sections of the laboring population.

Perrache, in a memoir he read before the Academy of Lyon in 1765, observed that whereas the ignorance of workers resulted in their poverty and arrested the progress of commerce, a well-directed technical education would help them overcome blind routine and would foster national prosperity.[179] In a second memoir dating from 1774

[178] H. Chisick, "Innovation in Popular Education."
[179] Perrache, "Réflexions sur l'éducation," (1765) A Ac. Lyon, mss. 147, fol. 137r.

he set forth a plan for a trades school that would teach grammar, history and arithmetic, and more specifically higher mathematics, commerce (which because of the nature of Lyon was expected to be the largest class), *dessin*, experimental physics and practical geometry.[180] There is no evidence to show that Perrache succeeded in founding this school, but an institution of the same sort had been functioning in Amiens for nearly twenty years.

In 1750 Jacques Sellier persuaded the municipal council of Amiens to support an *école des arts* in which he would teach without charge practical geometry, architecture (including specific skills for the building trades) arithmetic (including bookkeeping and weights and measures) and trades and manufactures to workers, artisans and whoever else was interested. The council, expressing its satisfaction at the prospect of more reliable clerks and better-trained artisans, continued to support the school until after the Revolution. Sellier maintained the trade oriented and utilitarian spirit of the institution, taking care to teach only so much of a subject as was necessary for his students' occupational needs and attempting to prevent them from developing a taste for the commercially valueless fine arts. In a manufacturing town such as Amiens, Sellier once wrote, one should breathe only the spirit of utility.[181]

Like Sellier and Perrache, Gourdin regarded ignorant workers and work by rote as economic liabilities. The *ouvrier automate* who is a slave to "blind routine" can become a positive danger to the state, for the mistakes that necessarily follow from his ignorance result in decreased production and diminish national wealth.[182] Having forcefully de-

---

[180] Perrache, "Project d'un Établissement d'Éducation relative aux sciences, au commerce et aux arts," (1774), A Ac. Lyon, mss. 147, fols. 87v-91r.

[181] ". . . l'on ne doit respirer que l'utile, surtout pour les gens du peuple, gens de travail" (Sellier, "Lettre au corps de ville," [1782], A Mun. Amiens, BB126[371], pp. 4-5).

[182] Gourdin, *De l'éducation*, fol. 97r.

scribed the dangers of ignorance among the laboring population, Gourdin wondered whether there might not be equally great objections to providing comprehensive occupational training for them. He asked:

> Mais en général l'ignorance de cette classe d'hommes n'est elle plus avantageuse que pre judiciable à l'Etat? En lui voulant apprendre à reflechir, à penser relativement au travail qui l'occupe, n'est il pas à apprehender que le rayon de lumiere que l'on veut diriger uniquement sur l'ouvrage, ne porte le jour dans tout l'atelier et n'en decouvre la misere? Sous le pretexte de rendre le pauvre plus habile ouvrier, il est bien à craindre qu'on ne lui fasse sentir tout le poid du malheur de sa condition, et que par conséquent on ne le porte au decouragement ou à la revolte?[183]

In reply to this question Gourdin readily admitted that any instruction "that tends, by cultivating a child's mind, to cause him to leave the place that nature has assigned him is always and absolutely as disadvantageous to him as it is harmful to the state, because it inverts the order of things."[184] But it was not, he argued, either occupational training or attendence at *petites écoles* that had this effect. As for writers who wished to close *petites écoles* to the people, they have seen the problem but have failed to understand it fully. Like Guyton and others, Gourdin asserted that it was the *collèges* and not primary or occupational instruction that produced the déclassés that the educated men of the eighteenth century so feared. To drive home this point the Benedictine used the following metaphor:

> Ainsi toute institution qui tend à porter dans la cabane du pauvre quelques rayons d'une lumiere étrangère à sa condition, y fait briller le feu terrible de l'eclair qui rend les ténébres et plus profondes et plus affreuses.

[183] Loc. cit.
[184] Loc. cit.

L'instruction au contraire absolument relative aux professions pour lesquelles il est né, ressemble au rayon
bienfaisant de l'astre du jour qui embellit, colore et viv-
ifie les objets qu'il éclaire.[185]

Thus, for Gourdin occupational training posed no threat
to society; the light it gives is steady and gentle, and its effect would be to render the working population more content, for:

En apprenant à l'ouvrier à raisonner les procédés de son
art, en lui enseignant le *pourquoi* de ses operations sa ma-
nipulation cesse d'être une routine purement mecan-
ique, elle lui devient intéressante, parce qu'elle a de quoi
piquer Sa curiosité et la satisfaire. il s'attache de plus en
plus à une profession qu'il a appris à estimer. Et
glorieux de faire continuellement l'essai de ses forces,
son esprit satisfait jouit avec tranquillité du fruit de ses
efforts. Le dégoût et l'ennui ne naissent que d'une situation pénible.[186]

Jaubert would have agreed heartily with these views. He
asked that the working population be held in higher esteem, and argued that artisans (*artistes*) be taught "to think
better for themselves."[187]

On the whole, Gourdin's views on occupational instruction can with justice be taken as representative of those of
the enlightened community. He was perhaps more optimistic than most in his expectation that the people would
not extend the critical habit of thought learned for occupational needs to other areas. But certainly he exemplifies the
widely held belief that education should be given according
to social standing and should prepare children for the occupations they were expected to exercise later in life.
Gourdin believed emphatically that knowledge not pertain-

[185] Ibid., fol. 97v.   [186] Ibid., fols. 97-98.
[187] Jaubert, "Introduction" to his *Dictionnaire raisonné universel des arts et
métiers*, quoted from JE, 1773 IV, 53.

ing to these occupations would best be avoided. Yet by conceiving the occupational instruction fitting for the people so broadly, he, Perrache, Bachelier, Sellier and others came to propose, and in some cases actually to put into practice, some extremely ambitious and far-reaching programs of education for the laboring population. Occupational need was the strongest argument in the arsenal of partisans of a broad curriculum for the lower classes, and many writers determined how much education would be fitting for the people primarily on the criterion of how much instruction was necessary in order to enable them adequately to exercise their trades, whether "sad" or otherwise.

PHYSICAL TRAINING

Philippe Ariès has said that concern with hygiene and physical education was an element introduced into discussions on education during the eighteenth century.[188] This contention finds support in the literature devoted to popular education, especially after 1770.

Even where authors did not go into detail about physical education, they often showed themselves aware of its importance. Gourdin, for example, in considering the people collectively as a "physical being," pointed out the general importance of physical education without making any specific suggestions.[189] Similarly, in reviewing a book on the physical education of the ancients, the *Journal encyclopédique* observed that it would be desirable if contemporaries were to introduce into their educational programs "the method of increasing the forces of the body together with the culture of the mind."[190] This wish did not go unheeded and had in fact been partly fulfilled at the time it was expressed.

[188] Philippe Ariès, *Centuries of Childhood*, trans. R. Baldick (New York, 1968), p. 133.
[189] Gourdin, *De l'éducation*, fol. 94v.   [190] JE, 1774 I, 200.

Rousseau had focused attention on the importance of physical education in the second book of *Emile*. Himself drawing on Locke and Montaigne, the *philosophe* advocated giving children a great deal of exercise and accustoming them to withstanding various forms of discomfort. Light clothing, exposure to cold, simple food, poor bedding, interrupted sleep, swimming—all these were to form part of a child's education, and were intended to safeguard his health and toughen him.[191] These two themes were taken up and treated in a similar manner by other educational theorists.

The author of *De l'éducation publique* prescribed the following formula to assure the health of children:

> Endurcir le peau à tous les tems; assouplir les muscles à tous les exercices; accoutumer l'estomac à tous les mets simples; voilà ce qui donnera aux enfans une santé ferme.[192]

Coyer was in agreement with these sentiments and favored a mildly Spartan regimen remarkably similar to that proposed by Rousseau in *Emile*.[193] Grivel thought it necessary to "accustom children early to a harsh life. . . "[194] and in all particulars subscribed to the views of the Abbé and the citizen of Geneva. But Grivel presented these ideas on physical education more fully and comprehensively than had most of his predecessors, for he followed the practice, increasingly common after 1770, of dividing his treatise into three sections, one dealing with the mind, a second with the heart and the third with the body.[195] Thus, after having been long neglected, physical training was ascribed a

[191] Rousseau, *Emile*, book II. This emphasis on physical training is also to be found in the essays of Montaigne and Locke on education, and was a generally accepted theme in the enlightened community.

[192] *De l'éducation publique*, pp. xv-xvi.

[193] Coyer, *Plan*, pp. 11-115.

[194] Grivel, *Théorie de l'éducation*, I, 348.

[195] Another example of this tendency is Perreau's *Instruction du peuple*.

place of equal importance with intellectual and moral instruction.

Eighteenth-century attitudes to physical education have little in common with contemporary ones, in which field sports and ball games play so large a part. During the age of Enlightenment, which was also an age of primitive demographic patterns, the desire to preserve the lives of infants and children by strict and even severe measures of personal hygiene left little room for the concept of physical education as sport. And if, as we have seen, the kind of physical training proposed for children in general was rough and arduous, that intended for the children of the laboring population was even more so. Their lot in life made it imperative that they not only receive such care and training as would conduce to their health, but also that they be inured to hardship and discomfort.

Goyon suggested daily cold baths during infancy and long, hard exercises during childhood to assure the health of the children of the people and to accustom them to the rigors of life.[196] Thélis proposed to train commoners in his school to the "hardest [*plus pénibles*] and most useful labors of the countryside. . . ."[197] Sellier was of the opinion that "the education of the common man [*des hommes du peuple*] must be firm and even a little harsh, it is necessary to be able to make of them at least good soldiers."[198] The author to place greatest emphasis on physical education, however, was Philipon.

Summarizing the goal of his proposed plan of popular education, Philipon wrote:

> . . . j'ai proposé de ne developper dans le peuple que les forces corporelles qui sont les seuls instruments de son pouvoir & de sa fortune, & d'éloigner soigneusement de

[196] Goyon d'Arzac, *Essais de Laopédie*, p. 22.
[197] Thélis, *Mémoire* II, 2.
[198] Sellier, "Lettre sur l'école de filiature" (1782). A Mun. Amiens, BB 126[370], p. 2.

> son esprit toutes ces connoissances qui ne font [qu'] exciter en lui les desirs inquiets, le dégoût de son état, les murmures contre la société.[199]

If Philipon expected physical training to take the place of subjects that might lead the people to question their condition, he was also concerned to toughen children of the laboring poor to the harsh life that they would have to lead on growing up. Cold baths, winter and summer, were recommended, and so were rough and even moderately dangerous exercises; for the people must learn to endure pain and risk danger. Food was to consist of only bread and water with fruit in summer and gruel in winter, for "sobriety which is a virtue for the rich is a necessity for the poor."[200] Children were to have only smocks and trousers to wear in order to "so harden their bodies that the various impressions of the air and the seasons will have no effect on them."[201] While in the school, students were to sleep without blankets, on benches, or on the floor. Philipon's principle, as he stated himself, was to diminish the needs of the children of the poor so as to better prepare them for a life of want.[202]

This overly pessimistic conception of physical education for the lower classes was attacked vigorously in the *Année littéraire*. The journalist observed acidly that there was little point in attempting to inure the people to hardship for "they are, unhappily, already only too exposed to it."[203] And as his evaluation of the condition of the people differed fundamentally from Philipon's, the critic continued:

> Il suppose que le peuple étant fait pour être misérable, c'est le rendre heureux, que de le former de bonne heure à la vie la plus dure. J'aime à penser que nous n'en

[199] Philipon, *Vues patriotiques*, p. 330.
[200] Ibid., pp. 88-89, 94-95 and 57.
[201] Ibid., pp. 63-64.
[202] Ibid., pp. 67-68, and 63.
[203] AL, 1784 I, 235.

sommes pas réduits à une pareille extrêmité. Qu'il seroit malheureux le peuple, dont le bonheur ne seroit appuyé que sur de semblables systêmes.[204]

By contrast, the *Journal encyclopédique* approved Philipon's book as a whole, and his treatment of physical education in particular.[205] It seems, too, that the opinion of the *pro-philosophe* journal was the more widely held.[206]

The emphasis on inuring the young to extreme conditions and to hardship was given a theoretical basis by, among others, Fourcroy de Guillerville, the younger son of a noble family who became an artillery officer, and served for twenty years in the colonies before returning to France to buy the post of *conseiller du roi* in a *baillage* of the Beauvaisis. In a work on physical education the second edition of which appeared in 1783, Fourcroy cited Locke to the effect that *"nos corps peuvent endurer ce à quoi ils sont accoutumés de bonne heure."*[207] This proposition of course follows from the basic tenets of sensationalist psychology, and if it was seldom stated outright, it nonetheless conditioned the views of most members of the enlightened community to physical education.

One of the forms of physical training designed to toughen infants and children that enjoyed wide popularity among theoreticians of education was the system of cold baths. Smollet caused Peregrine Pickle to undergo and benefit from this therapy, and later wrote a treatise on a related subject.[208] But the theory and practice of cold baths was not confined to boisterous novelists and their roguish creations. In an immensely influential book first published

---

[204] Loc. cit.

[205] JE, 1784 II, 210.

[206] See above, pp. 16-17.

[207] Fourcroy de Guillerville, *Les enfans élevés dans l'ordre de la nature ou Abrégé de l'histoire naturelle des enfans du premier âge à l'usage des Pères & Mères de Famille* (Paris, 1783), p. 27

[208] T. Smollet, *The Adventures of Peregrine Pickle*, J. L. Clifford, ed. (Oxford, 1969), pp. 28-29, and n. 1 to p. 28.

in 1761,[209] the celebrated Swiss doctor Tissot recommended cold baths daily, both winter and summer, and suggested that during warm weather infants be plunged indiscriminately into buckets, fountains, streams, rivers and lakes.[210] Strange to relate, it appears that most of Tissot's readers adopted or shared these opinions. Both Coyer and Grivel were partisans of this system.[211] Goyon called it a "powerful corroborative" and endorsed it warmly,[212] and Philipon also, we have seen, favored it. Fourcroy had seen this system in use, apparently with good effect, by the Indians of Saint-Domingue during his service there. He considered using it for his own son, but hesitated, both because the climate of France was so different, and because Madame de Guillerville had reservations about the idea. Fourcroy chanced, however, to come upon a copy of Tissot's *Avis au peuple*, and finding that the medical science of the Enlightenment corresponded with the folk medicine of a primitive people, needed only the prompting of the author of the *Avis*, with whom he corresponded, to undertake the experiment.[213] The result, Fourcroy reported, was gratifying.[214] Nor was the army officer turned judge alone in actually putting into practice this rather Spartan measure of childrearing. He asserted that he knew of at least one hundred other cases.[215]

Whether Tissot's system contributed to keeping the population growth that France experienced in the eighteenth century from becoming any greater than it was can-

[209] Tissot, *Avis au peuple*. The influence of this book is indicated by the facts that by 1779 it had gone through fifty editions, that it had been translated into German, Dutch, Flemish, English, Swedish and Italian ("Avis" of editor, 1779 edition), and that it is often cited by authors writing on popular education.

[210] Ibid., II, 63.

[211] Coyer, *Plan*, 20-25; Grivel, *Théorie de l'éducation*, I, 300-21.

[212] Goyon, *Essais de Laopédie*, p. 23.

[213] Fourcroy, *Les enfans élevés dans l'ordre de la nature*, pp. 38-40.

[214] Ibid., p. 75.

[215] Ibid., p. 94.

not be said. What is certain is that Tissot himself, Fourcroy, Coyer and Goyon expected it to have the effect of helping to arrest the process of depopulation that they believed was underway.

During the last two decades of the old regime a consensus of opinion on popular education emerged. It was generally agreed that the people should receive instruction in the three r's and in religion, together with a degree of training in subjects of occupational and domestic utility. Physical training also became an integral part of educational plans devised for the lower classes after 1770. This training was often designed with Spartan severity in order to inure the people to the harsh life they would have to lead.

The trend toward secularizing moral education, already under way in the 1760s, was continued, but, significantly, no writer consulted for this study thought that religion could be dispensed with in the education of the lower classes. Utility, and during the 1770s and 1780s, more especially patriotism, were the values that informed the cautious and partially secularized programs of popular education, while social control was a fundamental concern for almost all who approached the subject.

This summary of thought on popular education during the decades before the Revolution does not, on consideration, seem altogether satisfying. If the preceding chapters have, as I hope, adequately described what was being thought and written on the instruction of the lower classes during the Enlightenment, they in turn raise a new series of questions. Why did writers in the second half of the eighteenth century emphasize the specific aspects of popular education described above? Why such limited programs of education for the people? Why such emphasis on physical education? Why the concern with patriotism? Why, indeed, such ado about education at all? The answers to these questions cannot be determined by reference to socioeconomic conditions alone. Men's outlooks are formed by current opinions on nature and on man, but also by their hopes, fears and illusions. Only by examining the beliefs and anxieties, founded and unfounded, of members of the enlightened community can we come to a more satisfactory understanding of them and their thought.

CHAPTER IV

The Climate of Opinion in France: 1762-1789

A Crisis Mentality

After mid-century, and especially after 1770, educated Frenchmen came to feel that their society was functioning under stress, and even that it was in a state of crisis. And so it was. Historians have analyzed in great detail the nature and effects of the economic depression that set in after an extended period of prosperity in about 1770: the rise in prices, fall in real wages and series of bad harvests in these years; an increase in population so great that it began to outstrip the food supply; and a fiscal system that could not meet the demands made on it, thus bringing the country to the edge of bankruptcy. Taken together, these factors comprise the conjuncture of circumstances that created the preconditions for the Revolution of 1789. The second half of the eighteenth century has long, and with good reason, been regarded as the "crisis of the old régime."[1] The curious thing is that contemporaries give little indication that they were aware of a crisis arising from a conjuncture of socioeconomic and demographic factors, but a great deal to suggest that they believed themselves faced with another, fundamentally different, sort of crisis.

There was, it is true, considerable discussion of state finance and tax reform after mid-century, and a great and growing interest in agriculture. But far from showing awareness that population was growing faster than the supply of food, most contemporaries believed that the

---

[1] See Soboul, *La Crise de l'ancien régime*, for a thorough treatment of the crisis of the conjuncture.

population of France was in decline. The economic depression of the years after 1770 passed without much comment, perhaps because France was still so overwhelmingly agricultural a nation, and the forces determining the success or failure of the harvest were beyond human control. On the other hand, it was widely believed that France was radically corrupt, that the luxury enjoyed by a wealthy few rendered them effete and self-centered, that the rehabilitation of the idea of self-interest was destroying altruism and engendering an egoistic ethic, and that physical debility, moral depravity and widespread corruption were resulting in depopulation, and threatening the very fabric of society. Indeed, many contemporaries believed that their society was degenerate. Even so, they did not despair. They believed that new moral values would regenerate society, and that there was a means by which these values could be given general currency. Thus, though they thought themselves faced with a crisis of moral dissolution, the men of the later eighteenth century regarded themselves as equal to it.

Of the main assumptions that fed the crisis mentality of the last twenty years of the old regime, the first, the belief that France was facing depopulation, can be shown to have had little or no basis in fact, while the second, the conviction that French society was corrupt, cannot be verified. But this is of little importance. For men judge and act not according to absolute truths, but according to what they perceive and what they believe to be true or expedient. Without an examination of the beliefs and presuppositions that colored the climate of opinion in which the upper classes of French society lived under Louis XV, and more particularly under his successor, it will hardly be possible to appreciate the views of the enlightened community on education in general, and on the education of the lower classes in particular. Although the ideas that form the intellectual background to the works on education written in this period—depopulation, corruption, luxury, egoism, the decline of community spirit, degeneration and the moral virtue of the countryside—are all but inextricably intertwined, for purposes of analysis I shall treat them separately.

ELEMENTS OF THE CRISIS

Depopulation

To members of the enlightened community, population was a great good, and even, for many, an index of national well-being. Jaubert, for example, stated that nothing was more important than population, "since the power and wealth of empires depend on it."[2] In *The Wealth of Nations*, Adam Smith asserted that "the most decisive mark of the prosperity of any country is the increase in number of inhabitants,"[3] and Rousseau similarly believed that population was an accurate indicator of national power and wealth.[4] The *Dictionnaire universel des sciences* laid it down as a principle that the first rule of politics was that "the prosperity of a state derives from its population,"[5] while the *Encyclopedie méthodique*, after warning that prosperity rather than numbers was the essential point, asserted:

Tous les administrateurs cherchent à augmenter & à conserver le nombre de ceux qui la [population] com-

[2] Jaubert, *Des Causes de la dépopulation et des moyens d'y remédier* (London, 1767), p. 3.

[3] McNulty, "Adam Smith's Concept of Labor," p. 335.

[4] J. J. Spengler, *French Predecessors of Malthus: A Study in Eighteenth-Century Wage and Population Theory* (Durham, 1942), p. 347. This work is remarkable for its scope and immensely rich documentation. Though Spengler's chief concern here was not social theory, he nevertheless produced one of the fullest and best studies of this subject to date. See also L. Proal, "Les causes de la dépopulation et ses remèdes d'après Jean-Jacques Rousseau," in *La Grande Revue*, CII (1920), pp. 256-57.

[5] DUS, art. "Paysan," XXVI, 272.

posent. La vraie force de l'état consiste dans la multitude des habitans, & la politique indique les moyens de parvenir à ce but.[6]

So widely was it believed that a large population was an asset that, it was charged, the assertion that a government had increased its population was taken as praise and proof of its success, while decline in population was regarded as censure and an indication of bad government.[7]

The view that power and prosperity depended on population was so widely accepted at the time and appeared so obvious that it was often tacitly assumed, or mentioned in passing as an incontrovertible axiom of politics.[8] In the context of a preindustrial economy this is not an altogether unreasonable point of view. It also explains why contemporaries regarded the prospect of depopulation with such discomfort. And that many of them did hold this belief there can be little doubt.

Of the great *philosophes*, Montesquieu, Rousseau and Diderot believed that Europe was suffering depopulation, while only Voltaire held a contrary view.[9] He does not seem to have carried the majority of the enlightened community with him. In his book on population, Cerfvol asserted that "our uncertainty with respect to causes in no way destroys the reality of the effects. The human species

---

[6] EM, art. "Population," III, 671.

[7] DUS, art. "Population," XXXVI, 590. This passage reappears in the EM article on population, III, 669.

[8] Gourdin, for example, assumed that the doubling of the population was in itself desirable (*De l'éducation*, fol. 95v); Goyon de la Plombaine similarly put forward as one intended goal of a number of projects of reform he was proposing that they would increase population (*L'Unique Moyen de soulager le peuple, et d'enrichir la nation françoise*, Paris, 1775, p.v.); Robinet began an argument in favor of increasing population, "Comme la population est le premier degré de la puissance . . ." (DUS, art. "Paysan," XXVI, 272); and Lefebvre de Beauvray asserted in passing that it was unthinkable to deny that population was a good (DSP, art. "Population").

[9] A. Raymond, "Le problème de la population chez les encyclopédistes," in VS, XXVI (1963), pp. 1379-88.

is diminishing in number."[10] Fourcroy, who shared this conviction, stated dramatically that "depopulation has made itself felt in several European states to the point that it is no longer possible to hide the fact."[11] Jaubert, who accepted depopulation as a fact and sought only to explain its causes, cited decrees of the Parlements of Bordeaux and Dijon complaining of a decline in population.[12] La Chalotais, we have seen, complained that it was a pity to have so many students in a kingdom in which everyone was complaining of depopulation.[13] Coyer believed that the phenomenon was not of recent date, for he wrote that moral laxity (*mollesse de moeurs*) had long been depopulating the earth, and that it hardly contained one-fiftieth the inhabitants it had in the time of Caesar.[14] Depopulation was one of the ills that Goyon hoped education would help arrest.[15] Thélis was deeply concerned about the death rate among the peasantry, and repeatedly suggested that surgeons be kept in the countryside so as to provide medical aid for them.[16] The eminent Swiss doctor Tissot opened his widely read treatise on popular medicine with the statement that "the decrease in the number of inhabitants of this country [France] is a fact that strikes everyone, and which the censuses demonstrate."[17] Of course, the censuses, such as they were, showed no such thing. Still, Tissot was not without some justification for his claim, for the calculations of certain of his contemporaries did indeed purport to show that the population of France or of other European states had fallen.

[10] [Cerfvol] *Mémoire sur la population, dans laquelle on indique le moyen de la rétablir, & de se procurer un corps militaire toujours subsistant & peuplant* (London, 1768), p. 18.

[11] Fourcroy, *Les Enfans élevés dans l'ordre de la nature*, p. 25.

[12] Jaubert, *Des Causes de la dépopulation*, p. 2.

[13] See above, chap. II, n. 44.

[14] Coyer, "L'année merveilleuse," in *Bagatelles morales*, p. 43.

[15] Goyon d'Arzac, *Essais de Laopédie*, p. 9.

[16] Thélis, *Mémoire* I, 31; XII, 12-13; XVI, 7.

[17] Tissot, *Avis au peuple*, I, 1.

Cerfvol accepted Vauban's estimate of 18,700,000 people for the population of France in 1660. He assumed that at best a family would produce two surviving children, and that a certain proportion of these would never marry. On this basis he calculated that by 1769 the population of France would have fallen to 9,548,000, a decline of almost fifty percent over seventy years.[18] Similarly, the physiocrat Quesnay believed that the population of France had fallen from twenty-four million in 1650 to nineteen million in 1701, and then fell a further three million to sixteen million in 1714, remaining constant thereafter until 1750.[19] The author of a pamphlet entitled *Richesses de l'état* put the population of France at twenty million in 1700, and asserted that it had declined by a fifth in the following sixty years.[20] Discussing the population of Italy, Cantillon maintained that that country had only six million inhabitants in the eighteen century, whereas it had twenty-six million in antiquity.[21]

If the conviction that France was undergoing depopulation was extremely widespread, it was not universal. First, certain writers observed that there was little point in lamenting a diminution in the numbers of a people if those already in existence could not expect a decent standard of living.[22] Second, there were those, who, like Damilaville in

---

[18] Cerfvol, *Mémoire sur la population*, pp. 34-46.

[19] A. Landry, "Les idées de Quesnay sur la population," in *Revue d'histoire des doctrines économiques et sociales*, II (1909), p. 61.

[20] JE, 1763 VI-1, 39.

[21] [Cantillon] *Essai sur la nature du commerce en général* (London, 1756), p. 111.

[22] Thus, for example, Clément observed, "I do not know why there is so much talk about population. Are there not already enough poor and unhappy folk, enough unjust people [*méchans*] and wrongdoers on the earth?" (PDCV, art. "Population"). In reviewing an anti-*philosophe* work, the *Journal encyclopédique* wrote: "The numerous troop of half-baked political theorists cries, *population, population*; but this population, so ridiculously extolled by old bachelors, must be in proportion to the food that a country can produce" (JE, 1774 III, 434).

his rambling and contradictory article "Population" in the *Encyclopédie*, deduced the stability of world population from general principles. On the basis of his belief in the regularity of the laws of nature, Damilaville asserted that the population of the world had been, and could be expected to remain, stable.[23] And then, there are the facts.

A number of eighteenth-century pioneers in demography, principally Expilly, Messance and Moheau, published statistics to show that the population of France was neither falling nor so low as Cerfvol or Quesnay believed.[24] Nor were their works neglected. Lefebvre de Beauvray cited both Expilly and Messance to prove that the population of France was greater than was often argued,[25] and though the demographers were too late to be incorporated into the *Encyclopédie*, they do figure prominently in later reference works. The article "Population" of the *Dictionnaire universel des sciences* first recapitulates the Hume-Wallace debate on the relative populousness of the ancient and modern worlds, and concludes with Hume that the world has not suffered depopulation.[26] The *Encyclopédie méthodique* condenses this substantial section of Robinet's article into a brief, noncommittal paragraph, but then follows him closely in discussing the movement of population

[23] *Encyclopédie*, art. "Population," XII, 91. In this rambling and somewhat contradictory article, Damilaville first accepted Wallace's view that the population of the known world had declined since antiquity (ibid., p. 89). However, he then argued that since nothing was known of the population of the nonclassical world, one could make no generalizations about world population as a whole (ibid., p. 90). Not altogether consistently, Damilaville then devoted the rest of the article, which is far the greater part of it, to an examination of the causes of depopulation (ibid., pp. 91-103).

[24] Expilly's *Dictionnaire géographique, historique et politique des Gaules et de la France* appeared in six volumes between 1762 and 1770; Messance's *Recherches sur la population . . .* was first published in 1764; and Moheau's *Recherches et considérations sur la population de la France* was published in 1778.

[25] DSP, art. "Population."

[26] DUS, art. "Population," XXVI, 583-90.

in modern states. It is here that Expilly and the rest are cited to demonstrate that Europe was not in fact suffering from depopulation.[27] Yet even after having shown that the fear of depopulation was unfounded, and taking to task the "railers who raise an outcry about depopulation," the *Encyclopédie méthodique*, still following Robinet, again stressed that population was the basis of a state's power, and outlined a set of policies designed to assure and increase it.[28]

Even among those who were aware of the findings of contemporary demography, belief in depopulation died hard. What the *Dictionnaire universel des sciences* denied in its article "Population," it asserted to be true in its treatment of depopulation. The question of the relative populousness of the ancient and modern world is again broached, and this time decided in favor of the ancients. Having marshaled figures to show that ancient Egypt, Palestine, Greece, Italy and Gaul had greater population densities— in some cases four and five times greater—than eighteenth-century England, the author concluded that "history shows" that "in modern times the earth has lost considerable population."[29] The "fact" of depopulation established, the author went on to explain its causes. He recognized two principal physical agents of depopulation, change in climate over the centuries, and disease (particularly smallpox and venereal disease), but regarded these as insufficient to account for the "observed" change. A long list of moral causes, among which are included properly social and economic factors, is then adduced. It includes some twenty items, the first fourteen of which are treated separately. First comes religion, and a criticism, clearly inspired by Montesquieu, of the effects of Mohamedan polygamy and Catholic clerical celibacy on population. Then follow such items as harsh treatment of servants and

---

[27] Ibid., 592-93 and EM, art. "Population," iii, 668-70.
[28] Ibid., pp. 670-71.
[29] DUS, art. "Dépopulation," xv, 445-51.

beggars, the excessive severity of the criminal law, and the practice of keeping large numbers of servants. Primogeniture and large doweries are criticized for favoring the eldest children of wealthy families and forcing the rest into sterile bachelorhood. The lack of encouragement to marry, recourse to hired wet nurses, the large number of soldiers, the predominence of commerce which forces men to travel, neglect of agriculture, the size of modern states, luxury and corruption are all held to have deleterious effects on population. So, too, are the extent of poverty, mismanagement of institutions of relief for the poor, the tax system, religious persecution and warmongering kings. In combination these causes, the author concluded lugubriously, "have given such terrible blows to the population of the human species that it can no longer recover."[30]

Thus, in the midst of a period of great demographic expansion, and, furthermore, an expansion of which evidence was readily available, contemporaries continued to lament and fear depopulation. In something of an understatement, J. J. Spengler observed that despite the findings of Expilly, Messance, Moheau and others, the belief in a static or declining population "did not wholly disappear in the last quarter of the century."[31] Rather more forcefully, and on the whole justly, Ira Wade has described the eighteenth century as "an age haunted by the idea of depopulation."[32]

[30] Ibid., pp. 451-59. The treatment of depopulation is in substance the same in the *Encyclopédie* article "Population" and the DUS article "Dépopulation." Large parts of this article were in turn borrowed by the EM for its article "Dépopulation." The emphasis on moral and political factors is the same in all three cases, as is the assertion of the value and importance of population. The DUS, however, was more categorical about the actuality and extent of contemporary depopulation than the other two works.

[31] Spengler, *French Predecessors of Malthus*, pp. 77-78.

[32] I. Wade, "Poverty in the Enlightenment," in *Europaische Aufklarung; Studies Presented to Herbert Dieckmann*, H. Friedrich and F. Schalk, eds., (Munich, 1967), p. 317.

Why, despite good evidence to the contrary, the belief in depopulation persisted in the second half of the eighteenth century, is something of a problem. The explanation for it is by no means straightforward, and must take into account such varied factors as changing attitudes toward death, the assumption that the towns were draining the countryside and the widespread supposition that the causes of depopulation were fundamentally moral in character.

Today we approach the study of population with various kinds of mechanical computational equipment and graph paper, and in the case of eighteenth-century France, we are, despite certain regional anomalies,[33] impressed with the upward curves of the graphs we construct. The works of Expilly and the rest not withstanding, members of the enlightened community for the most part formed their impresssions of the demographic well-being of their society from the raw facts of demography, which is to say, from birth and death. It was death that impressed them.

For reasons that are not altogether clear, intellectuals in the second half of the eighteenth century seem to have been acutely aware of death, and particularly of infant mortality. On the basis of his own observations,[34] Fourcroy asserted with dismay that only half the children born reached the age of seven.[35] Now there was nothing new in

[33] In the countryside around Anjou, for example, the population gradually declined over the eighteenth century (Lebrun, *Les Hommes et la mort*, pp. 98-102), while the insecurity and poverty of the Auxois toward the end of the old regime, "does not give the impression of a real demographic expansion" (Robin, *La Société française en 1789*, p. 117). Though these cases are exceptional, it is worth pointing out that at least in some instances contemporaries could rightly adopt a pessimistic view of the state of the population by accurately observing conditions around them.

[34] Fourcroy says that he has studied "l'Histoire Naturelle des Enfans du premier age . . . dans la cabanne des pauvres paysans . . ." (*Les Enfans élevés dans l'ordre de la nature*, p. 62).

[35] Ibid., pp. 115-16 and 141-42. Cantillon stated that one of every two children dies before the age of seventeen (*Essai*, pp. 44-45) and Holbach, rather exaggeratedly, believed that only one of ten children born reached 30 (*Système social*, II, 140). Rousseau asserted that half the children who are

recognizing that a great many children died at a very early age. Philippe Ariès has shown that until the eighteenth century a high rate of infant mortality was taken for granted. Indeed, in parts of the country parents often did not trouble to attend the funerals of their infant children.[36] Ariès has also argued—and my sources confirm the contention—that only after 1700 did the concept of "necessary wastage" begin to disappear.[37] This is the crucial point.

Montaigne's attitude to the death of his own children was one of "indifference."[38] Infants tended to die infants: this was a pity, but it could not be helped.[39] Fourcroy's attitude to the high rate of infant mortality he observed was fundamentally different. He assumed that children who were born should, in the natural course of things, live to adulthood. Why did they not? Fourcroy's answer was that they were not properly cared for. He therefore took upon himself the role of an eighteenth-century Dr. Spock, and endeavored to instruct his contemporaries about the proper way of raising children.

The system of cold baths Fourcroy advocated, together with many others, has been discussed above. In addition to this measure, the army officer returned from the colonies denounced the practice of putting children into the care of hired nurses, of swaddling, and of boiling wheat flour with milk for use as pablum. A great number of children are

born die before reaching their eighth year (*Emile*, p. 259). These estimates, Holbach aside, in fact correspond quite closely to the findings of modern demographers. Summarizing the present state of knowledge concerning infant and juvenile mortality, P. Guillaume and J. P. Poussou write, "in the second half of the eighteenth century 30-45% of children did not reach their tenth year, the most common proportion being about 45%" (*Démographie historique* [Paris, 1970], p. 142).

[36] Lebrun, *Les Hommes et la mort*, p. 306.

[37] Ariès, *Centuries of Childhood*, p. 40.   [38] Ibid., p. 39.

[39] Lebrun describes the traditional attitude of parents toward the death of their infant children as one of "resignation before the inevitable" (*Les Hommes et la mort*, p. 305).

said to perish at the hands of hired wet nurses, the wheat pablum is said to be hard to digest and responsible for the death of many infants, and swaddling is ascribed "a distinguished place among the numerous causes of depopulation."[40] Better, Fourcroy advised, for mothers to breast feed their own children, and to leave infants free rather than swaddle them. Other authors, Rousseau among them, shared Fourcroy's concerns, and agreed with many of his criticisms.[41]

The point is not that these measures would necessarily have helped to lower the level of infant mortality, but that they were intended and expected to do so. It was to some degree the awareness of the high rate of infant mortality, but much more so the assumption that so many children were dying unnecessarily, that contributed to the widespread belief in depopulation.[42]

Complementing the belief that the population of Europe was decreasing in absolute terms was the conviction that the countryside was being depopulated by the towns. Indeed, while some authors denied that their society was suffering absolute depopulation, none questioned the view that the towns were draining the countryside. Whether ascribing the cause to the harshness of the peasant's lot, to

[40] Fourcroy, *Les Enfans élevés dans l'ordre de la nature*, p. 47.

[41] See *Emile*, pp. 254-55. Rousseau's criticism of swaddling was preceded by Tissot's (*Avis au Peuple*, ii, 80-81), and Tissot did not initiate this criticism (see the "Notes" to *Emile*, pp. 1304-05). Other critics of swaddling were Coyer (*Plan*, pp. 11-12), Grivel (*Théorie*, ii, 289), Goyon (*Essais de Laopédie*, p. 23) and Verlac (*Plan*, p. 119).

[42] There is, it will be noticed, a gap in the logic of this argument. No proof has been adduced to show that Fourcroy and his contemporaries believed that previous ages were in fact more populous, or had solved the problems of childrearing more successfully. As it happens, men of the eighteenth century did believe Europe to have been more heavily populated in antiquity (J. Huxley, "A factor overlooked by the *philosophes*: the population explosion," in VS, xxi [1963], p. 868). The widespread praise of Greek (especially Spartan) and Roman pedagogy also suggests that contemporaries believed the ancients to have reared their children more successfully than they.

luxury, which created a demand for artisans and domestics, to the church, which it was alleged drew workers away from productive occupations, to education, or to a combination of these factors, Sellier, Thélis, Crévier, Granet, Philipon, Gourdin, Coyer, Verlac, Baudeau and Lezay-Marnesia, all lamented the way in which countrydwellers were being attracted to urban centers.[43] Moreover, complaints of rural depopulation are to be found not only in the works of literary men, but also in reports of many intendants.[44]

Contemporaries were concerned about the draining of population from the countryside for a number of reasons. First, they saw that crowding, inadequate sanitation and bad air in towns tended to increase the incidence of disease and to raise the death rate, thus contributing to absolute depopulation. Second, rural depopulation implied the abandonment of agriculture, and the importance attached to agriculture at the time can scarcely be overestimated.[45] Third, it was nearly universally believed that while the countryside maintained a high standard of morality, the towns were the source of every form of vice and corruption. Thélis, Philipon, Coyer, Delacroix and Perrache were of one accord in asking that schools be established in rural settings so as to avoid the corruption of the cities,[46] and Rousseau in writing that men tend to be corrupted by large

[43] Sellier, A Mun. Amiens, BB 130³⁰, p. 3; Thélis, *Mémoires* I, 13; Crévier, *Difficultés*, p. 35; Granet, *Mémoire*, pp. 21 and 123; Philipon, *Vues patriotiques*, pp. 19 and 26; Gourdin, *De l'éducation*, fol. 101v; Coyer, *Plan*, p. 372; Verlac, *Plan*, p. 13; for Baudeau see above, chap. II, n. 168; Lezay-Marnesia, *Le Bonheur dans les campagnes*, p. 20.

[44] Hufton, *The Poor*, p. 97.

[45] "Population and agriculture are the bases of the prosperity of a kingdom" (AL, 1763 VII, 340). The influence of the physiocrats, which seems to have been very wide indeed, and the new emphasis on the "useful arts" which set in not long after mid-century would both have contributed to raising the esteem in which agriculture was held.

[46] Thélis, *Plan*, p. 20; Philipon, *Vues patriotiques*, p. 47; Coyer, *Plan*, pp. 281-82; Delacroix, "Mémoire," fol. 107r; Perrache, "Projet," fol. 87v.

gatherings and to degenerate in towns was expressing a sentiment that was general.[47]

This alleged moral depravity of the towns leads directly to the final reason contemporaries believed population was declining: they accepted the proposition that population depended directly upon morality. It is ironical, but nonetheless true, that Enlightenment population theory was too sophisticated to account for the facts with which it was faced. Malthus' brutally simple emphasis on the urge of men to procreate and the immediate and absolute dependence of a population on its food supply accounts for basic patterns of preindustrial demography fairly well; Montesquieu's emphasis on social, political and cultural factors does not. And of course it was Montesquieu, who believed that population proportioned itself to liberty, goodness of government, religious institutions and laws governing marriage and inheritance, whose views on population, as on so much else, exerted an immense influence on the Enlightenment.[48] Indeed, this ethicism is not peculiar to Montesquieu, but pervades the Enlightenment as a whole. Thus, when Holbach sought to explain the principles governing population growth he wrote:

[47] Rousseau, *Confessions*, p. 459. Others who held the cities up to moral obloquy and often idealized the countryside include: Sellier, "Lettre sur l'éducation des habitants de la campagne," p. 2; Grivel, *Théorie de l'éducation*, II, 379; Thélis, *Mémoire* v, 6; Berenger, *Les Quatre Etats*, pp. 15-16; Perreau, *Instruction du peuple*, pp. 22 and 43; Gourdin, *De l'éducation*, fol. 59v; Holbach, *Système social*, III, 128; and Gosselin, *Plan*, pp. 307-08. The rural *cahiers* of the Auxois presented the countryside as poor, not virtuous or productive; however, they did portray the towns as immoral and unproductive (Robin, *La Société française en 1789*, pp. 309-10). Warren Roberts has pointed out that the countryside was widely idealized in the literature of the later eighteenth century in his fine study, *Morality and Social Class in Eighteenth-Century French Literature and Painting* (Toronto, 1974), pp. 90-92.

[48] This influence is clear in the articles on population in the major encyclopedias discussed above. See also D. B. Young, "Libertarian Demography: Montesquieu's Essay on Depopulation in the *Lettres Persanes*," JHI, XXXVI (1975).

On vante à tout moment les avantages d'une grande population, & l'on cherche les moyens de la produire. Ne voit-on pas que par la nature des choses la population se proportionne à la bonté du Gouvernement, à la sagesse de ses loix, à la fécondité du sol, à l'industrie des habitans, à la liberté & à la sureté dont on jouit.[49]

Other writers were even more explicit than Holbach about the relation of morality to population. Jaubert, for example, stated, "A general rule: Depopulation is always relative to the corruption of morality [*le libertinage des moeurs*] . . ." and Cerfvol asserted flatly, "I should not find it difficult to demonstrate, by means of various censuses carried out in Europe, that population stands in proportion to morality, independently of any other factor [*mobile*]."[50] Depopulation was only one result contemporaries believed corruption and immorality would lead to; they were equally apprehensive of others also.

Corruption

Although it is probably true that there has never been an age that did not, at least to some extent, think itself corrupt, this belief seems to have been particularly strong in the second half of the eighteenth century. It was a proposition that did not need to be proved, but was so generally agreed upon that it could be referred to in passing as a truism. Almost all writers on education felt that corruption was widespread, and few failed to say so.

[49] Holbach, *Système social*, III, 34-35.

[50] Jaubert, *Des Causes de la dépopulation*, pp. iii-iv. Cerfvol, *Mémoire sur la population*, p. 30. In an imaginative recent article, A. McLaren was observed that:

> The threat brandished by both doctors and moralists as the ultimate punishment of the nation that did not protect the physical health and creative powers of its males was depopulation. The association of immorality and a declining population was maintained in Frenchmen's minds to a surprisingly late date ("Some Secular Attitudes toward Sexual Behavior in France: 1760-1860," FHS, VIII [1974], p. 621).

La Chalotais, after observing that the monasteries were full of monks and the *collèges* full of students, asked whether for all this, "is the world any better? is society better ordered? is corruption not as great and as widespread?"[51] Granet, without mentioning Rousseau, referred to the "celebrated question" of the corruption of morality by the sciences.[52] Agreeing that the society in which he lived was corrupt, Coyer found himself confronted with one of the great problems of pedagogy: how to teach morality in an immoral environment. He admitted that he had no solution, and wrote resignedly, "In the midst of this general corruption, how can the soul of a young man conserve its original worth? It must necessarily be corrupted and debased, in order to find itself at the level of society."[53] Crévier and Rivard were only too ready to concur that corruption was widespread.[54] For Formey, the century in which he lived was the "least estimable of all centuries," while Grivel too lamented the "funeste exemple du siècle."[55] Holbach, who was proud that his age was more enlightened than any previous period, admitted that it was also more corrupt. However, he stated defiantly, he preferred the "corruption" of his contemporaries to the "ferocity" of their predecessors.[56] It is not surprising to find that the *Année littéraire* complained that though there had never been so many books written on morality, nor had there ever been a less moral age; but one also finds substantially the same criticism in the *Journal encyclopédique*.[57] Both Lezay-Marnesia and Thélis believed that religion and morality were in decline, while Sellier found proof of corruption in coffee houses where youths gathered to play billiards, slander upstanding citizens, deny the great truths of religion, read novels (which he

---

[51] La Chalotais, *Essai*, p. 27.

[52] Granet, *Mémoire*, p. 122.   [53] Coyer, *Plan*, p. 358.

[54] Crévier, *Difficultés*, p. 59; Rivard, *Recueil*, p. 238.

[55] Formey, *Traité*, p. 121; Grivel, *Théorie de l'éducation*, I, 212.

[56] Holbach, *Système social*, I, 208.

[57] AL, 1762 v, 46; JE, 1773 I, 265.

qualified as "bad books") and generally, it seems, to spend thoroughly enjoyable evenings.[58]

One aspect of the corruption decried at this time was indeed related to bad books. This was the assumption that the new philosophy, and especially its rehabilitation of self-interest, had undermined morality. The *Année littéraire* made a particularly strong statement of this thesis. Referring the "works of our modern philosophers," the journalist wrote:

> . . . je le répète, les principes que ces Ouvrages contiennent ne peuvent qu'être funestes à la Nation qui les adoptera; leur effet nécessaire sera d'inspirer l'égoïsme, d'amollir les âmes, de corrompre les moeurs, de gâter les esprits, de répandre dans tous les citoyens une indifférence profonde pour la Religion, pour la morale & pour les devoirs de la société.[59]

Sellier denounced the "philosophy of the age" as the invention of "semi-learned and idle folk, libertines and people without morals."[60] Thélis complained of self-interest (*un intérêt particulier*), which he called "the sad fruit of false maxims," replacing public-mindedness, while Goyon lamented the evils which "egotistical philosophism caused the *Patrie* and humanity."[61] The charge that self-interest corroded public spirit, and especially patriotism, was one of the most common leveled against it.[62] More generally, Berenger denounced "the deadly effects of egoism," while Tschudy and Necker denied that self-interest could provide an acceptable basis for morality.[63] Gourdin, by contrast, accepted the importance and efficacy of self-interest

[58] Lezay-Marnesia, *Le Bonheur dans les campagnes*, p. 50; Thélis, *Mémoire* x, 12; Sellier, "Lettre sur l'éducation de la jeunesse de tous états," pp. 4-5.

[59] AL, 1783 ii, 164-65.

[60] Sellier, "Lettre sur l'éducation de la jeunesse de tous états," p. 1.

[61] Thélis, *Plan*, p. 16; Goyon d'Arzac, *Essais de Laopédie*, p. 36.

[62] See below, n. 175.

[63] Berenger, *Le Peuple instruit*, p. 15; Tschudy, "Mémoire sur la mendicité lu en séance le 6 fevrier 1773," B Mun. Metz, mss. 1467 v, fols. 28-29; Necker, *Opinions religieuses*, pp. 34-35.

as a motive, but insisted that the individual be taught to identify his own well-being with that of his society.[64]

The two other aspects of corruption most often and most vigorously denounced were luxury and *mollesse*. It is not easy to find an English equivalent for this second term. *Mollesse* denotes softness, slackness and weakness, but more than this it implies laxity, debility, effeminacy and enervation, and is opposed to the qualities of manliness, vigor and courage. At once causes and effects of the corruption in which contemporaries believed themselves (or more likely their neighbors) steeped, luxury and *mollesse* were often regarded as interdependent, and related to the ill of depopulation.

La Chalotais included luxury with debauchery of youth and lack of patriotism as causes of the low moral standards of large nations.[65] Coyer complained that luxury had "corrupted [*amolli*] morals to the extremities of the kingdom," and that his contemporaries had small souls in "corrupted [*amollis*] and sickly bodies."[66] In Jaubert's view, luxury deafened people to the "cry of nature" and resulted in weakening of moral fibre, neglect of duty and depopulation of the countryside.[67] Goyon complained that children did not get the care they should have because of prejudices connected with luxury and *mollesse*, and Thiollier adduced these same two factors to explain what he called "the weakness of the present generation."[68] Perreau believed that luxury was always harmful, Holbach qualified it as a "poison" and Durosoy as "deadly."[69] Philipon compared a European youth of fifteen, whom he designated a "child of luxury and *mollesse*" to a ten-year old Indian child, desig-

[64] Gourdin, *De l'éducation*, fol. 99v.

[65] La Chalotais, *Essai*, p. 6.

[66] Coyer, *Plan*, pp. 100 and 377.

[67] Jaubert, *Causes de la dépopulation*, pp. 39, 29-32, and 119-20.

[68] Goyon d'Arzac, *Essais de Laopédie*, p. 3; Abbé Thiollier, "Essai historique et Critique sur L'éducation Ancienne," A Ac. Lyon, mss. 147, fol. 71v.

[69] Perreau, *Instruction du peuple*, p. 21; Holbach, *Ethnocratie*, p. 125; Durosoy, *Philosophie sociale*, p. 26.

nated a "child of nature," and found the latter in every way superior to the former. He also justified some of his rather Spartan methods of childrearing by saying that they were not new, but had merely been proscribed by contemporary *mollesse*.[70] Thélis complained that he was living in an "age of *mollesse* and ignorance," and blamed luxury for draining the countryside, and turning productive peasants into domestics and artisans.[71] Those who, with Mandeville and Voltaire, regarded luxury as a positive good were a tiny minority.[72] Defense of it was almost always hesitant or qualified. The physiocrats, for example, favored luxury of the table, for they believed it stimulated agriculture, but condemned every other kind.[73] For Gourdin, luxury was only a necessary evil, while Lezay-Marnesia probably summed up moderate opinion on the issue in writing that "in moderation it is a good; in excess the greatest of evils."[74]

So great was the belief in corruption that a good many writers concluded that by comparison to the Gauls or their medieval forebears, eighteenth-century Frenchmen were degenerate. Comparing the French nobility of the time of Saint Louis and Henri IV to those of this own day, Verlac exclaimed, "How much it has degenerated!"[75] Berenger

---

[70] Philipon, *Vues patriotiques*, pp. 71 and 65.

[71] Thélis, *Mémoire* XIII, 10.

[72] See Gusdorf, *Principes de la pensée*, pp. 444-61. In his book, *L'Apologie du luxe au XVIIIe siècle* (Paris, 1909), Andé Morizé has shown that the tendency to regard luxury from an economic and social rather than a moral or religious point of view led to a significant rehabilitation of the idea in the first half of the eighteenth century. After 1750, however, this trend was arrested, if not reversed. This is not, however, the view of Labriolle-Rutherford who, laying emphasis on the rehabilitation of the passions in the eighteenth century and drawing exclusively on the major *philosophes*, finds the balance weighted in favor of the acceptance of luxury ("L'Evolution de la notion de luxe depuis Mandeville jusqu'à la Révolution," VS, xxvi [1963]).

[73] Spengler, *French Predecessors of Malthus*, p. 185.

[74] Gourdin, *De l'éducation*, fol. 95r-v; Lezay-Marnesia, *Le Bonheur dans les campagnes*, p. 4.

[75] Verlac, *Plan*, p. 50.

and Thiollier made similar comparisons and arrived at the same conclusions.[76] Coyer held that a reading of Tacitus showed that "mankind has degenerated in Europe," and Goyon de la Plombaine asserted that this degeneration was palpable.[77] After comparing the barbarians from whom the French were descended with his contemporaries, Philipon regretfully admitted that "one cannot hide from oneself the fact that our constitution has been prodigiously weakened."[78] Similarly, having shown how inferior a soldier of the eighteenth century was to a knight of the twelfth, Thélis invited the Duke of Charost to consider how "a long succession of generations of weakened men has, so to speak, debased [dégradé] the physical constitution of mankind."[79] Expressing the same idea in a different way, the Chevalier de Bruni likened the present generation to a tree, which in its decrepitude was incapable of producing good fruit.[80]

If these views, drawn for the most part from obscure authors, seem familiar to historians of the eighteenth century, this is not without good reason. They are all—the beliefs in depopulation, corruption and degeneration; the criticisms of luxury and mollesse, as well as the failure of mothers to nurse their children and the practice of swaddling; the awareness of a high rate of infant mortality; the idealization of the countryside and villification of the towns—to be found in Rousseau's Nouvelle Héloïse and Emile. One might try to explain the opinions of La Chalotais, Coyer, Thélis and the rest by arguing that they had read Rousseau, and had been influenced by him. While it is probably true that most of these writers had read Emile—and there are sufficient references to it to indicate

---

[76] Berenger, Les Quatre Etats, pp. 28-29; Thiollier, "Essai historique," fol. 71r.

[77] Coyer, Plan, p. 71; Goyon de la Plombaine, L'Unique Moyen, p. 21.

[78] Philipon, Vues patriotiques, p. 292.

[79] Thélis, Mémoire VII, 12.

[80] Ibid. III, 35.

that they had—such an explanation of the intellectual climate of the decades which preceded the Revolution is inadequate. It is inadequate, first, because it overlooks the fundamental fact that one man does not create a climate of opinion, and second, because it fails to explain why Rousseau's views appealed as widely as they did. The key to Rousseau's fame during his own life was not so much that he wrote with great imagination and skill, but that he expressed the fears, hopes and yearnings of a great many of his contemporaries.

In the context of the beliefs and opinions that colored the climate of opinion in France after 1750, one comes to see the emphasis that writers during that period placed on certain aspects of popular education in a different light. The people, it was agreed, were to be inured to harsh conditions because ultimately they would have to live in such conditions. But complaints of *mollesse* also led to demands for vigorous physical training, partly because it was believed that *mollesse* contributed to depopulation, and if children were pampered in their early years they would never reach maturity at all. The fear of depopulating the countryside helps account—and was often adduced as a justification—for the restricting of the education of the rural poor. The concern with moral corruption no doubt contributed to the tendency on the part of the spokesmen of the possessing classes to restrict the intellectual training of the people, and to emphasize moral instruction. Finally, the atmosphere of crisis in which books on education were written caused many of the views in these works to be given more extreme expression than they might otherwise have been.

Of the fact that an atmosphere of crisis, feeding on the beliefs in depopulation, corruption and degeneration, pervaded the intellectual atmosphere of the last decades of the old regime, there can be little doubt. In likening the condition of the countryside in the 1780s to a house on fire, Lezay-Marnesia clearly suggested the threat of catas-

trophe.[81] Goyon de la Plombaine looked upon extreme inequality in the distribution of the tax burden, which
amounted to insufferable oppression of the poor and productive classes, as the chief cause of the destruction of
great empires, and stated: "One cannot hide the fact from
oneself: we are threatened with similar misfortunes."[82] For
Thélis, too, things appeared to be coming to a critical pitch.
He wrote:

> On avoue que si les choses subsistent sur le pied sur
> lequel elles sont aujourd'hui, la corruption, en se for-
> tifiant & se répandant de toute part, deviendra telle, que
> dans les générations futures, elle entraînera nécessaire-
> ment la perte de notre constitution, & non plus seule-
> ment la décadence, mais la ruine de notre Empire. On
> sent que tout tend à s'isoler de plus en plus, qu'un intérêt
> particulier, triste fruit de faux principes & de fausses
> maximes, prend partout la place de l'intérêt public & du
> concours de volontés vers le bien général. On comprend
> que ce n'est qu'en formant au milieu de nous une géné-
> ration toute nouvelle, & en poussant toutes les volontés
> vers le même but par l'accord soutenu des mêmes prin-
> cipes, par une éducation commune, applicable dans ses
> modifications aux differentes classes de Citoyens, par
> des enseignements clairs & précis, par des leçons, par des
> institutions vraiment patriotiques & nationales que se
> répondent d'une extrémité du Royaume à l'autre, que
> l'on pourra venir à bout de rendre à l'état son ancienne
> splendeur, & à ses membres leur ancienne énergie.[83]

Thélis and the other writers cited above were not alone in
their doom-threatening prognostications and alarmism.
L. S. Mercier observed that the government was being in-
undated with all manner of plans and projects for reform
and improvement. These plans were written on the most
diverse aspects of government, yet, Mercier said, they had

[81] Lezay-Marnesia, *Le Bonheur dans les campagnes*, p. 10.
[82] Goyon de la Plombaine, *L'Unique Moyen*, p. 9.
[83] Thélis, *Plan*, pp. 16-17.

one thing in common: "All these projects say in substance: *if what I suggest is not done, France is lost.*"[84]

It is noteworthy that the warnings of the projectors of whom Mercier spoke, like those of Thélis and the rest, were conditional rather than categorical. It was their belief not that society was irrevocably doomed, but that if appropriate measures were not taken, it would be. The threat of serious social and political breakdown led many authors writing in this period to make extreme and sometimes extravagant claims. However, the fact that they believed it possible to avoid the worst by convincing the government to take appropriate measures explains the persistence of a good deal of optimism and the complete lack of apocalyptic and resigned pessimism; at worst they wrote off the present generation and placed their faith in the next one.[85] As I have argued above, though they were not unaware of the importance of economic and fiscal issues, contemporaries believed themselves faced with a crisis of moral dissolution, the chief elements and results of which were egoism, luxury, corruption, moral depravity, physical degeneration and depopulation. That they did not despair in the face of this alleged crisis was due to their belief that they had to hand the means of overcoming it. And of course since the ill perceived was a moral one, so too was the remedy. As alternatives to the insidious and harmful qualities they condemned they proposed a new set of values. The state or *patrie* was to act as a new principle of authority and a focus for common interests; beneficence and humanity were put forward as the key values in an altruist ethic; and education was seen as an agent of reform.

THE RESPONSE TO THE CRISIS

A Principle of Authority: Patriotism

Though the kind of nationalism that was so marked a feature of the nineteenth century was essentially foreign to

---

[84] Mercier, *Tableau de Paris*, chap. 447.
[85] As did Thélis; see above, n. 83.

the Enlightenment, it is generally recognized that na-
tionalist, or perhaps more correctly, patriotic sentiment
existed to a significant degree before the Revolution.[86]
Certainly this is the case if our perspective is that of the literature on education produced between 1762 and 1789.
Indeed, this literature and related works lead one to believe that the importance and role of patriotism in the Enlightenment have not been fully appreciated.

When Coyer published his dissertation on the people in
1755, there appeared with it another brief essay entitled
Dissertation sur le vieux mot patrie. No less than the former
work, the latter marked a turning point in the attitudes of
educated men toward a question of fundamental importance.

Coyer began his essay by observing that the word *patrie*
was not used by contemporaries; it was not considered polite. "State" and "kingdom" were used instead.[87] Yet, if
contemporaries were ignorant of the significance of the
patrie, the ancients had a very clear conception of its meaning. By consulting the classical authors, Coyer suggested,
one could learn,

> . . . le vrai sens du mot *patrie*. Sens magnifique sans
> doute; car on y lit qu'il n'y a rien de si aimable, de si sacré
> que la patrie; qu'on se doit tout entier à elle; qu'il n'est
> pas plus permis de s'en venger que de son père; qu'il ne
> faut avoir d'amis que les siens; que de tous les augures le

[86] Hyslop, in *French Nationalism in 1789*, p. 179, stated that a rebirth of
patriotism occurred during the electoral period preceding the Revolution. On this period see Boyd C. Shafer, "Bourgeois Nationalism in the
Pamphlets on the Eve of the Revolution," JMH, x (1938). Aulard traced
the history of patriotism in France back to the Renaissance, and followed
its development in the eighteenth century up to the reign of Louis XVI, at
which time, he argued, it gained greatly in importance (Aulard, *Le Patriotisme français de la Renaissance à la Révolution*, Paris, 1921, p. 65). R. R.
Palmer has suggested that patriotism was a part of the Enlightenment,
and that it had become a fairly common notion about forty years before
the Revolution ("The National Idea in France before the Revolution,"
JHI, I [1940], p. 96).

[87] Coyer, *Dissertation sur le vieux mot Patrie* (1755) in his *Oeuvres*, I, 168.

meilleur est de combattre pour elle; qu'il est beau, qu'il est doux de mourir pour la conserver; que le ciel ne s'ouvre qu'à ceux qui l'ont servie.[88]

The qualities which, for Coyer, characterize the *patrie* are first, a relative equality of conditions, and secondly, the rule of law. Ideally, the *patrie* admitted of varying degrees of wealth, but not poverty; it permitted variations in standing, but not oppression. And if the *patrie* allowed inequalities of wealth and status, it assured all "a kind of equality in opening to all the way to important positions."[89] The rule of law was both a guarantee of relative equality and a precondition to the existence of the *patrie*. Coyer, following Montesquieu, regarded the absence of law as the distinguishing feature of oriental despotisms,[90] and asserted that while a king was subject to the laws of his state, a tyrant's rule was that of brigandage united with authority.[91]

Having described the conditions that should obtain in a true state, Coyer went on to compare them with the situation in France. The comparison gave him the opportunity for a good deal of the sort of acid irony with which we are already familiar from his essay on the people. But there is little point in following the Abbé's bitter and brilliant social criticism. What is significant here is that Coyer has focused attention on the state as a principle of authority, and that other writers followed him in so regarding it.[92]

[88] Ibid., p. 170.   [89] Ibid., pp. 170-72.

[90] Ibid., p. 172. Coyer referred to Montesquieu as a "patriot" (ibid., p. 185).

[91] Ibid., pp. 173 and 176.

[92] Jaucourt borrowed extensively from Coyer's essay for his article "Patrie" in the *Encyclopédie*, but not so extensively as he had done for his article on the people. In this case Jaucourt copied only a few paragraphs verbatim from Coyer, organized his article independently from the essay, and by eliminating the bitterest of Coyer's social criticism (specifically, the image of society as a great cloth which the powerful had usurped to the detriment of the poor, and the description of French society divided into two separate and opposed "nations"), changed the tone and emphasis of the work markedly. Through Jaucourt, and having been modified to a

La Chalotais, for example, wished not only to take public education out of the hands of the Jesuits or any other order with ultramontanist inclinations, but also to make education the business of the state. Believing that the main task of education was to "prepare citizens for the state," he wrote:

> Je prétends revendiquer pour la Nation une éducation qui ne dépende que de l'Etat, parce qu'elle lui appartient essentiellement; parce que toute Nation a un droit inaliénable & imprescribtible d'instruire ses membres; parce qu'enfin les enfans de l'Etat doivent être élevés par des membres de l'Etat.[93]

This demand was to appear again and again, with many variations and with different degrees of intensity, between the time of the publication of La Chalotais' *Essai* and the outbreak of the Revolution. Guyton de Morveau laid it down as an "incontestable principle" that the government should control education.[94] Diderot incorporated this principle into his plan for a university in Russia.[95] Baudeau called for "a complete system of truly national education," and for an education that would be "truly patriotic."[96] Rolland looked to a nationally uniform education as a means by which a number of desirable reforms could be effected. Among its other virtues, the *parlementaire* saw a centralized system of education as "the only means of increasing the *love of one's country* [*la patrie*]."[97] Tschudy, we have seen, held a similar opinion.[98] For Coyer, education was the

considerable extent by him, Coyer's views on the *patrie* reached a wider public. The DUS reproduced the *Encyclopédie* article "Patrie" paragraph for paragraph, then added a number of pages of its own in the same vein. The *Encyclopédie méthodique*'s article "Patrie" is merely a copy of that of the DUS. The DUM also carries a much abridged but unmistakable version of Coyer's dissertation.

[93] La Chalotais, *Essai*, p. 17.   [94] Guyton, *Mémoire*, pp. 24-25.
[95] Diderot, "Plan," p. 520.   [96] *Ephémérides du citoyen*, 1765 I, 98.
[97] Rolland, *Compte rendu*, of 13 May 1768, p. 18.
[98] See above, pp. 126-27.

"foundation of the political edifice." He therefore did not hesitate to ascribe to the state the right to control education: "Have children reached the age of four? the *patrie* asks for them in order to make men of them."[99] Turgot looked to a nationally uniform system of education to create the kind of patriotism that had not been seen since antiquity, and Le Mercier de la Rivière felt that the task of public education was to create "only citizens."[100] Delacroix stated that his purpose in writing on education was to help "procure for the state well-instructed and truly useful citizens," and both the radical Holbach and the conservative Durosoy argued that the citizen was under an obligation to serve his *patrie*.[101]

Those actively engaged in some aspect of pedagogy showed as much concern with instilling national values as did theoreticians. Thélis believed that cosmopolitanism should be subordinated to the interest of the state. He agreed that the man of letters had a place in society, especially if he upheld morality and religion, and if he did not "renounce his *patrie* in order to be a citizen of the world."[102] Writing in the *Mémoires concernant les écoles nationales*, the Abbé Soulavie, an associate, correspondant or member of some sixteen French and two foreign academies and future Jacobin, criticized existing institutions of public education for producing savants but not citizens.[103] As eloquent as any discourse on patriotism is the motto that flew above the tents of the *écoles nationales*. It read simply "Tout pour la patrie."[104]

The view that one ought to give his all for the homeland,

[99] Coyer, *Plan*, pp. 4 and 15.
[100] Turgot, "Mémoire," p. 621 and Le Mercier, *De l'instruction publique*, p. 111
[101] Abbé Delacroix, "Mémoire sur les moyens que l'on pourroit employer pour perfectionner l'éducation de la jeunesse" (1762), A Ac. Lyon, mss. 147, fol. 104v. Holbach, *Système social*, III, 156; Durosoy, *Philosophie sociale*, pp. 55-56, 58 and 275.
[102] Thélis, *Mémoire* IX, 26.   [103] Ibid. VI, 5.
[104] Bachaumont, *Mémoires secrets*, 2 November 1779.

and that indeed the homeland was the all, spread during the decade of the 1780s. In this connection it is worth recalling Philipon's emphatic assertion that "*children belong more to the republic than to their parents.* . . ."[105] Goyon, who was generally more moderate than Philipon, would have left parents the liberty of educating their own children, "provided that the state does not suffer by it. . . ."[106] Delacroix asserted that children belonged "as much and even more" to the state than to their parents; Perrache noted approvingly that the ancient Greeks believed children belonged to the state; and Verlac would not have permitted parents to keep their children away from school on the grounds that "education is of greater importance to the nation [*patrie*] than to the parents."[107] In a like manner, but somewhat more graphically, Vauréal wrote that a child "should be offered to national education, to the altars of the *patrie*, like a lump of prepared clay that awaits the hand of the potter."[108] It would seem, then, that at the same time that the child was being integrated into the family, the state was beginning to challenge the right of the family to raise its children as it saw fit.[109]

ASPECTS OF PATRIOTISM: THE DEMANDS FOR STATE CONTROL, SECULARIZATION AND CENTRALIZATION OF EDUCATION

Associated with the idea of patriotism in works on education in our period were a number of interrelated ideas and demands. These include a marked preference for public as opposed to private education, a questioning of the capacity of churchmen to train citizens, and the demand for the creation of a centralized educational system.

Where the issue of private as opposed to public educa-

[105] Philipon, *Vues patriotiques*, p. 12.

[106] Goyon d'Arzac, *Essais de Laopédie*, p. 10.

[107] Delacroix, "Mémoire" fol. 105v; Perrache, "Réflexions," fol. 133r; Verlac, *Plan*, p. 105.

[108] Vauréal, *Plan*, p. 65.

[109] G. Snyders, *La Pédagogie en France au XVIIe et XVIIIe siècles* (Paris, 1965), pp. 295-98.

tion was raised, the latter was almost invariably preferred. The authors of *De l'éducation publique*, not surprisingly, regarded the emphasis traditionally accorded domestic education as misplaced. They observed that there was need for a system of public education, and asserted further that education should be a matter of state policy.[110] Similarly, Gosselin called for "a true plan of public and national education."[111] Formey, though he criticized seminaries and *collèges*, found the inconveniences involved in private education greater than those involved in public, and therefore preferred the latter.[112] Baudeau had no doubts whatever on this score. He would not have hesitated to "proscribe all private education. Public and common instruction is always preferable."[113] Coyer reasoned that as private education was possible only for a wealthy minority, public instruction was "absolutely necessary" for the nation as a whole.[114] Similarly, Philipon admitted that *collèges* were so bad that anyone with a choice would do well to prefer a domestic education for his children, but regarded a public education as the only kind suitable for the people.[115] Pernetti weighed the advantages and disadvantages of private and public instruction, and though on the whole favoring the public variety, suggested that the two could advantageously be combined.[116] Verlac would admit private education for girls, but not for boys.[117]

To the general consensus that public education was to be preferred to private education, there was one notable exception: Rousseau. *Emile* is a plan of education for a child whose family can afford a tutor. But if one reads the book carefully, one finds that Rousseau did not believe public education to be inferior to private instruction. On the contrary, he had too high an opinion of patriotism and public

[110] *De l'éducation publique*, pp. iii-iv.

[111] Gosselin, *Plan*, p. 39.

[112] Formey, *Traité*, pp. 130-38.

[113] *Ephémérides du citoyen*, 1765 I, 104.

[114] Coyer, *Plan*, p. 6.

[115] Philipon, *Vues patriotiques*, pp. 28-30.

[116] Pernetti, "Réponse," fols. 115-16.

[117] Verlac, *Plan*, pp. 117 and 24.

education to think his contemporaries capable of them. He wrote:

> L'institution publique n'existe plus, et ne peut plus exister, parce qu'où il n'y a plus de patrie, il ne peut plus y avoir de citoyens. Ces deux mots *patrie* et *citoyen* doivent être effacés des langues modernes.[118]

Rousseau was criticized by other writers who would not believe that their contemporaries could not at least aspire to a form of social and political organization in which they would be worthy of the title "citizen."[119] Worthy or not, Frenchmen were already using it, and on a grand scale.

Closely connected to the question of whether education should be private or public was the issue of who should be entrusted with so important a task. Most members of the enlightened community felt that only citizens could effectively give civic training. This was a roundabout way of saying that the various teaching orders of the Catholic Church were losing their vocation.

Morveau argued that only by taking instruction out of the hands of the church could education be put into harmony with the French state.[120] Though he bitterly denounced the Jesuits as subjects of a foreign sovereign and had harsh things to say about the "monastic spirit," La Chalotais regarded the Oratorians, because of their devotion to France, as worthy teachers.[121] Rolland, too, regarded the Oratorians, and with them the Benedictines, as good teachers, but cautioned that in most cases a member of a regular order would be "more attached to his order than to his *patrie*," and therefore incapable of providing a

---

[118] Rousseau, *Emile*, p. 250.

[119] Among Rousseau's critics on this point were Coyer (*Plan*, p. 7), and Vauréal, who wrote, "Je démontrerai contre le célèbre & trop sensible Jean-Jacques la possibilité & l'intérêt d'une éducation nationale" (*Plan*, pp. 20-21).

[120] Guyton, *Mémoire*, pp. 32-33.

[121] La Chalotais, *Essai*, pp. 19 and 16.

national education.[122] Coyer, who had once said that a
churchman's *patrie* was heaven, argued that as clerics were
not themselves citizens, they were unfit to train citizens.[123]
For similar reasons, Verlac stated flatly that clerics could
not teach civic morality.[124] Not surprisingly, in view of his
virulent anticlericalism, Holbach denounced priests as the
worst possible teachers of civic virtures.[125] There were,
however, two exceptions to this trend. Gourdin, who was a
member of an order that ran a number of *collèges*, argued
that priests were well suited to pedagogical functions, and
Philipon tended to favor clerics as teachers because he believed teachers should be unmarried.[126] Philipon would
not, though, have permitted monastic orders to take up
teaching functions,[127] and he further insisted that teachers
be state employed.[128]

A third aspect of the patriotic sentiment expressed in the
educational writings of the years between 1762 and 1789
was the desire for uniformity of instruction. It was widely
hoped that a single system of education for all of France
would produce a common morality and outlook, and not

[122] Rolland, *Compte rendu* of 13 May 1768, p. 26.
[123] Coyer, *Dissertation sur la patrie*, p. 174 and *Plan*, pp. 91-92.
[124] Verlac, *Plan*, p. 109.
[125] Holbach, *Système social*, III, 106-07.
[126] Gourdin, *De l'éducation*, fol. 100r. Philipon, *Vues patriotiques*, p. 39.
[127] Ibid., p. 35. Philipon here exhibits a very common eighteenth-
century attitude toward the church. He was critical of monks and nuns
who were cloistered (*clergé regulier*) but not of parish priests (*clergé séculier*)
or members of orders which took part in the life of the community, usually as teachers or nurses. A good example of this attitude is to be found in
the municipal council of the town of Montreuil in the diocese of Amiens.
The council wished to suppress the *soeurs grises* of their town because, "En
embrassant la vie contemplative et en se cloitrant, elles ont cessé d'être
temporellement utiles aux habitans qui les avoient appellés." What did the
municipal council of Montreuil intend to do with the revenues of the
soeurs grises once the order had been extinguished in their town? They
wished to establish several *Frères* of La Salle's order in order to take charge
of the education of the boys of the town (AD Somme, G 621[29]).
[128] Philipon, *Vues patriotiques*, p. 39.

least important, help end internal strife. Rivard, for example, looked to a uniform system of education as a guarantee of social peace. He wrote:

> Rien ne paroit plus à desirer dans un Royaume que l'union des esprits & des coeurs: sans elle la discorde & les guerres intestines regnent parmi les Citoyens. . . . Or, l'uniformité de l'éducation donnée à la Jeunesse, contribueroit infiniment à cette union si desirable. . . .[129]

Rolland also argued that only a uniform education could produce common manners, customs and usages throughout the whole kingdom, and to this end suggested making Paris the educational center of the country.[130] Thélis warmly approved the idea of uniform "national and patriotic institutions."[131] Making a concrete suggestion on how to achieve this much desired uniformity of manners and outlook, Baudeau proposed that a national council for education be established.[132] Turgot followed him in calling upon Louis XV to set up a council of the same sort, which was to control all institutions of learning from *petites écoles* to academies.[133] Goyon, too, proposed that municipal councils be organized to control schools locally, and that these councils be subordinated to thirty-two provincial councils which were to fall under the authority of a national council.[134] Le Mercier de la Rivière suggested to Gustave III of Sweden that in order to render instruction uniform, he have a set of texts composed for use throughout the whole of his kingdom.[135] Similarly, Sellier called upon the government of France to lay down a plan of studies that all public schools be obliged to follow.[136] These

[129] Rivard, *Recueil*, p. 86.
[130] Rolland, *Compte rendu* of 13 May 1768, p. 16.
[131] Thélis, *Plan*, p. 16.
[132] *Ephémérides du citoyen*, 1765 I, 102.
[133] Turgot, "Mémoire," p. 578.
[134] Goyon d'Arzac, *Essais de Laopédie*, pp. 17 and 29.
[135] Le Mercier, *De l'instruction publique*, p. 111.
[136] Sellier, "Lettre sur l'éducation des enfans du peuple," p. 7.

policies, if obvious today, were not so in an age when each
collège professor dictated a course of his own composition,
and each bishop designated the catechism to be used in his
diocese.

THE ACCEPTANCE AND APPEAL OF THE IDEA OF PATRIOTISM

While the idea of patriotism occupied an important place
in works on education which appeared between 1762 and
1789, it was not, of course, restricted to discussions of
pedagogy. Writing in 1762, Fréron observed that patriotism had become "the subject of an infinite number of
works," and that together with honor and zeal, "patriotism
has been awakened in all hearts and in all minds."[137] To
judge by the frequency with which the terms *patrie*, patriotism, nation, citizen and *concitoyen* appear in titles of works
published at this time and as epithets of approval in both
the traditionalist and progressive press, Fréron's observations were fully justified.

In 1762, for example, there appeared poems by Arnaud,
Colardeau and the Chevalier de Laures entitled respectively, "A la nation," "Le patriotisme" and "Les voeux d'un
citoyen à M. le Duc de Nivernois." The same year saw the
publication of various works of social and political criticism
with titles such as, *Les Vues d'un patriote, L'Amour de la patrie,
La Difference du patriotisme national, chez les François & chez les
Anglois*, and *Vues d'un financier patriote.* Though the Seven
Years War stimulated a number of these pieces, patriotic
sentiment and rhetoric did not die down after peace was
concluded. Lefebvre de Beauvray's *Dictionnaire social et patriotique* appeared in 1770, and was followed in the next two
decades by Dorat's poem, "Le nouveau règne. Ode à la nation (1774)," the *Oeuvres Complettes de M. de Chamousset, contenant ses projets d'humanité, de bienfaisance & de patriotisme*
(1783), *L'Ame des Bourbons, ou Tableau historique des princes de
l'Auguste maison de Bourbon . . . dédié à la Nation* (1783), and

---

[137] AL, 1762 I, 54; ibid., 1762 II, 127-28.

the *Projets de bienfaisance et de patriotisme pour la Ville de Bourdeaux* (1785). In 1787, Mathon de la Cour's, *Discours sur les meilleurs moyens de faire naître et d'encourager le patriotisme dans une monarchie*, which won the contest proposed by the Academy of Châlons-sur-Marne on this subject, was published, and so too, in the same year, was Dom Ferlus' oration, *Le Patriote chrétien*. Moreover, during these years, authors who wished to remain anonymous often signed themselves simply as "citizens." Some of those who adopted this practice include the author of an educational treatise, a critic of Mesmerism,[138] and the Abbé Baudeau, who had early begun entitling his works "Idées d'un citoyen sur : . ." and publishing them anonymously.

If there is much truth to the assertion that an "explosion" of patriotic sentiment occurred in the last decade of the old regime,[139] it is also true that the idea of patriotism and key terms associated with it had been revived well before the reign of Louis XV ended. The words "patriot" or "citizen" were routinely applied as epithets of commendation by both the *Journal encyclopédique* and the *Année littéraire*. Fréron or his collaborators, for example, described the author of a work on agriculture as "this patriotic writer," the author of a work on education as "this excellent citizen," and the compiler of a collection of moral anecdotes as "a good citizen."[140] For the *Journal encyclopédique*, the author of a history of Sumatra, which gave more attention to English politics than to the Far East, was, as well as a learned and profound writer, "a courageous patriot;" the author of a *Cours d'éducation* was an "estimable citizen;" and Chamousset, to whose projects of beneficence, humanity and patriotism reference has just been made, was "a citizen imbued with love of his *patrie*."[141] But

---

[138] *L'Elève de la Raison & de la Religion; ou Traité d'Education Physique, Morale & Didactique, par un Citoyen* (AL, 1774 II, 25). *Magnétisme animal dévoilé par un zélé citoyen françois*, JE, 1787 VI, 20.

[139] The term is Aulard's. *Le Patriotisme français*, p. 77.

[140] AL, 1762 VII, 15; AL, 1773 I, 335; AL, 1784 IV, 57.

[141] JE, 1762 V-1, 60; JE, 1783 I, 76; JE, 1783 V, 42.

perhaps the best indication of the degree to which the idea of patriotism had been accepted and generalized is the fact that the terms "citizen" and "patriot" came to be used virtually as synonyms for "person" or "man." Thus, children between the time they were weaned and age seven were "young citizens"; the indigent were referred to as "poor citizens"; men in positions of authority became "respectable citizens"; a young man who died trying to save a girl from drowning was designated a "brave citizen"; a retired sea captain who founded and endowed a charity school was referred to as "this worthy citizen"; and the French were ruled by "citizen Kings."[142] Indeed, so great was the power of patriotism after 1750 that men and women no longer fell victims to epidemics: "citizens" died instead.[143]

That the idea of patriotism gained wide currency in the second half of the eighteenth century, there can be little doubt. It has even been argued that "the idea of the *patrie* was possibly the dominant, as it was certainly the commonest, idea of all political thinkers in eighteenth-century France."[144] One of the harsher aspects of this patriotism is reflected in the following observation, which occurs in Coyer and was retained by all the dictionaries and encyclopedias that based their articles on the *patrie* on his essay:

> Brutus pour conserver sa *patrie*, fit couper la tête à ses fils, & cette action ne paroîtra dénaturée qu'aux âmes foibles. Sans la mort des deux traîtres, la *patrie* de Brutus expiroit au berceau.[145]

Brutus' renunciation of self and dedication to his *patrie*, as is well known, was given graphic representation by David

---

[142] AL, 1773 I, 334; JE, 1773 III, 111; JE, 1773 V, 251; JE, 1783 V, 331; JE, 1784 V, 339; AL, 1784 VI, 200.

[143] JE, 1784 VIII, 144.

[144] Alfred Cobban, "The Fundamental Ideas of Robespierre," in *Aspects of the French Revolution* (London, 1971), p. 141.

[145] *Encyclopédie*, art. "Patrie." These sentences, with a negligable variation in wording, are taken from Coyer, and were included in the DUS, EM and DUM articles on the *patrie*.

in 1789. A few years earlier, the great exponent of neoclassicism had painted a picture with a similar theme, the *Oath of the Horatii*, which has been described as "a clarion call to civic patriotism."[146] These paintings, like much of Coyer's dissertation, and even more so, Jaucourt's article, draw on and are inspired by the austere, even passionate patriotism of ancient Greece and more particularly, classical Rome. But together with this essentially state-oriented, harsh and classically inspired form of patriotism, one finds in Coyer's essay, and progressively more frequently in other writers as the century progressed, a gentler, more socially-oriented form of the idea. Both had important roles to play in the climate of opinion of the time.

In a discussion on method in the history of ideas, an outstanding French scholar has pointed out that "every living idea has a purpose, which is to say, a role and a place in a certain mental and ideological whole," and has emphasized the importance of determining the function of an idea in relation to the larger system of which it is a part.[147] An examination of the role or function of the idea of patriotism in the last decades of the old regime will go far toward explaining its sudden and striking popularization.

In France toward the middle of the eighteenth century, a reaction set in against the superficial and jejeune life of polite society. Hugh Honour sees in this reaction the source of the decline of rococo, and the rise of the severe,

[146] Hugh Honour, *Neoclassicism* (Bungay, 1968), p. 35. This growing nationalism was also reflected in the fine arts by demands for creation of a national gallery of French art, and for national subject matter in paintings and sculpture. The crown commissioned a large number of historical paintings and sculptures of outstanding Frenchmen, and the last four decades of the old regime saw an increasing number of national subjects exhibited in the yearly salons (James Leith, "Nationalism and the Fine Arts in France 1750-1789," VS, LXXXIX [1972]).

[147] Jean Ehrard, "Histoire des idées et histoire sociale en France au XVIIIe siècle: réflexions de méthode," in *Niveaux de culture et groupes sociaux*, p. 174.

moralizing neoclassical style.[148] Kingsley Martin, in a book that is still a classic, at least insofar as its treatment of ideas goes, suggested that by the 1760s a combination of factional strife within the church and the criticism of the *philosophes* had done much to discredit religion and spread scepticism.[149] The result was a sort of moral void. The void left by a discredited church was soon filled by an idealized concept of the state, as well as by a cult of nature and sentimentalism.[150] Only the former value interests us here.

The image of new values filling a void is in one respect misleading, for it suggests a sudden and complete change. If the rise of patriotism in the twenty or thirty years preceding the Revolution was swift, at least as far as cultural changes go, its victory was far from complete. Religion was not suddenly and definitively discredited during the eighteenth century, not even in the eyes of the enlightened community. Rather its standing as a moral principle was slowly eroded. Catholicism did not suddenly cease to be relevant to most educated Frenchmen: it became less relevant. Without disappearing, it was devitalized.

This change is reflected in the educational writings of the period. If Crévier asserted that religion took precedence over all else, including the state, and Holbach denied that Christianity and patriotism were compatible,[151] their opinions were extreme and unrepresentative. For most writers, it was the duty of the pedagogue to train his student to respect both religion and the state, and if they favored the one, they seldom criticized the other. Rivard, Guyton de Morveau, Formey, Gourdin, Perrache and Navarre all insisted that the purpose of education was to produce both good Christians and good citizens.[152]

---

[148] Honour, *Neoclassicism*, pp. 17-20.

[149] Kingsley Martin (J.P. Mayer, ed.), *French Liberal Thought in the Eighteenth Century* (New York, 1963), pp. 36 and 109.

[150] Ibid., p. 115, and Roberts, *Morality and Social Class*, chaps. v to vii.

[151] For Crévier, see above, n. 78; Holbach, *Système social*, ii, 3.

[152] Rivard, *Recueil*, p. 25; Guyton, *Mémoire*, p. 33; Formey, *Traité*, p. 6;

Navarre, in particular, wished to accommodate religion and national sentiment and institutions to each other. To this end he thought it necessary to discover "which would be the best means of inspiring the moral virtues in France in conformity with the character of the French, the Christian virtues according to the religion of the French, and the political virtues relative to the government of France. . . ."[153] Navarre's concern with nationalizing Christianity was soon to yield, however, to a greater emphasis on the state and an increasing indifference to religion.

Neither Le Mercier nor Turgot did more than touch on religion in their essays. Vauréal merely observed that one who fulfilled his family obligations and was faithful to his friends and to the principles of religion would be a good citizen; elsewhere, however, he held forth on the virtues of citizenship, and spoke of the "goddess of the *patrie*."[154] Verlac also neglected religion and emphasized the state.[155] Both Goyon and Philipon retained religious instruction in their curricula, but this instruction was fundamentally negative in nature. Neither writer was concerned with developing the Christian virtues as such. Similarly, religion had a place in the *Ecoles nationales*, but these schools were inspired primarily by enlightened beneficence and patriotism.

Because the Enlightenment is often held to be anticlerical, and because there was a tendency to neglect religious values in favor of national ones as the century progressed, it is necessary to point out that, certain dogmatic anticlericals such as Holbach aside, religion and patriotism were not regarded as incompatible. Indeed, where the issue was raised, quite the contrary opinion prevailed. Ferlus, for

---

Gourdin, *De l'éducation*, fol. 100r; Perrache, "Réflexions," fol. 138r; Navarre, le R. P., *Discours qui a remporté le prix par le jugement de l'académie des jeux floraux en l'année 1763 sur ces paroles: Quel seroit en France le plan d'étude le plus avantageux?* (n.p., n.d.), p. 17.

[153] Loc. cit.

[154] Vauréal, *Plan*, pp. 55 and 101.   [155] Verlac, *Plan*, p. 77.

example, went so far as to argue that "outside of the Christian religion there is no true patriotism."[156] Mathon de la Cour was in basic agreement. He wrote:

> . . . il est de la nature du patriotisme d'être désintéressé. . . . J'oserai meme le remarquer ici: le détachement des richesses que le législateur des chrétiens recommande si fortement à ses disciples, meme au sein de tous les avantages de la fortune, est précisément la caractère, qui élevant l'homme au dessus de tout ce que les richessess offrent de séductions, peut seul former les vrais citoyens.[157]

The argument that "true" patriotism is disinterested and compatible with the gentle and universalist side of Christian ethics brings to the fore one of the distinctive features of the patriotic sentiment of the old regime—its cosmopolitanism.

Most historians who have treated eighteenth-century patriotism have been struck by, and have commented on, the lack of narrowness and exclusiveness which are such central features of the nationalism of the nineteenth and twentieth centuries.[158] Aulard's description of the patriotism of Turgot and of the *philosophes* as "not only liberal and egalitarian, not only unifying, but humanitarian and internationalist"[159] can, with some qualification of the term egalitarian, be applied to the patriotism of the enlightened community as a whole. The demand that educators produce for France citizens who were to be "disinterested and indifferent to everything, except for the *Patrie*," and citi-

---

[156] Dom Ferlus, *Le Patriotisme chrétien, Discours prêché aux Etats de Languedoc en 1787* (Montpellier, 1787), p. 6.

[157] Mathon de la Cour, *Discours sur les meilleurs moyens de faire naître et d'encourager le patriotisme dans une monarchie, Qui a remporté le prix dans l'Académie de Châlons-sur-Marne le 25 août 1787* (Paris, 1787), p. 33.

[158] I have in mind here primarily the Western European and North American form of nationalism, not that of subject or oppressed minorities or of colonized peoples.

[159] Aulard, *Le Patriotisme français*, p. 68.

zens for whom "France is everything and everything else is nothing" was extremely unrepresentative.[160] It is curious that this distinctly chauvinistic statement should have come from a cleric; but it is significant, too, that it dates from 1763. Rare enough at that time, such opinions are hardly to be found in the following decades, while criticism of excessive or exclusivist patriotism is common.

Though the patriotism of the classical Greeks and Romans was important in reviving the sentiment in the eighteenth century, the devotion to the state exhibited by certain of Plutarch's heroes also met with criticism. Holbach, for example, referred to the Spartans as "monks armed by political fanaticism," and condemned Roman patriotism as "a hate sworn against other nations."[161] Similarly, Ferlus denounced exclusivist classical patriotism as a "misfortune for mankind" and further stated that such patriotism would result in "a war of interest, of passion and of egoism" in society.[162] For the *Encyclopédie* the most perfect kind of patriotism was that which presupposed a recognition of the rights of mankind and the respect of these rights for all peoples.[163] The *Journal encyclopédique* would have subordinated patriotism to *humanité* on the grounds that "before being citizens, we are men."[164] Mathon distinguished between "love of country" and patriotism. The former sentiment he regarded as an extension of man's egoistic impulse (*amour de soi*), and a generalized form of self-interest. Patriotism, by contrast, was rooted in man's altruistic impulse (*amour d'autrui*), was essentially selfless, and could be regarded as a virtue.[165] Indeed, for Mathon it was a particularly important virtue, for in his view "patriotism ultimately merits a large place in our esteem because it is

[160] Navarre, *Discours*, pp. 26 and 24.
[161] Holbach, *Systême social*, I, 41-42.
[162] Ferlus, *Le Patriotisme chrétien*, pp. 11-12.
[163] *Encyclopédie*, art. "Patriotisme."
[164] JE, 1763-II, 127.
[165] Mathon, *Discours*, p. 14.

related to all the social virtues, and is, so to speak, the measure and the guarantee of them."[166]

This emphasis on the relation of patriotism to the "social virtues" brings to the fore the fundamental fact that toward the end of the eighteenth century patriotism was primarily a social, and not, as it was in antiquity and was again to become, a political concept. In contrast to nineteenth-century nationalism which was forged in international conflict and essentially exclusivist, the patriotism of the Enlightenment was positively oriented toward assuring the well-being of the whole community,[167] and tended to regard other national groups, not as actual or potential rivals, but as part of a common humanity. Typically, the "patriot" of eighteenth-century France was a man who had done something to promote the common good, such as, for example, writing a book on agriculture, or education, or ethics, or who had performed a signal act of beneficence.[168] Soldiers were not, of course, denied the status of citizens and patriots, but the opinion of the time on the whole preferred examples of patriotism which conduced to social harmony to those which reflected conflict.

As a social value, the function of patriotism in the intellectual climate of the last years of the old regime was, above

[166] Ibid., p. 15.

[167] Mathon observed that, "in order to truly love one's *patrie*, one must be content with one's lot there" (ibid., p. 23), and for Jean Meerman, "the essential feature of Patriotism is to contribute to the good of the *Patrie* and to the happiness of those who are its members" (*Discours presenté à l'Académie de Châlons-sur-Marne en 1787. Sur la question qu'elle avoit proposée: Quels sont les moyens d'exciter & d'encourager le patriotisme dans une monarchie . . .*, Leiden, 1789, p. 10). Similarly, for the physiocrat Jean Auffray, economics was the most important science because it could promote general prosperity, and it was upon this prosperity that patriotism depended ("Discours sur les avantages que le patriotisme retire de l'étude et de la Pratique des Sciences Oeconomiques," B Mun. Metz, mss. 1349, p. 198). Conversely, it was often stated that the poor have no *patrie* (e.g. Voltaire, *Dictionnaire philosophique*, art. "Patrie"; Holbach, *Ethnocratie*, pp. 117-18; and *Encyclopédie*, art. "Population," XIII, 97).

[168] See above, nn. 140-42.

all, to overcome divisiveness, to unite the various classes, and to establish social harmony. One example of this can be seen in the use of the term "citizen," noted above. Poor citizens, respectable citizens, brave citizens, worthy citizens and even citizen kings have something in common. Remove the common denominator, which acts, at least on the level of ideology, as a cohesive force, and one is left with simply the poor, the respectable, the brave, the worthy, and the king. Not quite so comfortable a situation. Régine Robin seems perfectly justified in asserting that in a time when fear of social disaggregation was prominent, the term "citizen" was used "to obliterate distinctions of social reality."[169]

The desire to strengthen social bonds was expressed directly as well as by implication. Lezay-Marnesia, for example, apostrophized priests and *philosophes*, urging them to stop quarreling and to "unite under the standard of the *patrie*."[170] Similarly, Thélis lamented the fact that a self-serving corporate spirit had supplanted patriotism, and argued that the former feeling must be extinguished and the latter allowed to replace it.[171] Describing patriotism, Ferlus wrote:

> Il est une sagesse qui répand dans le corps politique, la force, la vie, & la santé, qui devient, quand elle se trouve en même-temps dans les Sujets & dans les Rois, l'appui inébranlable des Empires; c'est un lien commun qui unit le Chef aux Membres & les Membres entr'eux, les fait tous concourir au même but, en forme un corps parfait, dont elle est l'âme & le ressort.[172]

Mathon believed that the newly formed provincial assemblies would act as a cohesive force, and that, despite "the efforts of jealousy, the meanness of self-love, and the

[169] Robin, *La Société française en 1789*, p. 333.
[170] Lezay-Marnesia, *Le Bonheur dans les campagnes*, p. 53.
[171] Thélis, *Moyens proposés*, p. 3.
[172] Ferlus, *Le Patriotisme chrétien*, pp. 3-4.

intrigue of [self-]interest," they would not fail "to regenerate the nation, to form true citizens, to unite them all in one
same spirit by attaching them to the common good, and, so
to speak, cause patriotism and great talents to blossom
forth at the same time. . . ."[173] In writing of patriotism toward the end of the old regime, authors repeatedly used
terms connoting cohesion, such as "bind," "bond," "join,"
"unite," "common," "attach," and "cooperate," and frequently described the *patrie* as a family.[174] The value to
which they most commonly opposed patriotism was not
cosmopolitanism, but egoism,[175] and the values with which
they most often identified it were not glory and power, but
humanity and beneficence.

An Altruist Ethic: Humanité and Bienfaisance

Bienfaisance and *humanité* have long been recognized as
characteristic features of Enlightenment thought, and have
been accorded an important place in the process of secularization which occurred in the eighteenth century.
However, it is seldom realized how wide a currency these
ideas enjoyed in the late Enlightenment, how frequently
and in what varied form they were translated into action,
and how important a place they had in the social thought
of the time.

One valuable indicator of opinion during the later eighteenth century is the "news" item that appeared in certain
journals. For while they were for the most part devoted to
reviewing newly published books and pamphlets, these pe-

---

[173] Mathon, *Discours*, p. 6.

[174] The image of the *patrie* as a family occurs in Ferlus, *Le Patriotisme chrétien*, p. 4; DUS, "Discours preliminaire," I, vi; Baudeau, *Vrais pauvres*, p. 85; Coyer, *Dissertation sur la patrie*, p. 171; *Encyclopédie*, art. "Patrie," XII, 178, and other reference works based on it.

[175] Caraccioli, for example, complained that "l'intérêt personnel a to-talement éteint cet amour patriotique" (AL, 1763 II, 66), and the anony-mous author of *L'Homme sociable* stated that, ". . . ce qui . . . abâtardit tout-à-fait l'amour de la patrie, c'est cet égoïsme répandu partout. . . ." Quoted from JE, 1773 I, 21.

riodicals also carried various announcements, articles, letters and miscellaneous news stories. The news items, on the whole, fall into a number of categories. The first, which catered to the taste for the unusual and curiosity about the limits of nature, may be defined as sensationalist, and includes accounts of great crimes, extraordinary medical cases, unusual events, and various sorts of freak natural phenomena. Cases of unusual longevity or fertility, which reflect an interest in population, form a second category, and observations on natural science a third. A fourth category was devoted to stories of "human interest." Here various acts of kindness and public-spiritedness were presented under such rubrics as "Traits de bienfaisance, d'humanité et de patriotisme," or more simply, "Traits de vertus" or "Etablissemens utiles."[176]

While the *Année littéraire* remained true to its original conception and seldom published anything but book reviews, occasional articles, and certain kinds of advertisements, the *Journal encyclopédique* printed progressively more short news items. In the years 1762-63 it included only sixteen such items; in 1773-74 there were seventy; and in 1783-84, one hundred and eighty (see Figure 3). Of immediate interest here is the fact that the number of entries describing acts of beneficence and public-spiritedness rose from one in 1762-63 to thirty-six in 1773-74 to sixty-four in 1783-84.[177] Moreover, not only were moral anecdotes and

[176] Each rubric contains between one and half a dozen items.

[177] See fig. 3. In order to put these figures into perspective it will be useful to compare them with other elements of the climate of opinion of the time, such as balloon flights or mesmerism, to which Robert Darnton has drawn attention (*Mesmerism and the End of the Enlightenment in France*, Cambridge, Mass., 1968). Neither of these subjects figure in the "news items" just discussed, but articles and letters on them do appear in the periodical press of the time. Of 218 articles and letters (the distinction is fairly arbitrary, and hence they will be taken together) which appeared in the *Journal encyclopédique* in 1783-84, ten were devoted to mesmerism and forty-one to what was then called "aerostatics." Together these two subjects had fifty-one entries, while there were sixty-two items describing acts

FIGURE 3. NEWS ITEMS APPEARING IN THE *Journal Encyclopédique* DURING 1762-63, 1773-74 AND 1783-84*

	Human Interest	Bienfaisance	Population	Natural History	Obituaries	Buildings & Antiques	Totals
1762-63							
No Entries	11	1	1	2	1	-	16
% Entries	68.75	6.25	6.25	12.50	6.25	-	100.00
No. Pages	53.75	2.75	7	2.75	1.50	-	67.75
% Pages	79.34	4.06	10.33	4.06	2.21	-	100.00
1773-74							
No. Entries	25	36	1	7	-	1	70
% Entries	35.70	51.40	1.40	10.10	-	1.40	100.00
No. Pages	58.00	73.25	1.25	16.00	-	6.25	154.75
% Pages	37.48	47.33	.81	10.34	-	4.04	100.00
1783-84							
No. Entries	34	64	20	28	9	25	180
% Entries	18.90	35.50	11.10	15.60	5.00	13.90	100.00
No. Pages	82.75	188.00	13.75	36.00	32.25	17.25	370.00
% Pages	22.36	50.81	3.72	9.73	8.72	4.66	100.00

* Source: *Journal encyclopédique*, 1762-63, 1773-74 and 1783-84.

acts of generosity or self-abnegation retailed three and four at a time in journals, but they were also collected and published wholesale in anthologies. In 1769, for example, a *Tableau de l'humanité et de la bienfaisance ou Précis historique des charités qui se font dans Paris* appeared. A three volume compilation entitled, *Les Annales de la bienfaisance, ou les hommes rappellés à la bienfaisance par des exemples des peuples anciens & modernes qui ont donné des exemples d'humanité, de vertu, de générosité & c.* was published in 1773, and was followed the year after by the Abbé Poncol's *Dictionnaire de bienfaisance*. Even an almanach of deeds of benevolence and humanity entitled, *Etrennes de la vertu pour l'année 1784, contenant les actions de bienfaisance, de courage, d'humanité & c.*, was published, and both Fillassier's *Dictionnaire historique de l'éducation* (1784) and Berenger's *Le Peuple instruit par ses propres vertus* are no more than compilations, culled from history and contemporary journals, of stories, anecdotes and reports of brave or generous actions intended to inspire virtue.

Having seen that "traits de bienfaisance" and moral anecdotes enjoyed a considerable vogue toward the end of the old regime, it would be profitable to examine some of them to see precisely which aspects of the virtues of beneficence and humanity they held up to emulation. To this end we shall consider several representative anecdotes from Berenger's anthology and from the *Journal encyclopédique*.

A number of themes recur repeatedly in *Le Peuple in-*

---

of beneficence. These figures, however, cannot be taken at face value. During the two years in question, items on aerostatics took up just over three hundred pages in the *Journal encyclopédique* and mesmerism a further thirty pages, while "Traits de vertus" occupied about 290 pages. Thus, in terms of space allocated, Mesmerism and descriptions of balloon flights enjoy a slight advantage. Over time they do not appear to have done so. While the *Journal encyclopédique* carried thirty-six items on beneficence during 1773-74, there are no items on either mesmerism or aerostatics. Furthermore, there are indications that mesmerism and balloon flights lost in popularity once political ferment began later in the 1780s, but that beneficence remained as relevant as ever.

struit. The most persistent of these, the theme that virtue is always rewarded, is illustrated in the following two tales. A pretty and virtuous girl married a sailor, who soon after went to sea, leaving her with child. Her meager resources were quickly exhausted, so that she was obliged to approach a "bourgeois" (and there is some significance in the villain being so identified) for help. He would only agree to lend her money if she would compromise her virtue. At first the girl refused indignantly, but necessity left her little choice, and she resigned herself to her fate. However, before agreeing to the demands of her oppressor, she addressed a dramatic speech on her plight to her baby. Thereupon the heart of the "bourgeois" softened, and the girl both received the money she needed and preserved her honor.[178] A variation on the same theme tells how a girl bought a dirty, ugly and battered dog in order to save it from mistreatment by street boys. The dog saved the girl's life by awakening the house when a burglar with the avowed intention of murdering her had broken in. Whereupon Berenger rather heavy-handedly pointed his moral: ". . . so true is it that *a good deed is never lost.*"[179]

A second main theme is the importance of the virtue of loyalty. In one tale, a young man of good family lived so riotously that he squandered his whole fortune and was left in penury. One devoted servant nevertheless refused to leave him, and worked all day and begged at night in order to support him. Eventually the young man received an in-

[178] Berenger, *Le Peuple instruit par ses propres vertus, ou Cours complet d'instruction et d'anecdotes recueillies dans nos meilleurs auteurs* (Paris, 2 vols., 1787), vol. I, pp. 276-78.

[179] Ibid., I, 411-12. Tales of animals performing acts of beneficence, either for each other or for humans, are common at this time, and seem to have as their function to demonstrate that nature is itself and in its workings beneficent. The implication is that it is "natural" for man to be so, too. In his "Catéchisme," Tschudy asserted that man, because he is formed in the image of a Beneficent Creator, shares this propensity to beneficence (fol. 13v).

heritance, and insisted on sharing it with the servant.[180] Closely related to the theme of loyalty is that of gratitude. For example, a soldier was sentenced to death for indiscipline, and then reprieved at the request of the officer he had offended. When this officer was later imprisoned for debt, the soldier left his regiment and traveled to the jail to obtain the officer's release (the soldier shows his gratitude, and the officer's beneficence is rewarded); the officer, however, refused to put himself beyond the law, but gave the soldier a purse—despite the fact that he was in debtors' prison—for his trouble (the soldier's gratitude is rewarded).[181] Berenger also included in his anthology a number of sermons or moral exhortations, thinly disguised as advice given by virtuous fathers on their deathbeds to devoted children, to promote the more traditional virtues of piety, chastity, courage, honesty and industry. Both exemplary tales and moral exhortations generally end with the characters in extremely awkward postures—someone is inevitably on his knees, or at someone else's feet—and there is scarcely one which is not copiously watered with tears of joy or gratitude.

Though there are no major differences in the nature or the themes of the *traits de bienfaisance* which appeared in the periodical press and Berenger's moral anecdotes, there are, nevertheless, certain differences in emphasis that are not unimportant. Since Berenger was essentially editing a textbook on morality, he strove for universality of appeal and uniformity of tone. Furthermore, it was immaterial to Berenger whether the anecdotes he presented had actually occurred or not, so long as they were morally edifying.[182] Periodicals, on the other hand, reported as *traits de bienfaisance* events or deeds that had in fact taken place, and often

[180] Berenger, *Le Peuple instruit*, I, 94-95.
[181] Ibid., pp. 65-66.
[182] Berenger lists the sources on which he has drawn, and these include periodicals and works of literature. Ibid., "Avertissement."

included in their accounts details of no lasting interest, or which had no value to the moralist. To the historian, however, they are particularly valuable, for they provide a good deal of information on the practice of beneficence in the final decades of the old regime.

Early in 1783 the *Journal encyclopédique* reported the following series of events. A certain fruitseller (*marchande fruitière*), Mme. Menthe by name, worked in a market of Paris. Her husband, a coachman, had been ill for over a year, so that the burden of supporting their ten surviving children—they had had eighteen altogether—fell principally on her. The sister of Mme. Menthe had amassed a sum of four thousand *livres*, and when she died, left this sum to an acquaintance, completely ignoring her hard-pressed sister. Mme. Menthe consulted a lawyer to see if the will could be annulled, but was told that it had been made out in due form, and could not. The last remaining child of her sister, a boy of five, was present at the interview with the lawyer, and Mme. Menthe decided to take her nephew home and care for him, observing that this was one part of the succession that would not be disputed her, and that her sister's acquaintance would probably send the child to a *hôpital* to be rid of him. The lawyer remonstrated with her, pointing out that her family was already greater than her means. Mme. Menthe replied simply, "The poor thing didn't ask to be born, and someone must feed him; God will help."[183]

The Mme. Menthe's story up to this point had been printed in the *Journal de Paris*, and had aroused the compassion of a number of people who had sent the editors of that journal money to the sum of 168 *livres* for the poor but virtuous woman. In presenting the money to her, the editors of the journal pointed out that it was "less the very natural sort of assistance that might be provided to help her feed her ten children, than the reward for her act of

[183] JE, 1783 i, 518-20.

humanity and charity toward her nephew." They also underscored the point that "sooner or later every good deed is rewarded." Mme. Menthe of course showed herself greatly moved, and stated her intention to use the money to pay off her debts, observing that "one is always rich enough when one has his health and owes nothing."[184]

Mme. Menthe seems to have caught the imagination of the public. Several months after its initial item, the *Journal encyclopédique* reported a meeting of freemasons of the lodge La Candeur, in which Mme. Menthe and her family figured prominently. They were presented in a *tableau vivant*, "the virtuous Mme. Menthe" seated on a "magnificent throne," her children grouped around her, and her adopted nephew at her feet. The marquis who presided over the meeting explained the meaning of the tableau to the audience, and at the most moving point of his discourse a countess crowned Mme. Menthe with a "civic crown." A marquise presented her with a "rich purse," and a second countess gave her a layette for the baby she was expecting, her nineteenth. The masons had also clothed the entire family at their own expense, and had undertaken responsibility for the education of the adopted nephew.[185] A further entry on the Menthe saga reports that Mme. Menthe had given birth to her nineteenth child, and that the curate of the parish was its godfather and a baroness its godmother. Moreover, the editors of the *Journal de Paris* had passed on to her a further 440 *livres*.[186]

The moral that this item seeks to illustrate is one with which we are already familiar from Berenger: virtue is rewarded. There is, however, a significant difference in the way the reward is conferred in the two sources. In Berenger's moral anecdotes the person who has benefited from an act of beneficence finds a way through his or her own particular abilities, or is enabled by a turn of fortune to repay, usually with enormous interest, the original act of

[184] Ibid.   [185] JE, 1783 III, 131-32.   [186] Ibid., pp. 333-34.

kindness. The reward for the act of beneficence is immediate and personal. In the case of the *Journal encyclopédique* report, by contrast, the rewarding of beneficence has become a social matter. People who did not know Mme. Menthe sent her money anonymously; editors of a prominent journal undertook to pass this money along to her; and a lodge of freemasons further contributed to the family's well-being, and rather more strikingly, dramatized and publicized what they considered an outstanding act of "humanity and charity." Now, while the account of Mme. Menthe's act of beneficence and its many rewards is particularly striking, it is in no way unrepresentative. In the last fifteen years or so of the old regime, the more literate and affluent sections of society not only extolled the virtues of humanity and beneficence, but practiced them too. In order to do so more effectively, they organized and joined committees and clubs. They also sought to stimulate people to virtue through contests and rewards, both material and honorific.

An examination of other *traits de vertus* which appeared in the *Journal encyclopédique* during 1783 shows that the sentiment of beneficence was capable of inspiring serious attempts at the relief and improvement of the poor as well as signal acts of kindness. A certain "virtuous citizen," for example, donated 15,000 *livres* to set up a fund for the benefit of inmates of debtors' prisons; his initial donation was increased by members of the public to over 85,000 *livres*, and the fund freed more than 1,700 prisoners.[187] In Dijon, the rising price of grain and increasing unemployment led the intendant of Burgundy to establish an *atelier de charité* to provide work for those who needed it. The intendant reduced his own expenses, and contributed the savings to the cost of running the *atelier*. He also provided from his own pocket a lump sum of 2,000 *livres* for it, and some local chartreux made a similar contribution.[188] In

[187] JE, 1783 I, 517-19.   [188] Ibid., pp. 520-23.

Toulouse a number of lawyers set up a system of legal aid for those who could not afford to pay for it.[189] Another scheme which anticipated a feature of our modern social services, a pension fund for aged workers, was begun in Paris. However, there were only twelve of these pensions, they were conferred by a committee of a voluntary association, and they could not be claimed before age 80.[190] Many more examples, both of this nature and of acts of personal kindness could easily be adduced. Yet one cannot help remarking that while the intentions of those who undertook these schemes were laudable, and while they in some cases achieved positive results, their efforts were pitifully inadequate to the objective situation they confronted.

The formation of ad hoc committees and societies to carry out programs of aid and charity for the poor indicates that members of the enlightened community saw that it was necessary not only to practice beneficence on a personal level, but also to organize so as to act more methodically and effectively. Lodges of freemasons sometimes, as in the case of Mme. Menthe, helped the virtuous poor, but during the 1780s a number of philanthropic societies, whose purpose was simply to extend as much relief on as a wide a scale as possible, were formed. Sellier was a corresponding member of the Philanthropic Society of Strasbourg, and Thélis a full member of the Paris Society. Members of the Philanthropic Society of the capital paid an annual membership fee of 100 *livres*, and were called by the *Journal encyclopédique* "ces actionnaires de la bienfaisance."[191] The money was used to support the poor. Residents of Bordeaux and Lyon wrote to the Paris Society in 1784 asking for copies of its statutes, and expressed the desire to set up similar institutions.[192] In the event, it does seem that a network of philanthropic societies was established in the larger towns of France in the five years pre-

---

[189] JE, 1783 v, 330-31.
[191] JE, 1784 iv, 341.

[190] Ibid., pp. 526-27.
[192] Loc. cit.

ceding the Revolution. Unfortunately very little is known of these organizations, a systematic study of which would cast a good deal of light on the theory and practice of an important Enlightenment value.

A significant feature of the *traits de vertus* published in the *Journal encyclopédique*, as well as in other periodicals, is that they were often extracted from other journals. The editors, it seems safe to suggest, were motivated less by the need to fill space than by the desire to give as wide a currency as possible to these morally edifying and reassuring events in order to propagate and generalize the values they embodied. Another means of stimulating moral rectitude which was favored at the time was to offer prizes for good or exemplary conduct over an extended period, usually a year. The prizes were sometimes honorific, sometimes quite substantial. In Copenhagen, for example, a private society offered an annual prize of 150 *livres* to the member of the lower classes (*bas peuple*) who had performed the most meritorious action during the year.[193] In Guyenne a curate founded a prize of 30 *livres* for the peasant in his parish who had most successfully cultivated his land.[194] Four "prizes of merit" of unstated worth were established by a seigneur on his estates in 1783. They were awarded for "respect for parents and the elderly, assiduity at work and respect for religion." The girl who won the first prize was crowned by the bishop of the region.[195] A similar sort of contest took place in the village of Romainville, where a special "fête de la Rosière" was established to honor the girl who was most distinguished for her "irreprochable morals." Any woman between eighteen and thirty was eligible, and the choice was made by a vote of heads of families and former winners of the contest. In 1783, thanks to the generosity of the Duke d'Orléans, the prize was a life annuity of 200 *livres*.[196] But perhaps the most common kind

[193] JE, 1783 I, 331-32.
[195] JE, 1783 VI, 149-50.
[194] Ibid., pp. 130-31.
[196] JE, 1783 V, 149-50.

of prize awarded for good conduct or exemplary morals was a dowry. Raynal provided a dowry of 300 *livres* for the "most virtuous and most hard-working girl" in the French colony of Berlin.[197] In Paris six girls of the parish of Saint Roch were married in 1783 with dowries of 1,000 *livres* each, which they had been awarded for good morals and fulfillment of their duties, both religious and other.[198] A lodge of freemasons of Marseilles dowered one girl from each of the five parishes of the town, chosen by the curates, with 300 *livres* each, and in Toulouse, two male workers recognized as "honest and hard-working" were dowered with 150 *livres* each by the canons of the metropolitan church.[199]

The popularity of the dowery as a prize for virtue is probably connected both with the concern about falling population and with the view that bachelorhood was an egotistical, not to say antisocial or unpatriotic, state. Be that as it may, it should be clear that the virtues of beneficence and humanity were not restricted to the realm of ideas alone.

The moral implicit in these accounts of beneficence, generosity, humanity and kindness is clear. They attempt to show by example rather than precept that there is good in men, and that regardless of the social level at which one finds oneself, one is capable of performing acts of kindness as well as of finding oneself in need of them. It is noteworthy that there is no egalitarianism and no blurring of social categories in these tales and news items. The virtue of the poor who benefit from acts of kindness is gratitude and acceptance of their condition; and that of the wealthy to perform acts of beneficence (though when the poor did so, they were held up as examples of exceptional virtue). I have come across no examples of acts of beneficence that help a person to rise above his condition. These moral

[197] JE, 1783 IV, 527-28.
[198] JE, 1783 V, 150.
[199] JE, 1784 V, 139-40; JE, 1783 V, 149.

anecdotes exhort the reader to fulfill the obligations of his *état*, and they seek to smooth and improve relations between classes at a time of very real social tensions. One can, of course, easily belittle what Mornet has called the "tearful and beribboned beneficence" of the period,[200] but one can hardly deny that it represents an attempt, albeit a pathetically inadequate one, to deal with the social disjunction caused by the crisis of the conjuncture, and misperceived as a moral crisis.

That this interpretation of the meaning of the moral anecdote and its function is not altogether fanciful is apparent from the way contemporaries regarded the virtue of beneficence. Beneficence, for them, provided the element of good will and cooperation without which society could not continue to function. It was a value that, against the centrifugal forces of poverty and the concept of self-interest, worked to bind one man to his fellow, and each class to the rest. Fréron referred to beneficence as, "this celestial virtue which [if there were no villains] might make mankind a people of brothers and friends."[201] Holbach asserted:

> Le bon citoyen est celui que est utile à son pays, dans quelque classe qu'il se trouve placé: le pauvre remplit sa tâche sociale par un travail honnête, ou dont il résulte un bien solide & réel pour ses concitoyens: le riche remplit sa tâche lorsqu'il aide le pauvre à remplir la sienne; c'est en secourant l'indigence active & laborieuse, c'est en payant ses travaux, c'est en lui facilitant les moyens de subsister, en un mot, c'est par sa bienfaisance que le riche peut acquitter ses dettes envers la Société. C'est donc en détournant l'esprit des citoyens riches des fantaisies insensées & nuisibles du luxe & de la vanité, pour le porter vers la bienfaisance utile à la Patrie, que le Législateur établira chez lui l'harmonie sociale, sans laquelle il ne peut y avoir de félicité pour personne.[202]

[200] Mornet, *La Pensée française au XVIIIe siécle*, p. 154.
[201] AL, 1774 I, 259.   [202] Holbach, *Ethnocratie*, p. 140.

Like patriotism, beneficence had as its ultimate purpose the achievement of "social harmony."[203]

By the late 1780s, beneficence had, at least for some, ceased to appear merely as a useful virtue, and had become a social necessity. Thus Necker wrote:

> . . . dans l'état actuel des sociétés, il est devenu impossible de se passer de ces vertus [i.e., vertus bienfaisantes]. Il ne suffit plus d'être juste quand les loix de propriété réduissent à un étroit nécessaire, le plus grand nombre des hommes, & que le moindre accident vient déranger encore leurs foible ressources: ainsi, je ne crains point de dire que telles sont les inégalités extrêmes établies par ces loix, qu'on doit aujourd'hui considérer l'esprit de bienfaisance & de charité, comme une partie constitutive de l'ordre social. . . .[204]

It is curious that Necker, who saw more clearly than most the economic and institutional roots of the crisis that France was facing, should have proposed as an antidote only the institutionalization of a moral value.

An Agent of Reform: Education

Though during the second half of the eighteenth century many members of the enlightened community believed that they faced a crisis of moral disaggregation, they did not think it to be insuperable. In patriotism they had found a principle of authority, in humanity and beneficence the main features of an altruist ethic, and in education the means by which these new values could be inculcated, and the groundwork laid for a better society. Education, it was hoped, would play a major role in arresting depopulation, regenerating morality, fostering national unity and reinforcing social order. Such confidence

---

[203] Berenger wrote: "Le prince doit être la providence sensible de ses Peuples, le principe de l'harmonie sociale, & comme l'esprit qui fait penser & mouvoir ce vaste corps politique" (*Les Quatre Etats*, p. 49).

[204] Necker, *Opinions religieuses*, p. 105.

in the efficacy of education no doubt seems exaggerated. Indeed, it could only be ascribed these Herculean tasks on the assumption that its powers were virtually unlimited. This assumption came to be made with increasing frequency as the century progressed.

During the 1760s few writers insisted on the potential power of education. The authors of *De l'éducation publique*, Navarre, Baudeau and Granet made no improbable claims for the efficacy of instruction. Guyton, Rolland and Tschudy all expected education to make significant contributions to society, but only La Chalotais, Rivard and Formey assumed its social significance to be very great. La Chalotais asserted that the power of education had been proved by experience. He exclaimed:

> Que ne pourroit point une institution formée par les loix & dirigée par des exemples! Elle changeroit en peu d'années les moeurs d'une Nation entière; chez les Spartiates, elle avoit vaincu la nature même.[205]

Toward the end of his essay, La Chalotais painted a glowing picture of the benefits that would result from a well directed educational system.[206] Rivard saw in education a means of reforming morality and encouraging social peace.[207] Despite his belief in the radical corruption of man, the Jansenist pedagogue could assert that "almost all good and evil result from a good or bad education."[208] The author of the preface to Formey's *Traité d'éducation* argued that if men would realize that education begins at birth and act accordingly, this principle "would change the face of the whole world."[209] The child is after all no more than a "soft wax" that can be worked in any way one chooses.[210]

[205] La Chalotais, *Essai*, p. 5.
[206] Ibid., pp. 143-46.
[207] Rivard, *Recueil*, pp. 255 and 387.
[208] Ibid., p. 239.
[209] Editor's preface to Formey's *Traité*, p. v.
[210] Ibid., p. vii.

Though Formey's treatise was written in 1762, it was not published, and the preface not written, until 1773. This was also the year in which Helvétius' *De l'Homme* appeared posthumously. In this book Helvétius applied the premises of Lockean psychology to education and concluded that its powers were virtually unlimited. In Helvétius' own words: "L'éducation peut tout."[211]

As it happens, the number of claims put forward for the unlimited power of education increased after this date. It is unlikely that this was necessarily the result of people having read Helvétius' book. Rather, I suggest, Lockean psychology and Condillac's rendering of it were being widely diffused in these years. The conclusion followed of itself. Be that as it may, statements very much like Helvétius' "Education is all-powerful" became more common after 1773. Pernetti stated that all faults can be ascribed to education, for "elle fait tout."[212] Gourdin admitted that education depends on legislation, but then added, "and it is education that makes men."[213] Both the conservative Durosoy and the radical Holbach agreed on this point. The one-time Jesuit asserted that "Nature only roughs out men, it is education that completes them," and the *philosophe* wrote, "One can [through education] make of man whatever one wishes."[214] Goyon began his *Essais de Laopédie* by observing that if education were responsible for virtues and vices, and thus for the welfare of nations, it should be of great interest to governments.[215] And of course his entire essay is predicated upon this assumption. Philipon stated on the first page of his *Vues patriotiques* that:

. . . l'être raisonnable devient par l'éducation, ou l'instrument du crime, ou l'ornement de la vertu. C'est

---

[211] This brief statement serves as the title of chap. 9, book x of *De l'Homme*.

[212] Pernetti, "Réponses," fol. 6r.

[213] Gourdin, *De l'éducation*, fol. 10r.

[214] Durosoy, *Philosophie sociale*, p. 281; Holbach, *Systême social*, I, 12.

[215] Goyon d'Arzac, *Essais de Laopédie*, p. 1.

l'éducation seule qui fait l'homme; il n'est jamais que ce qu'elle veut qu'il soit.[216]

Turgot, who was no armchair philosopher, but controller general of France, maintained that a properly organized system of education would in ten years change the face of the country.[217] For the *Année littéraire*, education was a particularly important subject because "on it alone depends the glory of empires and the happiness of households."[218] The *Journal encyclopédique* wrote with respect to a proposed plan of educational reform, "It is perhaps, we dare to say, the only means of forming virtuous men, faithful citizens, and true scholars."[219] Perrache argued that education alone had produced the multitude of great men which had flourished in classical Greece, and Beguillet described the power of education as "immense," "infinite" and "incalculable."[220] One might well expect more moderation from those who had first-hand experience with some aspect of education. But one does not find it. By 1787 Sellier had been teaching for over thirty years, yet he could assert: "Men are only what they are made."[221] For Thélis, too, "it is education that makes men."[222] Thélis' associate, the Chevalier de Bruni, stated that education was "the surest source of public felicity," and further maintained that this view was universally held: "Philosophers, scholars, legislators, all agree on this truth."[223] In point of fact, there were those who dissented from this view. They were, however, a small minority. The assumption that education had

[216] Philipon, *Vues patriotiques*, p. 1.

[217] Turgot, "Mémoire," p. 580.

[218] AL, 1773 II, 127.

[219] JE, 1773 V, 396.

[220] Perrache, "Projet," fol. 86v; E. Beguillet, *Considérations générales sur l'éducation adressées à l'auteur des "Reflexions détachées . . ."* (Bouillon, 1782), pp. 6-7.

[221] Sellier, "Lettre sur l'éducation de la jeunesse de tous états," p. 1.

[222] Thélis, *Plan*, p. 10.

[223] *Mémoire* III, 28.

virtually unlimited powers was the rule toward the end of the eighteenth century, and criticism of it the exception.[224]

Obviously, the faith of the enlightened community in the power of education was exaggerated. Education did not have in the eighteenth century, and does not have today, the power that Helvétius, Philipon and the others attributed to it. Why then did the great majority of educated men agree that it did? The reasons are three-fold.

First, the thesis of the unlimited power of education did not appear implausible in the intellectual climate of the time. I have suggested above that Lockean psychology was one of the foundations of Enlightenment thought, and that Locke's epistemology lent itself naturally to a theory of education. In conceiving the mind of man at birth to be a *tabula rasa*, or in the suggestive metaphor of Formey's editor and a number of others, a ball of soft wax,[225] sensationalist psychologists implied the virtually unlimited malleability of human nature. And from the unlimited malleability of human nature to the unlimited power of education is but a short step. If the child is soft wax in the hands of the educator, it follows that the educator can shape him as he chooses. This conclusion, in the form of statements to the effect that "it is education alone that

---

[224] The thesis of the unlimited power of education was called into question in an anonymous article entitled, "Réflexions détachées sur les Traités d'Education" which appeared in the *Mercure de France* of March 1782. A refutation to this article appeared within a few weeks in the same journal. Beguillet drew inspiration for his book from this debate, arguing in favor of education and against heredity (or "nature"). Thus if the thesis of the almost unlimited power of education was attacked, it did not lack defenders. Among the *philosophes*, Diderot offered a guarded criticism of this thesis. See his "Réfutation suivie de l'ouvrage d'Helvétius intitulé *De l'Homme*," in *Oeuvres*, II, 315-20.

[225] The image of the child as wax in the hands of the educator occurs in Durosoy, *Philosophie sociale*, p. 278, and Pernetti, "Réflexions," fol. 3v, while a slight variation of this image, likening the child to clay, is used by Vauréal (see above, n. 108).

makes the man" (Philipon), and "men are only what they are made" (Sellier), was widely drawn.

The second reason that members of the enlightened community held the powers of education to be so great must be sought in the climate of opinion of the last decades of the old regime. Believing themselves faced with a crisis which was in its origins and character moral, it was logical that they should have recourse to a moral agent to overcome it. To be sure, one ought not to overlook or minimize the more practical efforts made by members of the enlightened community to come to grips with worsening socioeconomic conditions. They advocated programs of administrative, fiscal and penal reform, seriously discussed issues such as mendicancy and abandonment of infants, founded agricultural societies in an attempt to improve French farming practices, made donations to charity, organized systems of poor relief, and not only praised, but practiced the virtue of beneficence on an impressive scale. They were, in short, neither unaware of, nor unmoved by, economic depression and social tensions. But the fact remains that where we today see the crisis of the conjuncture, they saw a crisis of moral dissolution. Perhaps they interpreted a socioeconomic crisis as a moral one for the same reason that their pious contemporaries regarded epidemics as a divine visitation, and responded with prayers and processions. They were faced with forces beyond their control, and, for the most part, beyond their comprehension. Only by ethicizing them could they understand them.

The third reason that educated Frenchmen believed the powers of education to be virtually unlimited is a simple one. They wanted to. The authors on whom this study is based were churchmen, army officers, professional educators, and members of the legal professions. A quarter of them were nobles, and a great many enjoyed the prestige conferred by membership in the academies. Their incomes, in most cases, would have consisted in various combinations of fees for professional services, benefices, revenues from landed property, and *rentes*.[226] These members of the enlightened community were not only part of the intellectual elite of their day, but of the social and economic elites as well. As such, they had a strong interest in overcoming the problems their society faced. And they would have had every reason for wishing to solve them within the framework of the old regime. While most members of the enlightened community wished to improve and to reform society, they wished to do so gradually and without dislocation. The particular appeal of education lay in the fact that it was believed capable of effecting important reforms slowly, safely, and without calling into question the social relations and economic conditions upon which the old regime was based.

[226] See F. Ford, *Robe and Sword* (New York, 1965), chap. 8, and M. Vovelle and D. Roche, "Bourgeois, Rentiers and Property Owners," in J. Kaplow, ed., *New Perspectives on the French Revolution: Readings in Historical Sociology* (New York, 1965).

CHAPTER V

The Impasse: Images of the People and the Limits of Reform

THE attitudes of the enlightened community toward the people and popular education went much deeper than the response to a crisis, even an extended one. These attitudes were predicated on an accurate evaluation of the economic role of the lower classes, and ultimately upon the assumption that there existed a "people-condition" that was as necessary as it was wretched. The democratic and egalitarian strain of Enlightenment thought was opposed not only by a current of elitism inherited from the seventeenth century,[1] but also by the socioeconomic conditions that had generated that elitism. But before drawing any conclusions from the belief in the necessity of a people-condition among members of the enlightened community, it would be well to examine the evidence for the existence of such a belief.

TOWARD REDEFINITION: THE POVERTY-STRICKEN AND PRODUCTIVE MASSES

The dictionaries published during the first half of the eighteenth century, we have seen, often defined the people as those who were neither noble, bourgeois nor *honnêtes gens*, and emphasized their ignorance and turbulence. Writers treating the lower classes after 1750 were both more specific and more positive. They explicitly recognized the poverty of the people,[2] and they came to ac-

---

[1] Snyders, *La Pédagogie en France*, pp. 400-10.

[2] Thus, for example, Le Mercier addressed the laboring poor as, "you, who born of poor parents, possess no manner of property" (*De l'instruction*

knowledge and to respect their productive role in society.

Because of their poverty, the people were generally regarded as belonging in the "last ranks," the "last classes" or the "last degree" of society.[3] But this was not to say, as the dictionary of the Académie did, that the people were the "least considerable part of the community." Formey, Tschudy and Baudeau, who relegated the people to the bottom of the social scale, stated respectively that the lower classes formed "the greater part of nations," "the most numerous and the most useful classes of the state" and "the largest and most useful portion of the nation."[4] This recognition that the poor made up the bulk of any nation was widespread.

Crévier calculated that the people, whom he equated with the peasantry and the poor, formed ninety-five percent of the population of France.[5] Frédéric de Castillon, a teacher and member of the Berlin Academy, referred to the people as the "greater part of the nation."[6] Beguillet stated that "the man of the third estate, the man of the people, the man of the countryside, really forms in every country the body of nations."[7] Goyon agreed that the people "truly compose the body of the nation," and added that they were the power of the state.[8] Thélis spoke of the people as "the most numerous class of citizens, and the most worthy, after all, of our interest, by reason of its wretchedness [misère] and the services which it renders us and which we repay so badly, and by reason of its vast ex-

publique, pp. 48-49), and Necker defined the people as those who were without property or special talents (Opinions religieuses, p. 52). On this shift see above, chap. I, pp. 45-75.

[3] Formey, Traité, p. 22; Tschudy, "Mémoire sur la mendicité," fol. 15v; Baudeau, Ephémérides, 1765 I, 103.

[4] Formey, Traité, pp. 24-25; Tschudy, "Mémoire sur la mendicité," fol. 15v; Baudeau, Ephémérides, 1776 III, 20-21.

[5] Crévier, Difficultés, pp. 12-13.

[6] Krauss, Est-il utile de tromper le peuple? p. 22.

[7] Beguillet, Considérations, p. 17.

[8] Goyon d'Arzac, Essais de Laopédie, p. 1.

tent, which includes the greatest part of the nation.[9] Similarly, in making an announcement about its essay contest on popular education, the Academy of Châlons-sur-Marne referred to the people as, "the most numerous and most useful part of the nation."[10]

Compared to the new awareness of their economic importance, the recognition that the people were the majority in any country played only a minor role in their rehabilitation. The lower classes were now identified with specific occupations, and their collective contribution to the life of the state was acknowledged. Thus, the people ceased to be seen primarily as *canaille*, and came to be looked upon, first and foremost, as "gens de travail."[11] La Chalotais placed the social categories *laboureur* and *artisan* in apposition to the term people.[12] Formey and Verlac retained these categories, and added that of servant to their definitions of the lower classes.[13] Philipon ignored domestics, but mentioned peasants, workers and soldiers as the groups which constituted the popular classes, while Goyon, we have seen, included both merchants and indigents in his definition of the people.[14] An anonymous member of the Academy of Lyon stated that the "last classes of society" were composed of peasants (*agriculteurs*) and artisans, and Gourdin made the same identification in almost the same words.[15]

Though the occupations of the people were humble ones, their worth and importance were coming to be appreciated. The authors of *De l'éducation publique* asserted that without artisans, peasants and soldiers the state could not subsist.[16] Perrache referred to the people as an "essen-

[9] Thélis, *Plan*, p. 17.   [10] AD Marne J 48[8].
[11] Sellier, Letter to the Municipal Council, 23 December 1782. A Mun. Amiens, BB 162[371], pp. 4-5.
[12] La Chalotais, *Essai*, p. 25.
[13] Formey, *Traité*, p. 22; Verlac, *Plan*, p. 103.
[14] Philipon, *Vues patriotiques*, p. 7; see above, chap. III, n. 11.
[15] "Pensées sur l'éducation," fol. 49r; Gourdin, *De l'éducation*, fol. 94v.
[16] *De l'éducation publique*, p. 159. Jaubert makes a similar claim in his *Eloge de la roture*. See above, chap. I, n. 99.

tial part of the state," and dividing society into two groups, the people and the better-off, asserted that the former were "the base and the support" of the latter.[17] This appreciation of the vital role that the lower classes played in society grew as the century progressed. Having been described as malicious and seditious in the first half of the century, the people now had more favorable modifiers applied to them. They were said to be useful, and even precious.

Sellier said that the lower classes of the towns (*peuples des villes*) were "a very numerous and most useful class of men," and referred to the peasantry as "the most useful and most neglected class of men . . . the most docile and the most hardworking."[18] Goyon spoke of the people as "the most numerous and most useful portion of humanity."[19] Fréron observed that the lower classes were "so useful and often so unhappy."[20] Verlac referred to the people as "useful to society," and noted that they had been scorned until the time at which he was writing.[21] The *Dictionnaire universel* spoke of the poorest citizens as "the most truly useful to the state," and asserted that a "miserable peasant" was much more useful to society than the greatest seigneur.[22] Tschudy called propertyless day laborers "very useful men" and "the nerve of agriculture" but did not press his point because, he said, their utility was generally recognized.[23] Baudeau referred to the peasantry as "this class of citizens, the most useful to the *Patrie*" and as "the most precious portion of the state."[24] De l'Averdy called the poor

[17] Perrache, "Réflexions," fol. 130r. Coyer similarly referred to the people as "le soutien de l'état," in his "Plaisir pour le peuple," *Bagatelles morales*, p. 68.

[18] Sellier, "Lettre sur l'éducation des habitants de la campagne," p. 1.

[19] Goyon d'Arzac, *Essais de Laopédie*, p. 1.

[20] AL, 1784 I, 218-19.

[21] Verlac, *Plan*, pp. 18-19.

[22] DUS, art. "Privilège," xxvi, 26, and ibid., art. "Paysan," xxvi, 272.

[23] Tschudy, "Mémoire sur la mendicité," fol. 25v.

[24] Baudeau, *Vrais pauvres*, p. 103; *Ephémérides*, 1766, iii, 28.

"this precious portion of subjects."[25] Philipon asserted
that if the people were disdained by the frivolous and oppressed by the powerful, they were nonetheless "the most
precious part of humanity" for the wise man.[26] The author
of a work on abandoned infants spoke of "the precious
class of the people,"[27] and in an announcement about an
essay contest on the best moral education for the people,
the Academy of Amiens referred to them as "this precious
class of society."[28] It is not difficult to understand why the
people were found to have such great worth in the eyes of
their social superiors. The latter had come to see them as
"those whose labor is indispensibly necessary."[29]

PERSISTENCE: *Classes Laborieuses, Classes Dangereuses*

Coyer, Jaucourt, Thomas and the others had, it appears,
succeeded to a large degree in impressing on their contemporaries an awareness of the debt the rest of society
owed the laboring population. But if this awareness of the
economic role of the people was widespread, it by no
means resulted in the elimination of the current of mistrust
and fear which the lower classes traditionally inspired. The
people were seen as useful, necessary, even precious; but it
was not forgotten that they were a potential threat.

Lezay-Marnesia described a famine in northeastern
France which resulted in many peasants immigrating to
Hungary on the basis of a rumor that land was to be had
there. This example, he observed, "proves that the people,
when abandoned to itself, can easily take an extreme

[25] De l'Averdy, *Compte rendu concernant les bourses*, p. 4.

[26] Philipon, *Vues patriotiques*, p. 6.

[27] "Mémoire sur cette question: Quelles sont les moyens compatibles
avec les bonnes moeurs d'assurer la conservation des bâtards, et d'en tirer
une plus grande utilité pour l'Etat? Ouvrage qui a remporté le prix de la
Société Royale des Sciences et des Arts de Metz en 1787," B Mun. Metz,
mss. 1350, p. 11.

[28] AD Somme, D 148, p. 336.

[29] Formey, *Traité*, p. 22.

course of action.[30] We have seen that Thélis was well aware of the conditions in which the rural poor lived, and believed for reasons of humanitarianism and utility that the possessing classes should take a benevolent interest in them. However, he also thought that the progress of irreligion and the corruption of morality could not help but weaken "the spirit of subordination" and therefore suggested that "it would be particularly useful to have a regular corps of troops composed of nobles, able to impose this spirit on the people, whether in the towns or in the countryside."[31] Finding potential danger in a physiological rather than a mental state, Verlac described a man whose wife and children were hungry and crying for bread. Should he not be able to give them any, Verlac asked, "is his despair not to be feared?"[32] Similarly, Jaubert observed that "reduced almost to nothing by the continuation of its wretchedness, despair leads it [the people] to violent excesses which are always dangerous for society."[33] Philipon noted simply that "it is not the well off [*citoyens aisés*] who trouble the state."[34] But he too was aware that extreme poverty (*misère*) rather than innate perversity led the lower classes to trouble the peace so dear to the well-fed and possessing minority.[35] Fear of the people recognizing and understanding their condition and a resulting war of poor against rich "by principle" was the keynote of Necker's *Opinions religieuses*.[36] In Holbach we find both a sympathetic recognition of the effects of poverty on the poor and typically classical denunciations of their turbulence. On the one hand, the *philosophe* stated that indigence "causes the heart to wither or incites it to fury" and that the despair and crimes of the people were a direct result of their *mi-*

[30] Lezay-Marnesia, *Le Bonheur dans les campagnes*, p. 9.

[31] Thélis, *Mémoire* x, 12.   [32] Verlac, *Plan*, p. 78.

[33] Jaubert, *Des Causes de la dépopulation*, p. 148.

[34] Philipon, *Vues patriotiques*, p. 76.

[35] Ibid., p. 125.

[36] Necker, *Opinions religieuses*, pp. 94-95.

sère;[37] on the other hand, he described the lower classes as "scatterbrained, inconstant, imprudent, impetuous, subject to fits of enthousiasm" and, because of their ignorance, the instruments of troublemakers.[38] They could not safely be admitted to full citizenship, which, in his view should remain the prerogative of property owners.[39]

In the eighteenth century, as in the nineteenth, the association *classes laborieuses, classes dangereuses* was made. The significant point, however, is less that authors writing after 1750 retained something of the fear and suspicion of the lower classes prominent in the dictionaries of the first half of the century, but that they recognized the productive role of the people.

THE CONDITIONS OF EXISTENCE: *Misère* AND *Peine*

If the lexicographers of the first half of the century remained silent about the basic facts governing the lives of the lower classes, after mid-century this omission was more than made good. Goyon, Philipon and Perreau all regarded manual labor as a distinguishing feature of the people.[40] Other writers were more specific. Necker stated that the lower classes were "obliged to have 'recourse to rough work . . . in which only physical strength is required."[41] No one believed that such work was easy or pleasant. La Chalotais described the occupations of those engaged in manual trades as "sad."[42] In Rivard's eyes the labors of the peasantry (*gens de campagne*) were "hard [*pénibles*] and regarded as scarcely honorable," while the anonymous author of the *Pensées sur l'éducation* stated that

[37] Holbach, *Ethnocratie*, p. 119; *Système social*, III, 34-35.
[38] Ibid., pp. 24 and 32.
[39] Ibid., II, 51-52.
[40] For Goyon and Philipon, see above, chap. III; Perreau, *Instruction du peuple*, p. 13.
[41] Necker, *Opinions religieuses*, p. 52.
[42] La Chalotais, *Essai*, p. 26.

the people were "subjected to rough and constant labor."[43] Granet asserted that cabin boys and workers of the arsenal were subject to "a service as hard [*pénible*] as it is necessary."[44] Goyon observed that the lower classes were commonly exposed to "perilous, hard [*pénibles*] and unceasing labors," while Perreau noted that even women of the people were obliged to perform "harsh [*pénibles*] physical labor."[45]

Though their work was hard and their hours long, the lower classes gained little from it, and it was recognized that they lived continuously on the edge of subsistence. Stanislaus Auguste stated that peasants generally received a wage that at best prevented their dying of hunger.[46] Verlac asserted that the people lived in "indigence and infamy."[47] Necker saw that the greater part of society was reduced to the "bare necessities."[48] Sellier, writing in 1787, pointed out that many did not have even that. He observed that "workers without property whose salaries do not increase and cannot increase lack their most urgent necessities, they die of hunger and cold."[49] Philipon characterized the situation of the people as "absolutely precarious."[50] Tschudy, who we have seen was fully aware of the condition of the rural poor spoke of the "cold poison of indigence," and Thélis referred to day laborers as "unfortunates" who had to work unprofitable land in order to wrest a bare livelihood from it.[51] For as long as their health was good and no natural catastrophes occurred, they could

[43] Rivard, *Recueil*, p. xl; "Pensées sur l'éducation," fol. 49r.

[44] Granet, *Mémoire*, pp. 132-33.

[45] Goyon d'Arzac, *Essais de Laopédie*, p. 22; Perreau, *Instruction du peuple*, p. 165.

[46] Quoted by Granet, *Mémoire*, p. 120.

[47] Verlac, *Plan*, pp. 18-19.

[48] Necker, *Opinions religieuses*, p. 105.

[49] Sellier, "Letter to Necker" (1785), A Mun. Amiens, BB 130[30], p. 2.

[50] Philipon, *Vues patriotiques*, p. 216.

[51] Tschudy, "Mémoire sur la mendicité," fol. 15r; Thélis, *Mémoire* XII, 11.

supply their basic needs. But it took very little to plunge them into the direst poverty:

> . . . une intémperie, une indiscretion, un accident; & quand ils échapperoient à ce qui ménace tous les hommes, ils n'échapperont pas à une viellesse prématurée, qui absorbe presque toujours le fruit de plusieurs années, & les dévoue, avec leur postérité, à la misère & aux besoins.[52]

To judge from the frequency with which the terms *misère, peine* and their derivatives were used to describe the condition of the lower classes, it was widely recognized that the vital threshold between subsistence and intense poverty was crossed all too often.

The *Dictionnaire universel* described the *bas peuple* as "crushed with *misère*."[53] Guyton de Morveau observed that "*misère* and debasement seem to be attached to the harshest [*plus pénibles*] forms of labor."[54] Granet quoted Mandeville to the effect that the way of life of the poor was "laborious, wearisome and *pénible*."[55] Goyon, Philipon and Gourdin all used the word *misère* to describe the conditions in which the people lived, and Thélis stated that day laborers commonly lived in "the greatest *misère*."[56] Sellier believed that *misère* was the inevitable and often unmerited lot of the laboring poor.[57] Verlac characterized the condition of the people as one of "fatigue, *peine* and poverty," while Necker described the lives of the poor as *pénible*, monotonous and *misérable*.[58]

[52] Ibid., p. 12.

[53] DUS, art. "Dépopulation," xv, 454.

[54] Guyton, *Mémoire*, p. 44.   [55] Granet, *Mémoire*, p. 11.

[56] Philipon, *Vues patriotiques*, pp. 9-10; Goyon d'Arzac, *Essais de Laopédie*, p. 1; Gourdin, *De l'éducation*, fol. 102r; Thélis, *Moyens proposés*, p. 18.

[57] Sellier stated that while prices had risen by a quarter between 1780 and 1785, salaries had remained unchanged. The rich, he said, were unaffected by this, but propertyless workers suffered cold and hunger as a result. He then went on to criticize the liberal thesis that need is a spur to industry ("Letter to Necker," pp. 1-2).

[58] Verlac, *Plan*, p. 103; Necker, *Opinions religieuses*, p. 169.

What did it mean to be subject to *misère* in eighteenth-century France? Authors treating the lower classes do not leave this question entirely to the imagination. *Misère* meant that families of ten people were often obliged to live, together with whatever animals they might own, in a single small room.[59] It meant being inadequately clothed and often going barefoot.[60] Extreme poverty obliged parents to set their children to work "as soon as they could walk," and it was recognized that the normal development of children suffered as a result of this practice.[61] *Misère* meant, in the forceful expression of Coyer, being overwhelmed by work and devoured by hunger.[62] Overwork and undernourishment were indeed the two most salient features of the wretchedness of the people.

The first of several causes of illness among the people listed by Tissot was overwork (*épuisement*). The Swiss doctor suggested, logically enough, that rest was an adequate cure for this condition, but added immediately, "often it is impossible."[63] An unsuccessful contestant to the essay contest proposed by the Academy of Châlons-sur-Marne for 1779 adduced six factors to explain why the childhood of the people was so often spoiled. This list complements Tissot's comments on the causes of illness among the poor, and reads: (1) the *misère* of the parents; (2) lack of good food during pregnancy; (3) excessive and forced work during pregnancy; (4) illness which the impossibility of procuring proper care for renders continuous; (5) incontinence on the part of the husband; (6) abandonment of the mother during childbirth, or the incompetence of the attendants.[64]

Thus, when members of the enlightened community

---

[59] Tissot, *Avis au peuple*, I, 35.

[60] *De l'éducation publique*, pp. xiv-xv.

[61] Ibid., p. 165; Tissot, *Avis au peuple*, II, 37. Gourdin stated that it was common practice in the countryside to have children work at tasks for which their strength was inadequate ("De l'éducation," fol. 94v).

[62] Coyer, *Plan*, p. 111.

[63] Ibid., p. 29.   [64] AD Marne, J 48².

spoke of *misère*, they had in mind wretchedly inadequate housing and clothing, child labor, illness, overwork and undernourishment. It will be noticed, however, that though the word *misère* was used widely to describe the condition of the people, only a very few writers cared to spell out what this term implied. The subject, after all, is an unpleasant one. But that most writers were fully aware of the implications of the word *misère*, and of the condition of the people, is clear from the figures of speech they use to describe the lower classes.

The concept of servitude is evoked by a number of metaphors. Coyer referred to day laborers as convicts (*forçats*), and Baudeau spoke of the despair of peasants reduced to begging after having worked for twenty years "like convicts."[65] Necker believed that if a secular principle of morality were adopted, it would become necessary to separate the people from the citizens and hold them in servitude like the helots of Sparta.[66] Both Formey and Baudeau spoke of the people as slaves, and compared their condition to that of negroes in the colonies.[67] In this connection Chamfort's aphorism, "The poor are the negroes of Europe," comes to mind.[68]

If images of man's servitude to man are most appropriate to describe the condition of the lower classes, they were not on that account most used; the more emotionally charged comparison of man to beast occurs far more frequently. So great does the debasement of the laboring poor seem to have been in the eyes of their social superiors that implicity—and sometimes explicitly—even their humanity was questioned. Formey stated that the poor in *hopîtaux* were treated as mere cattle (*un vil bétail*), and that the occupations of the laboring poor reduced them almost to the

---

[65] Coyer, *Plan*, p. 111; Baudeau, *Vrais pauvres*, p. 100.

[66] Necker, *Opinions religieuses*, p. 104.

[67] See above, chap. 11, nn. 103 and 161.

[68] Chamfort, *Produits de la civilisation perfectionnée; Maximes et pensées, caractères et anecdotes* (Paris, 1968), p. 168.

level of beasts of burden.[69] Voltaire wrote in the privacy of his notebooks, "The people is between man and beast."[70] Montlinot asserted that kennel dogs of great lords were treated better than mendicants; Ferlus complained that though Christianity regards rich and poor as equals, the former often treat the latter as "the most vile animals"; and the author of the article "Population" in the *Encyclopédie* accused certain of the wellborn of using their fellow men in a way in which they would have been reluctant to use animals.[71] Lorinet referred to a beggar as an "animal" and "a being formerly human."[72] Bruni observed that just as animals gathered to feed, the poor were obliged to meet together to receive instruction.[73] The amiable Arthur Young spoke of stable boys as an "execrable set of vermin," and of a waitress in an inn as an "animal."[74] Le Mercier de la Rivière asserted that men in ignorance were on a lower level than even animals, for they were deprived of both the instinct that guides animals and the reason that directs men. In this condition they were more miserable and more difficult to control than either.[75] Here we may recall Baudeau's peasant indignantly proclaiming, "We no longer wish to be worse than beasts of burden," and the anguished question: "Are we animals?" that Coyer put into the mouths of the laboring poor. His answer, we have seen, was, "People! that may be."[76]

[69] Formey, *Traité*, pp. 225 and 23.

[70] Payne, *The Philosophes and the People*, p. 29.

[71] Montlinot, *Discours*, p. 7; Ferlus, *Le Patriotisme chrétien*, p. 26; *Encyclopédie*, art. "Population."

[72] Krauss, *Est-il utile de tromper le peuple?* p. 54.

[73] Thélis, *Mémoire* III, 14.

[74] Arthur Young, *Travels in France during the Years 1787, 1788 and 1789*, J. Kaplow, ed. (New York, 1969) pp. 9-10.

[75] Le Mercier, *De l'instruction publique*, p. 23.

[76] See above, chap 1, pp. 62 and 54. The same metaphors appear in other literary sources treating the people in eighteenth-century France. See, for example, the citations Taine has taken from writers of memoirs and journalists in the section "Le Peuple" of his *Ancien régime*.

Changing Attitudes: Sympathy and Idealization

It is doubtless true that kindhearted men and women have always commiserated with the poor. Johan Huizinga, for example, has pointed out that pity for the poor was a common theme of late medieval literature, but that this pity was limited to the realm of sentiment.[77] The sympathy of certain members of the enlightened community went beyond mere commiseration. Many felt that the lot of the people was not entirely their own fault, and that the workings of nature or the inefficient or unjust organization of society added to their burdens. Thélis and Tschudy in particular gave concrete and highly detailed accounts of the situation of the laboring population. Both men described the resources of day laborers, the amount of employment they needed to live, the amount they might in the normal course of things expect to receive, factors influencing wages, variations in the price of grain and exactions to which the lower classes were subjected.[78] Further, both were acutely aware of the utter precariousness of the lives of rural laborers, and saw that the economies of such families could be smashed by the merest accidents, such as sudden illness or a bad harvest. "The day laborer," Tschudy wrote, "has always and by his very condition [*Etat*] had one foot in the class of mendicants."[79] Indeed, given the situation of rural laborers, it was astonishing, the Baron said, that there was not far more mendicancy than already existed. This was "a real paradox, for which I [Tschudy]

[77] Huizinga observed that "this pity, however, remains sterile. It does not result in acts, not even in programmes, of reform. The felt need of serious reform is wanting to it and will be wanting for a long time. In La Bruyère, in Fénelon, perhaps in the elder Mirabeau, the theme is still the same; even they have not got beyond theoretical and stereotyped commisseration" (*The Waning of the Middle Ages*, trans. by F. Hopman, Harmondsworth, 1968, pp. 60-61).

[78] Thélis, *Plan*, pp. 25-26; Tschudy, "Mémoire sur la mendicité," fols. 22-25.

[79] Ibid., fol. 25v.

can only find the solution in the extreme sobriety and in the precious virtues of these despised men."[80] According to Thélis' calculations, it was impossible for a day laborer with children to support his family, even at the level of bare subsistence.[81] Thus, having turned from a predominently ethical approach to poverty, Tschudy and Thélis were able to replace moral condemnation and literary lamentation with close observation and hardheaded analysis. Their sympathy for the laboring poor, which was great, was not sentimental, but informed.

Because they were seigneurs of wealth and standing, Tschudy and Thélis were not obliged to restrict their social criticism to the level of theory alone. Both men engaged in projects to improve the conditions of tenants on their estates. Tschudy, who criticized large-scale farming and enclosures and defended the right of the rural poor to the commons, let only so much land to a peasant as he could farm and charged him a smaller rent than he had previously charged *fermiers*. The result, the Baron claimed, was to increase his own revenue and to provide an honest living for a hundred families where before there had been a few rich *fermiers* and a great many wretched day laborers.[82] Thélis put into practice a scheme to absolve his peasants from the *corvée*, and raised poor children in schools in which they received lessons, worked and were fed.[83] If most other members of the enlightened community were unable to experiment with various forms of relief for the poor on their own estates, they nevertheless followed these two liberal nobles in their analyses of poverty and in their sympathy for the laboring poor.

In Gourdin's view the poverty the people suffered resulted from factors beyond their control. He observed that "the needs of the people triple in winter, and their earnings almost always diminish in the same proportion as their

---

[80] Loc. cit.   [81] Thélis, *Plan*, pp. 25-26.
[82] Tschudy, "Mémoire sur la mendicité," fols. 17-20.
[83] See Chisick, "Innovation in Popular Education."

needs increase."[84] And, the Benedictine noted, the rigors of nature were complemented by the inequity of a legal system whose voice "scarcely makes itself heard in the palace of the rich and powerful, [but which] thunders in the hovel of the poor."[85] Turgot stated that the working population (*classes laborieuses*) was overtaxed, and Jaubert, Berenger and others agreed with him.[86] Goyon rejected the idea of a general tax to finance the school system he proposed on the grounds that "the people are already so overburdened." Better, he thought, to have the rich pay for the education of the poor, whom he designates "children ill-treated by fortune and policy."[87] Formey observed that in theory princes were made for their subjects, but in fact the reverse was true and the poor often suffered as a consequence.[88] More generally, Montlinot asserted that even in the best of governments "everything weighs on the people" and spoke of the "burden which crushes the people."[89] As contemporaries seem to have been fully aware of the *misère* and oppression to which the people were subject, it is surprising that they often idealized the lower classes, and especially the peasantry.

An idealized peasantry, whose greatest virtue was to live in close proximity to a highly idealized nature, offered in its assumed health, robustness, simplicity and moral rectitude a convenient foil to supposedly corrupt and overfed townsmen. Baudeau praised "good artisans full of honor and charity that one finds in large numbers in the poorest classes, but those least corrupted by luxury, vanity and the irreligion of our century. . . ."[90] Grivel held that men in the

---

[84] Gourdin, *De l'éducation*, fols. 95-96.

[85] Ibid., fol. 99v.

[86] Turgot, "Mèmoire," p. 594; for Jaubert and Berenger see above, chap. I, pp. 64-67.

[87] Goyon d'Arzac, *Essais de Laopédie*, p. 36.

[88] Formey, *Traité*, p. 202.

[89] Montlinot, *Discours*, pp. i-ii.

[90] Baudeau, *Vrais pauvres*, pp. 77-78.

countryside were "closer to nature" than those in towns, and that althought the former might be rude (*grossiers*), they preserved the simplicity and sincerity of "the first ages."[91] Philipon argued that because the people were closer to nature, they had less pretensions and more sensibility than other classes.[92] Goyon based his opinion that the peasantry was less corrupt than other sections of society on identical reasoning.[93] Tschudy emphasized that "we have shown in this class of men [the people] virtues of which superior orders are incapable," and Berenger stated that if one wished to find the repository of morality, he must look in the thatched cottages of the poor.[94]

Comfortable intellectuals praised the illusory health of the lower classes no less than their supposed morality. The authors of *De l'éducation publique*, Coyer, Tissot and Perreau all admired the health of the people, and attributed it in part to the simplicity of their food and their eating habits.[95] Durosoy believed the people were exempt from vapors, apoplexy and indigestion, and observed, as if to emphasize what fine health they must enjoy, that some of them lived to a hundred.[96] Similarly, Perreau stated with confidence that "folk much occupied with business rarely enjoy as good health as country folk."[97]

Perreau not only believed that the people enjoyed good health, but also that, for a variety of reasons, they had greater peace of mind then the rich, whom, he said, were "more harrassed [*tourmenté*]."[98] Holbach said that the people were free from boredom (*ennui*) and that this was

[91] Grivel, *Théorie de l'éducation*, II, 378-79.

[92] Philipon, *Vues patriotiques*, p. 221.

[93] Goyon d'Arzac, *Essais de Laopédie*, p. 3.

[94] Tschudy, "Mémoire sur la mendicité," fol. 31v; Berei.ɡ‿i, *Le peuple instruit*, p. x.

[95] *De l'éducation publique*, pp. xiv-xv; Coyer, *Plan*, pp. 44-45; Tissot, *Avis au peuple*, II, 39; Perreau, *Instruction du peuple*, p. 14.

[96] Durosoy, *Philosophie sociale*, p. 34.

[97] Perreau, *Instruction du peuple*, p. 14.

[98] Ibid., pp. 9-10.

for them a great piece of good luck.[99] Goyon believed that
the people's proximity to nature was a compensation for
their otherwise wretched lot, and offered the opinion that:

> . . . par un dédommagement bien favorable des peines et
> des maux de sa condition, il ignore ou Connoit bien
> moins des raffinemens d'une fausse délicatesse et les
> Caprices d'une mode meurtrière.[100]

In like fashion, Fourcroy argued that the harsh life which
the rural poor led was far healthier than the life style of
rich bourgeois, and that this made the pregnancy and labor
of peasant women easier than that of more comfortable
women in the towns. These considerations, Fourcroy
claimed, provided a "real compensation for poverty."[101]

Thus, toward the end of the eighteenth century the
people were seen as poor, underfed, and oppressed; but
they were also believed to be natural, virtuous and free
from the vices of the wealthy. It is as if the moral virtues
and the supposed health of the people were expected to
compensate for the wretchedness of their condition, and
perhaps, at the same time, ease the consciences of their social superiors. For if, as I will attempt to show, members of
the enlightened community could hardly conceive of a radical improvement in the lot of the people, it was only logical
to try to compensate them for the wretchedness they would
have to endure indefinitely.

THE ELITISM OF THE ENLIGHTENMENT: THE VIABILITY OF THE OLD REGIME AND THE PEOPLE-CONDITION

If the people, and especially the peasantry, were
idealized because of their supposed simplicity, good health
and proximity to nature, nowhere was it suggested that the
laboring poor were capable of governing themselves, or of

[99] Holbach, *Système social*, III, 84.
[100] Goyon d'Arzac, *Essais de Laopédie*, p. 3.
[101] Fourcroy, *Les Enfans élevés dans l'ordre de la nature*, pp. 150-51.

taking part in the government of the country. Indeed, where the question of the political competence of the people was raised, quite the contrary opinion prevailed.

Guyton de Morveau was concerned primarily with assuring a sound education for the ruling classes, for it was they who "necessarily guide or lead astray the multitude which follows after them."[102] In precisely the same fashion, Coyer would have had "children of distinguished families, designated to lead the others," educated in one kind of school, and "the people, who must be led" educated in another kind.[103] Turgot, who noted that the lower classes were overburdened, endorsed a system of local government based exclusively on landed wealth, the chief effect of which would have been to exclude the propertyless from participation in local politics.[104] Perreau observed that because the people had not the leisure to think and were easily led astray, "it is therefore necessary to think, to observe for them, and to show them clearly the route they should take and that which they should avoid," while Frédéric de Castillon referred to the people as "those who need to be led."[105] It will be recalled, too, that Berenger's advice to the people in 1789 was not to meddle in politics but to trust to the good will and ability of their betters.[106]

That the preceding statements reflect an elitist point of view will not be denied. It may, however, be suggested that elitism was contingent, not fundamental, to Enlightenment thought. This is to say that members of the enlightened community recognized the condition of the people for what it was, and concluded, sensibly enough, that men whose occupations reduced them, in Formey's graphic phrase, almost to the level of beasts of burden, were inca-

[102] Guyton, *Mémoire*, p. 12.   [103] Coyer, *Plan*, p. 282.
[104] Turgot, "Mémoire," pp. 583-88.
[105] Perreau, *Instruction du peuple*, p. 84; Krauss, *Est-il utile de tromper le peuple?* p. 23.
[106] See above, chap, I, n. 111.

pable of looking after their own affairs, let alone of sharing the responsibilities of government. This, substantially, is the view of one student of eighteenth-century French literature, who, having analyzed the essay contest proposed by the Academy of Berlin on the subject, "Is it useful to mislead the people?" concluded that "for the philosophy of the Enlightenment there exists only an enlightened and responsible elite which must gradually raise to its level the ignorant people."[107] In like fashion, James Leith has argued that "the highest hope of the proponents of mass education was for a generally enlightened citizenry," and Peter Gay has assumed that the *philosophes* wished to "transform silent subjects into self-reliant citizens" and that they sought to do so by means of education.[108] Gay even calls this "the logic of enlightenment."[109] Yet on examination, the writers consulted for this study do not bear out these assertions.

The authors on whose works I have drawn did not discuss directly the possibility of raising the people to their own level. One can, however, form quite a clear idea of their opinions on this question by examining their reactions to the proposal that the people be given a broad, liberal education which would put them, intellectually at least, on a par with their social superiors. Members of the enlightened community were remarkably consistent in describing the effects that such an education would have on the laboring poor: they regarded it as "dangerous."

We have seen above that a number of writers felt concern at the prospect of the poor getting "too much" education. The "politiques" against whom Terrisse argued warned of the dangers and inconveniences of popular education. Rolland feared that the fruits of an incomplete education would be "crude and dangerous" but believed

[107] Jean Biou, "Est-il utile de tromper le peuple?" in *Images du peuple*, p. 195.
[108] Leith, "Modernization, Mass Education and Social Mobility," p. 228; Gay, *The Enlightenment*, II, 498-99.
[109] Ibid., p. 499.

that a "complete education" should remain the prerogative of a small elite. The curate of the Diocese of Troyes felt that any instruction beyond the four r's would turn the head of a peasant and render him dangerous. Goyon found that too much education was to be feared when it passed "fitting limits," and Philipon could think of nothing more dangerous than learning in the hands of the people. Gourdin observed that working class children who received an extended education were "often dangerous," and Pernetti expressed the same opinion in almost the same words.[110] Perreau feared that peasant children who had been to *collèges* would return home to "sow dangerous opinions," and thought that it was "very dangerous" for an artisan to provide his sons with a secondary education.[111]

Other writers not so far cited to this effect also regarded the education of the laboring poor as potentially dangerous. Granet, for example, believed that learning (*Les Connoissances*) was harmful to the people, for "never sufficiently complete to enlighten them, it can only discourage them and lead them astray."[112] Even the education given by La Salle's order was, in Granet's eyes, "useless and dangerous."[113] Bachelier, the director of the *école de dessin* of Paris, looked upon a literary education as necessary for those intended for the church or bar, but "dangerous" for those who will not find themselves in those two classes.[114] Sellier had doubts about even *écoles de dessin*. Children attending these schools, the master of the *école des arts* of Amiens observed, were liable to become "bad painters, or rather do-nothings, useless folk, to say no more."[115] Thélis asserted that it was "dangerous" to give soldiers and offi-

---

[110] See above, chap. III, pp. 148-54.

[111] Perreau, *Instruction du peuple*, p. 23.

[112] Granet, *Mémoire*, p. 122.

[113] Ibid., p. 130.

[114] J. J. Bachelier, *Discours sur l'utilité des écoles élémentaires en faveur des arts mécaniques. Pronouncé par M. B . . . à l'ouverture de l'Ecole Royale gratuite de Dessein, le 10 Sept. 1766* (Paris, 1766), p. 13.

[115] Sellier, "Lettre sur l'éducation des enfants du peuple," p. 6.

cers the same education, and Beguillet, who was no obscurantist, observed that it was not a good thing for education to spread too far, and that its excess [*surcharge*] would be "infinitely dangerous."[116]

What was the danger that so many members of the enlightened community saw in extending a broad education to the lower classes? The answer to this question is not so simple as one might at first expect. The possessing classes no doubt feared that the underprivileged might take cognizance of the injustices to which they were subject and attempt on their own initiative to rectify them. But there are, I believe, more profound factors at work here also. These are first, the nature of Enlightenment social and political thought, the conservatism of which has perhaps been underestimated, and second, the economic conditions of the period, in which the people played so large and sad a role.

One of the areas in the history of the Enlightenment that most needs attention is social thought. Refracted through the works of conservatives who regarded the French Revolution as an evil and the Enlightenment as partly or wholly responsible for it, or through those of liberals seeking the origins of the ideas of liberty and democracy, treatment of social ideas in the eighteenth century has tended to be abstract and polemical.[117] Too much time and energy have gone into debating the virtues and vices of liberty and equality in the Enlightenment and the Revolution, and too little attention has been paid to the preliminary work that must precede such discussions if they are to prove fruitful. If we know what we mean by liberty, equality and democracy today, do we know what the men of the eighteenth

---

[116] Thélis, *Mémoire* VII, 13-14; Beguillet, *Considérations*, p. 37.

[117] The tendencies to link the Enlightenment with the Revolution and to emphasize the views of the great *philosophes* have had an unfortunate effect in this regard. However, among older scholars Mornet in particular must be excepted from this criticism, while among more recent students of Enlightenment social thought, so too must Payne, Boss, Weintraub and a number of others.

century meant by them? Have we carefully and fully enough studied how these terms were defined at the time, and have we reintegrated them into their social context? Do we know, for example, how far the liberties of the individual and of groups were thought to extend? Was liberty thought to be incompatible with privilege, or could the two subsist together? Or again, if it was believed that men were by nature equal, was this philosophical truth held to have any immediate social significance, or was it vitiated by another key idea of the time, that of the social contract? Did natural equality preclude social inequality? Did it necessarily come into conflict with the idea of hierarchy? Could not equals be subordinate to one another?

These questions require long and careful study. However, if the writers on whom I have drawn are at all representative, the answers, when they come, will not be so clearcut as those given by traditional treatments of Enlightenment social thought. Most of these writers accepted both the institutions and values of the old regime, such as hierarchy, privilege and subordination, and the key values of Enlightenment thought, such as liberty and equality. It cannot be too strongly emphasized that the great majority in the enlightened community thought their society both viable and just and were prepared to defend both its institutions and ideology. If, at the same time, they adhered to the new values of the Enlightenment, this is in no way contradictory, for they used these new ideas not to challenge or undermine the old regime and its institutions, but to reform, reinforce and improve them. The monarchy, the special status of the clergy and nobility, and the principle of hierarchy were universally accepted, or very nearly so. What were criticized and condemned were abuses such as arbitrary exercise of power, absentee bishops, *abbés commendataires*, nobles who enjoyed privileges but accepted no responsibilities or performed no service, or the pride of men who believed that their rank entitled them to despise those lower than themselves in the social scale.

Though to illustrate the above statement would call for a separate study, it would be instructive to see how these generalizations were given particular form in at least one case. Perhaps the best example is the notion of equality and the antithetical ideas of hierarchy, rank, subordination, and *état* (condition).

The fundamental equality of all men, taken from a secular perspective, is one of the great ideas generally, and on the whole correctly, identified with the Enlightenment. Certainly there is no lack of authors in this study who ascribed to this view. Formey referred to the "primitive equality" of all men, Perreau asserted that all men were naturally equal, the thoroughly conservative Durosoy stated that the poor were by nature the equals of the rich, and Thélis originally wanted the nobles in his schools to work and exercise with the commoners to teach the former that "all men are born equal."[118] If it seems that such assertions of equality preclude acceptance of the values of hierarchy and rank, such phrases as "primitive equality" and "natural equality" should put us on our guard. For what was fitting in the state of nature was not necessarily thought to be so in society. Durosoy defined one's station or *état* as "a constant manner of being, a fixed style of life, a position which does not change with that which changes around us or in us"; and he asserted that it was desirable in any social system that "everyone should be in his *état* and in his place."[119] Later in his career, Thélis wrote that "although our principles are invariable, and our respect for equality is still the same, we nevertheless know that we owe something to the distinction of ranks, without which a monarchical state could not subsist."[120]

Virtually all members of the enlightened community

[118] For Formey, see above, chap. ii, n. 103; Perreau, *Instruction du peuple*, pp. xi-xii; Durosoy, *Philosophie sociale*, pp. 135-36; Thélis, *Idées proposées*, p. 36.

[119] Durosoy, *Philosophie sociale*, pp. 193 and 197.

[120] Thélis, *Mémoire* vi, 2.

joined with Thélis in both respecting equality and in recognizing the legitimacy of the "distinction of ranks." A fine
example of this tendency occurs in the discussion of moral
education by the anonymous author of *De l'éducation
publique*:

> Enfin Ce Cours de morale devroit être accompagné d'un
> Coup d'oeil Sur Les différens états qui Composent La
> Société; tous Sont utiles; nul ne doit être méprisé; il faut
> inspirer Les égards, et La Soumission Sans bassesse, dûs
> aux Rangs Les plus elevés dans L'ordre Civil, mais Sur-
> tout une Sorte de respect tendre et Compatissant pour
> Les rangs inférieurs, et surtout pour les malheureux
> honnête [*sic*]; Ce Seroit Suivi d'une instruction Sage et
> moderée Sur la liberté et L'égalité naturelles des hom-
> mes.[121]

Beyond an assertion of the "natural liberty" of man, no
writer encountered in this study was willing to go. Not even
the more daring thinkers believed that theoretical equality
could be given practical application. Jaubert, for example,
assumed that the destruction of rank, condition and *état*
would result in anarchy, and called, not for the destruction
of hierarchy, but for a hierarchy of merit to replace the
existing hierarchy based on birth.[122] Holbach shared this
opinion, even asserting that, "A perfect equality among
members of society would be a real injustice."[123] Since
some men are more able and useful than otherss, in Holbach's view they deserved more consideration and a higher
status. In the *Discourse on the Origins of Inequality*, Rousseau
distinguished between natural or physical inequality on the
one hand, and moral or political inequality on the other,
and found only the latter reprehensible. Elsewhere, however, he shows himself a firm advocate of the retention of
traditional privileges and social distinctions. It was, for

[121] "Pensées sur l'éducation," fol. 53r.
[122] Jaubert, *Eloge de la roture*, pp. 26-27.
[123] Holbach, *Système social*, I, 140.

example, desirable in Rousseau's view to "contribuer autant qu'on peut à rendre aux paysans leur condition douce,
sans jamais leur aider à en sortir."[124] Thus, if the particular
criterion on which a hierarchy should be established was
sometimes questioned, the basic need for a hierarchical
structure of society was not. Virtually all writers consulted
accepted the proposition that there were stations or *états*
(usually providentially designated) in life, and to judge
from their insistence that the lower classes be given only
such education as was suited to their place in the social
scale, they agreed with Durosoy that it was desirable for
men to remain in the stations to which they were born.

Since they did not intend to advocate greater equality in
practice, it may be asked, why did so many writers draw attention to theoretical equality? The reason, I suggest, is
that while they admitted the practical necessity of inequality in any large society,[125] they wished to point out that
one's rank or *état*, especially in the case of the high born,
was not a natural right, but the result of a compact,
whether implicit or explicit, on which men agreed when
they entered society. Like all agreements, it had two sides,
conferring both rights and obligations. Members of the
enlightened community did not on the whole call into
question the rights of the upper echelons of the social
hierarchy—to which they for the most part themselves belonged—but they did insist that those in positions of power
had responsibilities, and that it was their duty to fulfill
them. Emphasizing the original equality of all men was a

Rousseau, *Julie ou La Nouvelle Héloïse*, book v, letter 2. Both Crocker
in his article, "Rousseau and the Common People," and Roberts, *Morality
and Social Class*, pp. 89-90, have brought attention to Rousseau's social
conservatism.

[125] Tschudy, for example, asserted that, "The inequality of conditions is
the very essence of monarchy . . ." ("Mémoire sur la mendicité," fol. 15r).
See also above, n. 120. Again Montesquieu's immense influence on his age
makes itself felt. See *De l'esprit des lois*, book x, chap. 3. Régine Robin has
called the idea of the "limits of equality" one of the key ideas of the eighteenth century (*La Société française en 1789*, p. 232).

way of reminding people of quality that acceptance of responsibility, performance of service and practice of beneficence toward their fellows and ultimate equals were the condition of rank.[126] Though the concept of equality is alien to the ideology of a system based on orders and privilege, it was not drawn on by members of the enlightened community to call the society and ideology of the old regime into question, but to make them work.[127]

The second reason that members of the enlightened community would not countenance seeing the people broadly educated lies even deeper than the first, and in part determined it. I submit that in the years preceding the Revolution, as indeed throughout the old regime, the great majority of educated Frenchmen assumed the necessity of a "people-condition" the chief characteristics of which were unrelenting toil and unending poverty. Such, they recognized, was the lot of the "greatest and most useful part of the nation" and such, they believed, it must continue. This assumption was the great *non-dit*, the generally unspoken but universally understood presupposition on which the entire debate on popular education rested.

In the introduction to his *Epître*, Thomas stated that he would consider the people "in its labors, in its virtues and in the portion of happiness to which it might attain."[128] He himself did not regard the limits of the potential happiness of the masses as very wide, and others who addressed themselves to this matter were no more optimistic. Coyer, for example, believed that poverty was necessarily the lot

[126] Durosoy informed the rich that a poor person "is your fellow man, he has the right to be your equal" (*Philosophie sociale*, p. 96), and Baudeau pointed out that while society necessitated ranks and conditions, all men were originally equals (*Vrais pauvres*, p. 187).

[127] Harry Payne, while recognizing the elitism of the *philosophes*, has justly pointed out that theirs was a responsible elitism (*The Philosophes and the People*, pp. 48 and 190).

[128] Thomas, *Epître au peuple*, p. 5.

of the great majority in most societies. In an ideal state, he admitted, this would not be so, "but in the constitution which is so general, in which the few possess all while the multitude has only its arms, it is necessary that there be many unfortunates."[129] Montlinot was no more optimistic than Coyer about the possibilities of eventually distributing the wealth and burdens of society more evenly. He asserted that "it is too true that by the very organization of political societies inequality of wealth is the natural effect of wealth itself, and that extreme wealth in one class necessarily results in extreme poverty [*l'extrême misère*] in another."[130] Necker, too, shared this view, and his reasons for doing so were even more explicit. To explain why the great majority of men could always expect to live at the level of bare subsistence, the Swiss banker hit upon a formula very closely resembling the iron law of wages enunciated by liberal economists. He explained with relation to the laboring poor that "their competition and the dominion of wealth reduce the salary of this numerous class to the barest necessities."[131] Nor did Necker regard this situation as the result of a passing crisis, but as "the inevitable effect of our civil and political legislation."[132]

Other writers who failed to analyze the socioeconomic causes of poverty were agreed about its basic inevitability. Not uncommonly they described it as a disease inherent in the body politic. Fontenelle, for example, spoke of the lives of the people as "one long malady."[133] Perreau wrote with unusual honesty:

> Je ne prétends pas dire au pauvre qu'il ne souffre pas d'être pauvre; mais comme je ne puis changer sa situa-

---

[129] Coyer, *Plan*, p. 5. [130] Montlinot, *Discours*, p. i.

[131] Necker, *Opinions religieuses*, pp. 52-53.

[132] Ibid., p. 53. This statement is introduced by the conditional "if," but it is clearly Necker's understanding that such is the case.

[133] Quoted in Paul Hazard, *The European Mind*, trans. J. L. May (Cleveland and New York, 1967), p. 293.

tion absolument, pas plus que celle d'un malade qui se plaindroit devant moi d'un mal que je ne pourrois guérir, je lui indique des consolations qui peuvent le soulager & adoucir ses peines. . . .[134]

In a like manner, the committee on mendicity of the constituent assembly explained that "poverty is a malady inherent in every large society; a good constitution and a wise administration can diminish its intensity, but nothing, unfortunately, can destroy it completely. . . ."[135] Regardless of the form of social or political organization, the report continued, the unequal distribution of property would prove "a necessary and permanent principle of poverty."[136]

This assertion that whatever a legislator might do, poverty would remain the lot of the great majority of mankind brings us to the heart of the matter. For it is an acknowledgment that only fundamental economic change, and not political measures, could substantially alter the lives of the masses; and it is also an admission that no such economic change was expected. And indeed, how could it be? In order seriously to entertain the idea of abolishing the people-condition, members of the enlightened community had first to conceive of the possibility of an economic system in which machines replaced men as the basic units of production. They had, in other words, to forsee the longterm effects of industrialization over fifty years before the process had begun in France.[137] The authors consulted here were pragmatic men, not visionaries. They expected

[134] Perreau, *Instruction du peuple*, pp. 11-12.

[135] Hufton, *The Poor*, p. 19.

[136] Loc. cit.

[137] J. L. Talmon has asserted that "there is no more baffling feature in French eighteenth-century social philosophy than the almost total lack of presentiment or understanding of the new forces about to be released by the Industrial Revolution" (*The Origins of Totalitarian Democracy*, New York, 1970, p. 59). In that the changes that the Industrial Revolution was to effect had not yet occurred, it is not surprising that they went unnoticed.

their civilization to continue functioning more or less as it had done for the past thousand or two thousand years. That is, they expected a majority of men to join their efforts to those of domesticated animals to produce food and goods; and they expected a minority to continue to benefit from their efforts. From the perspective of the eighteenth century, this was not an unreasonable expectation. Guyton de Morveau reasonably believed that "the torch of philosophy will always remain extinguished" among the "rough men" who inhabit the countryside; Diderot could reasonably expect the masses never to reach an intellectual level at which they could discard the old sop of religion; and Voltaire could reasonably assert that propertyless laborers would never have the time or ability to instruct themselves.[138]

These authors, I think, would have agreed with Condorcet that men are born neither stupid nor mad, but become what they are by virtue of the conditions in which they live.[139] They certainly did not believe that the laboring poor were by heredity incapable of thinking and acting reasonably. Rather they assumed that the conditions in which the people lived would continue to preclude their doing so for the forseeable future. The *philosophes*, no less than lesser- and less-known members of the enlightened community, regarded poverty as "the necessary and acceptable condition of most men."[140]

When they confronted the issue of popular education, members of the enlightened community were faced with a dilemma. They were caught between the demands of their ideology on the one hand, and the imperatives of the economics of underdevelopment on the other. The dilemma was resolved by compromise. The people were neither to

[138] Guyton, *Mémoire*, p. 15; Diderot, "Plan," p. 517; Mortier, "Voltaire et le peuple," p. 143.
[139] *Est-il utile de tromper le peuple?* p. 74.
[140] Payne, *The Philosophes and the People*, p. 146.

be left in ignorance, nor enlightened. A middle path was to be found between these extremes, and this middle path was an education fitting to one's place in society.

There is, I think, a meaningful distinction to be drawn between enlightenment and education. To "enlighten" implies developing a critical, secular and analytic habit of mind, allowing the mind to encounter all known facts and letting the argument lead where it may. Ultimately, perhaps, enlightenment implies liberation. Education, on the other hand, may be regarded as the teaching of skills or beliefs, whether true, false or merely expedient. It is in this rather narrow sense that most members of the enlightened community understood education, at least for the lower classes. To the question "Should the people be enlightened?" virtually all spokemen of the Enlightenment answered with an emphatic "No." To the question "Should the people be educated?" they responded with a reserved "Yes." The education that members of the enlightened community proposed for the lower classes was intended to improve their health, teach skills suited to their *état*, and to enlist their minds and hearts for religion and for the *patrie*. Such an education was intended not to liberate the people, but to increase their efficiency and to control them.

To the statement that members of the enlightened community did not wish to see the lower classes educated in such a way as would develop their critical faculties, there are two exceptions. Strictly speaking, neither occurs within our period, but as one comes from one of the great figures of the Enlightenment and the other was quite uninfluenced by the Revolution, they should not be overlooked.

The only well-known *philosophe* to push the logic of the Enlightenment to its just conclusion, untroubled by socioeconomic implications, was Condorcet. A gentle, speculative man, he showed himself more idealistic and more generous—some would say less practical—than other members of the philosophic family in demanding that or-

dinary men and women be given an education that would,
as well as preparing them for the practical side of life, teach
them to rely on their own unaided reason. In a work that is
often regarded as the testament of the Enlightenment, he
wrote:

> . . . on peut instruire la masse entière d'un peuple de tout
> ce que chaque homme a besoin de savoir pour
> l'économie domestique, pour l'administration de ses af-
> faires, pour le libre développement de son industrie et
> de ses facultés; pour connaître ses droits, les défendre et
> les exercer; pour être instruit de ses devoirs, pour les
> bien remplir; pour juger ses actions et celles des autres
> d'après ses propres lumières, et n'être étranger à aucun
> des sentiments élevés ou délicats qui honorent la nature
> humaine . . . pour se défendre contre les préjugés avec
> les seules forces de la raison. . . .[141]

It is worth noting, however, that this passage occurs in the
last book of the *Esquisse*, that expressing the author's hope
and trust in the future.[142]

The second writer to favor enlightening rather than
merely instructing the lower classes was the author of a
piece written in response to the essay contest on the subject, "The simplest means of procuring for the people the
education necessary to improve its morals," proposed by
the Academy of Amiens for 1791. The author, who wrote
in Latin, was clearly either a cleric or an extremely pious
layman. In making his case for the education of the lower
classes he used a number of arguments with which we are
now familiar. He pointed out, for example, that once educated the people were more socially useful, and that educa-

[141] J.A.N.C. de Condorcet, *Esquisse d'un tableau historique des progrès de
l'esprit humain* (Paris, 1971), p. 263.
[142] On Condorcet's view of the people, see Isabelle Vissière's articles,
"Le peuple d'après Condorcet: classifications et images," *Structure et fonction du vocabulaire social dans la littérature française* (Halle, 1970) and
"L'emancipation du peuple selon Condorcet," in *Images du peuple*.

tion could be used to make the lower classes accept their lot.[143] Socioeconomic considerations were not, however, his primary concern. He revealed his point of view in referring to the people as "our brothers and sisters in eternal life" and in asserting that, like other men, they are creatures "divinely endowed with reason."[144] The anonymous Latinist further insisted that "it is not with vain purpose that God has endowed these people with the power of reasoning, nor is he indifferent to the way in which his gifts and his creation are used," and that men are, for all eternity, "responsible for the consequences of their actions."[145] From these premises he deduced the obligation of cultivating the rational and critical faculties of the lower classes. And while he did not expect the people to acquire "the highest knowledge of all the sciences," he vigorously denounced the policy of keeping the poor in ignorance so as to control them.[146] In the pious author's view, it was desirable to arouse the curiosity of students and it was pointless to have them commit to memory things that they did not understand.[147] Furthermore, it was the duty of teachers to "elicit the thought and reasoning powers of the pupils" and to "inculcate the necessity of rational thought on every possible occasion."[148] He even hoped that through education members of the lower classes might become "men of a nobler order."[149] More in harmony with others who treated popular education during the Enlightenment, our Latinist asserted that "the instructor must always take care that he does not blind them [his pupils] with too much light."[150] He went on to say, however, that although it was essential that their education be gradual, "through the twilight the

---

[143] *Responsio ad Problema propositum ab illustrissima Academia Scientiarum atque artium quae Ambiani est, quaenum sint simplicissimae rationes quibus viliori plebi institutio ad horum mores emendandos necessaria praebeatur*, AD Somme, D 153[79], p. 3.

[144] Ibid., pp. 2-3.   [145] Ibid., p. 3.

[146] Ibid., p. 1.   [147] Ibid., pp. 6-7 and 10.

[148] Ibid., p. 3.   [149] Ibid., pp. 2-3.

[150] Ibid., p. 3.

people should be brought out of the thickest darkness into the clear light of day."[151]

This emphasis on the moral and spiritual well-being of the people and the readiness to lead them into the "clear light of day" recall the views of Rivard and Crévier, but of no other author who wrote on popular education before 1789. Thus, we find at the end of this study, as at the beginning, that, the significant exception of Condorcet aside, those most ready to see the people broadly educated and even enlightened were pious Christians. They could adopt this point of view because, as I have argued above, their basic premises differed from those of more secular and enlightened writers. The overwhelming majority of the members of the enlightened community, from the great *philosophes* to members of provincial academies and minor legal officials, basing themselves on secular and utilitarian criteria, were too practical and realistic to believe that it was either possible or desirable to enlighten the people.

It may appear paradoxical to suggest that the movement we know as the Enlightenment did not care to enlighten the greater part of humanity. In fact, there is no paradox here at all. Members of the enlightened community never thought the masses capable of philosophy, or that society could continue to function if the people ceased to be subject to the people-condition. They believed, on the contrary, that the enlightened attitude of mind should be restricted to a small minority. This point of view is illustrated by Voltaire when he wrote, "it is not the working man who should be educated, but the worthy bourgeois"; and by Granet, when he proposed that charity schools for the poor be closed, and the library of the *collège* of Toulon be opened to the public once a week, for the benefit of *honnêtes gens.* [152]

[151] Loc. cit.

[152] Quoted from Mortier, "Voltaire et le peuple," p. 143; Granet, *Mémoire*, pp. 151-52.

Conclusion

In the preceding pages we have seen that popular education was the subject of considerable discussion during the second half of the eighteenth century. We have found that far from demanding that the lower classes receive extensive instruction that would allow them to develop a critical outlook and reach intellectual maturity, the great majority of the enlightened community wished to see them taught to read, write and count, and given a measure of physical, occupational and moral training. The purpose of this instruction was thoroughly pragmatic, being aimed at economic utility on the one hand, and social peace on the other. A current of obscurantism persisted through the Enlightenment, and even those who thought it proper that the laboring population receive a basic education wished to keep that education within what they regarded as acceptable limits. While asserting in theory that all men were equal, members of the enlightened community looked upon the people as fundamentally different from themselves in function and social standing.

The particular form the debate on popular education took during the second half of the eighteenth century in France was influenced by a number of factors that were not necessarily intrinsic to it. Lockean psychology and its sensationalist premise, from which the assumption was derived that education was virtually all-powerful, was, of course, directly relevant. But this conclusion was drawn in an atmosphere of crisis and may never have been reached, or at least not so often stated or so fully elaborated, in more tranquil times. Certainly the forms that the discussions of physical and moral education took were deeply influenced by the prominent beliefs in depopulation, corruption and the nefarious consequences to be expected from an ethic that legitimized self-interest. The popularity of education as an agent of reform is in part explained by the fact that as a means of change it was both gradual and peaceful. Members of the enlightened community, for the most part well integrated into the ruling elites of the time, believed in, and were committed to, maintaining the organization and institutions of the old regime. A model of change that did not call into question existing social or political structures had particular appeal for them. Finally, the entire debate on popular education rested on the assumption that there existed a people-condition, necessitated by an economic system requiring endless and brutalizing labor on the part of the great majority of men and women.

In concluding a work, one likes to feel that all aspects of the problem investigated have been analyzed and satisfactorily explained. Unfortunately, the present writer can make no such claim. The subject of popular education and attitudes toward the lower classes might profitably be traced back into the seventeenth century, and could, further, be pursued into the nineteenth century. For the issue of the instruction of the people was not definitively treated by the ruling classes of France and Europe in the fifty or sixty years before 1789, but remained a subject of intense interest and animated discussion for a good part of the nineteenth century. The French Revolution did not finally end the condescension, mistrust and hostility with which the wealthy and leisured viewed the laboring population. The treatment of the question in the Enlightenment is best viewed not as marking the resolution of the debate on popular education but rather as a phase, though an important one, of a more comprehensive debate extending back perhaps to antiquity and continuing well into the nineteenth century and, in one form or another, into our own.

It has been shown that in their attitudes toward educating the peasantry or lower classes, the revolutionaries of 1789-93 were remarkably conservative, wishing to see the working population provided with a degree of economic- and trade-oriented instruction, but not with anything approaching a liberal education, or instruction that might lead a peasant to abandon the land, or a worker to become disgruntled with his place in society.[1] In these attitudes one recognizes a marked continuity with the main ideas on popular education formulated during the last half-century of the old regime. There also continued to be those in the nineteenth century who, whatever they thought of providing the lower classes with occupational or moral instruction, firmly opposed their being given a broad education. Madame de Genlis, herself a product of the old regime, wrote in 1804:

> Je ne crois pas qu'il fut bon, en supposant que cela fut possible, d'éclairer et de perfectionner l'esprit des gens du peuple. . . . On verrait sur la terre une étrange confusion et de terribles soulèvements si l'on pouvait établir parmi les hommes une parfaite égalité de lumières; heureusement que ce souhaît de la philanthropie philosophique ne sera jamais exaucé.[2]

In a speech before the English House of Commons in 1807, Davies Giddy used this same argument from social dislocation to dissuade his colleagues from supporting popular education.[3] Summarizing the evolution of opinion on the instruction of the lower classes in England up to 1867, the Victorian scholar W. B. Hodgson wrote:

> The inconveniences of total darkness were more and more recognized, and the advantage of, at least, a sort of twilight state of mind was more and more perceived; but

---

[1] M. Edelstein, "Mobilité ou immobilité paysanne? Sur certaines tendances conservatrices de la Révolution française," AHRF, xlvii (1975).

[2] Mme. de Genlis, *Souvenirs de Félicie*, quoted in Grosperrin, "Faut-il instruire le peuple?" p. 167.

[3] Silver, *The Concept of Popular Education*, p. 23.

it may well be questioned whether the noonday blaze of knowledge was not more dreaded by the educational patrons of the lower classes than even the midnight blackness of total ignorance. . . .[4]

The issue of popular education in nineteenth-century France has, to my knowledge, not been extensively explored. Studies dealing with or touching on this question in England and Germany, however, indicate that there was no dramatic shift away from the terms in which the subject was debated in the eighteenth century.[5] The question remained how much and what kind of education the lower classes should receive, and restricting the instruction of the laboring population to certain acceptable areas remained a principal concern of nineteenth-century authors. Indeed, one could, without serious distortion, apply Professor Hodgson's summary of the progress of the debate on popular education in nineteenth-century England to eighteenth-century France.

It would, of course, require a separate study adequately to analyze the debate on popular education in the nineteenth century. To consider the subject briefly, though, may lend perspective to the treatment of the question during the Enlightenment. It is striking to note, first, that into the nineteenth century, and indeed into the twentieth, the notion of the people as irresponsible children or brutes has persisted. Flaubert, for example, has one of his characters wonder whether progress can be achieved other than through the efforts of an elite, and exclaim, "Le peuple est mineur, quoi qu'on prétende!"[6] For Fourier the condition of the lower class was "worse than that of wild animals."[7] In

[4] Ibid., p. 24.

[5] See Silver, ibid., and Gagliardo, *From Pariah to Patriot*.

[6] Gustave Flaubert, *L'Education sentimentale: histoire d'un jeune homme* (Paris, Garnier-Flammarion, 1971), p. 389.

[7] Fourier, *The Utopian Vision of Charles Fourier: Selected Texts on Work, Love and Passionate Attraction*, translated and edited by J. Beecher and R. Bienvenu (Boston, 1972), p. 147.

her autobiography, Simone de Beauvoir recalls that her Catholic training had taught her to respect all individuals, no matter how humble their condition;[8] but on the other hand, she found personal contact with the peasantry in her youth distasteful, and in reporting a comment made by her father, revealed a deep-seated disdain for the laboring poor. She writes:

> Whenever I went with Mama to call on grandfather's tenant-farmers, the stink of manure, the dirty rooms where the hens were always scratching and the rusticity of their furniture seemed to me to reflect the courseness of their souls; I would watch them labouring in the fields, covered in mud, smelling of sweat and earth, and they never once paused to contemplate the beauty of the landscape; they were ignorant of the splendours of the sunset. They didn't read, they had no ideals: Papa used to say, though quite without animosity, that they were 'brutes.'[9]

In the nineteenth century, as in the eighteenth, and in many places still today, the objective conditions in which the lower classes live call to mind animal images and metaphors. The question then arises, did men in the nineteenth century commonly share the opinion, which predominated in the eighteenth, that the people were bound by the weight of economic necessity to remain in an inferior condition?

Fourier believed that social conditions could and should be radically transformed, and that the fact human beings were reduced to living at or below the level of animals was a horrible historical accident susceptible of rectification. Socialists in general—and the nineteenth century saw the growth and proliferation of an influential and multifaceted socialist movement—believed that social conditions could

[8] Simone de Beauvoir, *Memoirs of a Dutiful Daughter*, J. Kirkup trans. (Harmondsworth, 1976), p. 191.
[9] Ibid., p. 130.

be radically transformed so as vastly to improve the quality of life of ordinary men and women. Yet this assumption, which had been made by utopian theorists centuries before, and which, I believe, became so widespread as to be predominant by the end of the nineteenth century, did not yet command general assent by its midpoint. There were, of course, narrow minded men and reactionaries who equated any substantial improvement in the condition of the laboring population with the subversion of society, but there were also progressive and generous thinkers and writers who could not conceive of economic conditions improving to the point that ordinary workers would be able to lead full and rounded lives. In an essay written in 1831, John Stuart Mill observed:

A large portion of the talking and writing common in the present day, respecting the instruction of the people, and the diffusion of knowledge, appears to me to conceal, under loose and vague generalities, notions altogether fallacious and visionary.

I go, perhaps, still further than most of those to whose language I so strongly object, in the expectations which I entertain of vast improvements in the social condition of man, from the growth of intelligence among the body of the people; and I yield to no one in the degree of intelligence of which I believe them to be capable. But I do not believe that, along with this intelligence, they will ever have sufficient opportunities of study and experience, to become themselves familiarly conversant with all the inquiries which lead to the truths by which it is good that they should regulate their conduct, and to receive into their own minds the whole of the evidence from which those truths have been collected, and which is necessary for their establishment. If I thought all this indispensable, I should despair of human nature. As long as the day consists but of twenty-four hours, and the age of man extends but to threescore and ten, so long (unless

we expect improvements in the arts of production sufficient to restore the golden age) the great majority of
mankind will need the far greater part of their time and
exertions for procuring their daily bread.[10]

Mill thus expected that the great majority of men would
indefinitely have to base their opinions on authority rather
than their own reason, and relegated the aspiration that
economic conditions would ever permit the enlightenment
of the working population to parentheses, within which it is
wistfully associated with the restoration of the "golden
age."

The economic conditions that led Mill to despair of the
working class ever being fully enlightened led Tocqueville
to assume that "all mature societies contained a very substantial reservoir of poverty, and therefore large numbers
of men whose share of the advantages and values of society
ranged from meager to nonexistent."[11] Tocqueville, who
nowhere hesitates to manifest his low opinion of the
masses, argued that poverty was endemic and essential to
society, and not merely contingent upon modes of organization. Considering popular attempts at reform during the
Revolution of 1848, he wrote:

> The people had first endeavored to help itself by chang-
> ing every political institution, but after each change it
> found that its lot was in no way improved, or that it was
> only improving with a slowness quite incompatible with
> the eagerness of its desire. Inevitably it must sooner or
> later discover that that which held it fixed in its position
> was not the constitution of the government but the unal-
> terable laws that constitute society itself; and it was natu-

[10] John Stuart Mill, "The Spirit of the Age," in *Mill's Essays on Literature
and Society*, J. B. Schneewind, ed. (New York, 1965), p. 40.

[11] A. de Tocqueville and G. de Beaumont, *Tocqueville and Beaumont on
Social Reform*, translated and edited by S. Drescher (New York, 1968).
Drescher's "Introduction," p. xix.

ral that it should be brought to ask itself if it had not the power and the right to alter those laws, as it had altered the rest.[12]

Though Tocqueville speaks of the "unalterable laws that constitute society" and Mill emphasizes the conditions of production of his day, both assume, and attempt to explain, a people-condition. Mill's version of the lot of the lower classes is brighter perhaps than, say, Philipon's, and it may be that Tocqueville's talk of unchangeable social laws is more explicit and sophisticated than the views of Terrisse or Tschudy, but the essential notion is the same, and this explains why Mill's and Tocqueville's conclusions about popular education do not differ fundamentally from the consensus reached on the subject during the Enlightenment. Similarly, Michelet, in his remarkable little book *Le Peuple*, first published in 1846, expresses a whole range of opinions and ideas characteristic of the late Enlightenment, and assumes that society would indefinitely be composed of a number of classes, of which the people would continue to be one. As so many eighteenth-century writers had done, and for substantially the same reasons, he suggested that education be provided for all, but that its scope vary with the means and time at the disposal of each student.[13] Basic economic realities and the organization of society did not make it appear likely in the first half of the nineteenth century, any more than it had done in the eighteenth, that the working population could be freed from lives of unending labor, labor so demanding and wearing that it was incompatible with the development of their intellectual and spiritual faculties. It is worth noting in this connection that the Industrial Revolution, with its concomitant, the factory system, did not initially suggest to contemporaries that the working classes stood to gain by

[12] A. de Tocqueville, *The Recollections of Alexis de Tocqueville*, A. Teixeira de Mattos trans., J. P. Mayer, ed. (New York, 1959), pp. 78-79.
[13] Jules Michelet, *Le Peuple*, P. Viallaneix, ed. (Paris, 1974), p. 230.

the introduction of mechanization. In formulating the iron law of wages, liberal economists seemed to promise that workers could expect indefinitely to live within the framework of a people-condition, and Tocqueville can reasonably be construed to have believed that the existence of a "brutalized dependent class" was a "necessary consequence of the industrial system."[14] Thus, socialists and communists aside, political and social thinkers in the first half of the nineteenth century seem to have been quite as pessimistic as their predecessors of a century earlier about the possibility of fundamental social improvements, and hence of the feasibility or desirability of extending the scope of the education of the laboring population.

In summarizing the findings of his study of attitudes toward the German peasantry in the eighteenth and the first part of the nineteenth centuries, John G. Gagliardo writes with respect to education:

> At the same time, that instruction should impress upon him [the peasant] that his proper role as citizen lay in the efficient performance of his work and in certain moral attitudes which expressed an essentially submissive posture toward social and political authority and privilege. An important novelty of this proposed instruction, however, was that submissiveness in the above sense was to be the result of conscious consent stemming from understanding. It was not to be the submissiveness of the slave, or much less of the dumb and bewildered beast, but that of a man who willed submission to his duty because he understood the nature and importance of his social function and the mutual dependence of all the various groups which went to make up the society in which he lived.[15]

[14] Drescher, "Introduction" to *Tocqueville and Beaumont on Social Reform*, p. xv.
[15] Gagliardo, *From Pariah to Patriot*, p. 289.

The above passage calls to mind Tschudy's assertion that "the people more enlightened would be, if it were possible, even more submissive; or its reasoned submission would at least be more certain."[16]

Perhaps the most striking feature of the notion of considered or reasoned submission is the belief on the part of those who held it that such submission was in fact reasonable, and that if members of the lower classes were to think carefully about how best to further their own interests, they would find that there was no better way of doing so than to perform the tasks that were expected of them and to respect the law. That Tschudy and others could take so optimistic a view of the social order of their time followed, of course, from the fact that they believed that French society was necessarily, and would indefinitely remain, hierarchical. When a society is divided into parts, each must perform its allotted task, or the whole will suffer. Though the men of the Enlightenment were keenly interested in social engineering, they were, on the whole, sincere in believing that the maintenance of order was in the interests not only of society as a whole, but also and more particularly of the lower classes. And indeed, the notion of reasoned submission was not an unreasonable postulate in a formally hierarchical society in which a high degree of socioeconomic differentiation was inevitable, and inequality of status juridically sanctioned.

For the duration of the old regime and, as the statements of Mill and Tocqueville show, well into the nineteenth century, the assumption that society was essentially hierarchical prevailed, and with it the belief that certain men and women should be prepared for, and should carry out, certain kinds of tasks. The idea of equality began in some places and on some levels to replace the notion of hierarchy in social thought toward the end of the eighteenth century, but did not, I suggest, achieve widespread or general

---

[16] See above, chap. II, n. 173.

acceptance until the later nineteenth or the twentieth century, depending on the place and circumstances. It was not enough for the French Revolution to proclaim equality as one of its ideals—a study of the practical and theoretical limitations on equality as understood by the revolutionaries would be instructive—nor was the appearance of the factory system sufficient to undermine the notion of hierarchy and cause it to be replaced by that of equality. Without going into the question of the degree to which hierarchy remains a principle in any highly differentiated and integrated system, or the problem of the de facto persistence of hierarchy and elites in societies which formally adhere to egalitarian ideologies, I would like to suggest that agrarian and industrial societies are in a position to begin to realize a measure of social equality only when they have solved technological problems so effectively that they free most individuals from specific economic or productive roles and from residence in given locations. Most workers or farmers in industrialized countries today are closer in income, life style and cultural orientation to their employers or social superiors than was the case with their eighteenth century counterparts. Juridicial and political equality, which are in any case modified by circumstances, follow and are made possible by deeper economic and social changes. Formally, equality has now become a more useful social principle than hierarchy.

If there was considerable continuity in the debate on popular education from the eighteenth through the nineteenth century, this is not to say that there was nothing distinctive in the way the problem was handled during the last half-century or so of the old regime. But there is not, I think, a single factor that distinguishes attitudes toward the education of the lower classes in the French Enlightenment. Rather, a number of factors must be taken together so as to set off enlightenment views of the subject from those of the periods that preceded and succeeded it.

In contradistinction to the seventeenth century, in which education in general and popular education in particular were dealt with from a religious point of view and by ecclesiastical personnel, the eighteenth century largely secularized the question. To be sure, pious men and women continued to show concern for, and to write on, education down to, and into, the Revolution, but the terms in which discussion of the subject was carried out in the eighteenth century were essentially secular, putting social and economic considerations before all others. Again unlike the seventeenth century, and perhaps, too, unlike later periods, the eighteenth century had an excessive faith in the power of education as an agent of reform. But like the men of the seventeenth century, those of the eighteenth conceived of their society as a hierarchy, and, most probably, assumed that all "advanced" or "civilized" societies had necessarily to be formally hierarchical. That presupposition is not widely shared today, and sets Enlightenment social theory off from that of the later nineteenth and twentieth centuries. However, on its most basic conviction about popular education, namely, that the lower classes were to receive a "fitting" education, and that what was fitting was determined on social and economic criteria, the Enlightenment and our own age appear to be in broad agreement.

Members of the enlightened community were, after all, very much like our own politicians and administrators, hard-headed, practically-minded people, and neither the ones nor the others would sanction programs devoted to moral and spiritual improvement, the pursuit of knowledge for its own sake, or the development of a critical and independent outlook in the great majority of the population, at least if such programs could not be justified in economic or administrative terms. Politicians of all parties, administrators and even many educational theorists today speak of education in terms of training students in marketable skills and at lower instructional levels, of socialization.

To be sure, primary education, and especially that for the lower classes is far wider and its apparatus more extensive today than it was two hundred years ago. But that this implies a greater measure of generosity or liberality in contemporary social values is probably not a just conclusion. The fact that we were born into a more sophisticated society that necessitates a higher level of instruction is an accident, not a virtue. It is curious, but nevertheless seems to be the case, that the view that it is neither feasible nor desirable to enlighten the greater part of mankind is part of our heritage from the Enlightenment. But if this is so, it does not allow us to look with condescension on men who, with resources infinitely inferior to our own, came to conclusions on popular education in principle similar to those still maintained today.

Bibliography

PRIMARY SOURCES

Manuscript Scources

Archives Nationales
F^{17} 1196^{32} Inventory of library of C.A.P. de
                        Thélis
T 93   Personal papers of Thélis
T 1669^{49} Personal papers of Thélis

Bibliothèque Nationale
Ancien fonds   Goyon d'Arzac, *Essais de*
français,   *Laopédie, ou Mémoire à l'Academie de*
22048   *Châlons-sur-Marne en reponse à cette*
                question: Quel seroit le meilleur plan
                d'éducation pour Le Peuple?

Archives De La Marine
G 86   Plans and prospectuses for lessons,
                courses and schools

Archives Départementales
Marne
J 48   Documents relating to the essay
                contest proposed by the Academy of
                Châlons-sur-Marne for the year
                1779 on the subject, "Quel seroit le
                meilleur plan d'éducation pour le
                peuple?"

Rhone
C 78   Ecole de travail of Saint-Etienne
C 169   Ecole de travail of Saint-Chamond

Somme

C 33[1]   Sellier, J., "Mémoire sur la Mendicité et sur les moyens d'entretenir les chemins publics en abolissant la corvée"

C 1547[2]   Sellier, J., "Lettre sur l'éducation des enfants du peuple" (1783)

C 1547[6]   Sellier, J., Letter to the Intendant of Amiens (1783)

C 2074[6]   Sellier, J., "Lettre sur l'éducation des habitants de la campagne"

C 2074[7]   Sellier, J., "Lettre addressée à Mgr. l'Evêque d'Amiens sur l'éducation de la jeunesse de tous états" (1787)

D 152   Sellier, J., Memoirs and letters, post 1789

D 153[79]   Anonymous, *Reponsio ad Problema propositum ab illustrissima Academia Scientiarum atque artium quae Ambiani est, quaenum sint simplicissimae rationes quibus viliori plebi institutio ad horum mores emendandos necessaria praebeatur*

G 621   Soeurs Grises of Montreuil

Archives Municipales
Amiens

BB 126[370]   Sellier, J., "Lettre sur l'école de filiature" (1782)

BB 126[371]   Sellier, J., "Lettre au corps de ville" (1782)

BB 130[30]   Sellier, J., "Lettre à M. Necker" (1785)

Rouen

Fonds de   Terrisse (Abbé), *Examen de la*
l'Académie   *question s'il est utile ou préjudiciable*
(uncoded)   *au bien de l'Etat que les gens de la*
                  Campagne sachent lire et écrire (1746)

Toulon
    GG 54   Granet, *Mémoire sur l'éducation publique
                     dans le ressort de la sénéchaussée de
                     Toulon* (1764)

Bibliothèque Municipale de Metz
    mss. 1349   Auffray, "Discours sur les avantages
                     que le patriotisme retire de l'Etude
                     et de la Pratique des Sciences
                     Oeconomiques" (1769)
    mss. 1467[3]   Tschudy, "Catéchisme de morale fait
                     pour des enfans agés de 8 à 9 ans où
                     se trouvent les grandes principes sur
                     la justice, le courage, la bienfaisance,
                     la formation des sociétés" (1771)
    mss. 1467[5]   Tschudy, "Mémoire sur la mendicité"
                     (1773)
    mss. 1350   Anonymous, "Mémoire sur cette
                     question: Quelles sont les moyens
                     compatibles avec les bonnes moeurs
                     d'assurer la conservation des
                     bâtards, et d'en tirer une plus
                     grande utilité pour l'Etat? Ouvrage
                     qui a remporté le prix de la Société
                     Royale des Sciences et des Arts de
                     Metz en 1787"

Archives de l'Académie de Lyon
    mss. 141   Anonymous, "Reflexions sur la
                     difference que la naissance produit
                     parmi les français"
    mss. 147   Pernetti (Abbé), "Réponse aux
                     questions d'un père sur l'éducation"
                     (1775)
                     ———, "Discours sur les avantages de
                     l'histoire relativement à l'éducation"
                     (1762)

Anonymous, "Pensées sur l'éducation"

Thiollier (Abbé), "Essai historique et Critique sur L'éducation Ancienne" (1762)

Perrache, "Réflexions sur l'Education" (1765)

———, "Projet d'un Etablissement d'Education relative aux sciences, au commerce et aux arts" (1774)

Gourdin (Père), *De l'éducation physique et morale considérée relativement à la place qu'occupent, et que doivent occuper les Enfans dans l'ordre de la Société* (1780)

Delacroix (Abbé), "Mémoire sur les moyens que l'on pourroit employer pour perfectionner l'éducation de la jeunesse" (1762)

Printed Sources

Alembert, J.I.R. de, and Diderot, D., eds., *Encyclopédie ou Dictionnaire raisonné des sciences, des arts et des métiers*, 28 vols., Paris, 1751-72

Anonymous, *Dictionnaire de l'Académie Françoise dédié au Roy*, 2 vols., Paris, 1694

———, *Dictionnaire raisonné de plusieurs mots qui sont dans la bouche de tout le monde, et ne présentent pas des idées bien nettes*, Paris, 1790

———, *De l'éducation publique*, Amsterdam, 1763

———, "Lettre sur l'éducation physico-morale des enfans de la campagne," *Annonces, Affiches et avis divers de Picardie, Artois, Soissonnais et Pays-bas François*, 1771

———, *Projet d'éducation tardive* (n.p., n.d.)

———, "Projet en faveur des petites écoles de la Campagne," *Journal de la Ville de Troyes & de la Champagne Méridionale*, 1784

————, "Réflexions détachées sur les Traités d'Education," *Mercure de France*, March, 1782

————, "Sur l'Education, en réponse aux Reflexions détachées sur les Traités d'Education, insérées dans le Mercure du Samedi 2 Mars," *Mercure de France*, March 1782

Bachaumont, L. P. de, *Mémoires secrets pour servir à l'histoire de la république des lettres en France depuis MDCCLXII jusqu'à nos jours, ou Journal d'un observateur*, 36 vols., London 1777-89

Bachelier, J. J., *Discours sur l'utilité des écoles élémentaires en faveur des arts mécaniques. Prononcé par M. B . . . [achelier], à l'ouverture de l'Ecole Royale gratuite de Dessein, le 10 Sept., 1766*, Paris, 1766

Bastide, J. F., *Dictionnaire des moeurs*, Paris, 1773

Baudeau, N., "De l'éducation nationale," *Ephémérides du Citoyen ou Chronique de l'Esprit National*, 1765-66

————, *Idées d'un citoyen sur les besoins, les droits et les devoirs des vrais pauvres*, Amsterdam, 1765

Beguillet, E., *Considérations générales sur l'éducation adressées à l'auteur des "Reflexions détachées sur les Traités d'éducation," Insérées dans le Mercure de Fevrier de la présente année 1782*, Bouillon, 1782

Berenger, L. P., *Les Quatre États de la France*, n.p., 1789

————, *Le peuple instruit par ses propres vertus, ou Cours complet d'instruction et d'anecdotes recueillies dans nos meilleurs auteurs*, 2 vols., Paris, 1787

Borelly, J. A., *Plan de réformation des études élémentaires*, The Hague, 1776

Cantillon, *Essai sur la nature du commerce en général*, London, 1756

Cerfvol, *Mémoire sur la population, dans laquelle on indique le moyen de la rétablir, & de se procurer un corps militaire toujours subsistant & peuplant*, London, 1768

————, *Le Radoteur, ou Nouveaux mélanges de philosophie, d'anecdotes curieuses [et] d'aventures particulières*, 2 vols., Paris, 1777

Cerveau, R. (Abbé), *Nécrologe des plus célébres defenseurs et confesseurs de la vérité du dix-huitième siècle*, 2 vols., n.p., 1760

Chantréau, P. N., *Dictionnaire national et anecdotique*, Politicopolis [sic], 1790

Chicaneau de Neuville, D. P., *Dictionnaire philosophique ou Introduction à la connoissance de l'homme*, Paris, 1762

Clément, J.M.B., *Petit dictionnaire de la cour et de la ville*, Paris, 1788

Colomb, *Plan raisonné d'éducation publique pour ce qui regarde la partie des Etudes*, Avignon, 1762

Condillac, E. B., "Discours Préliminaire" to the *Cours d'études pour l'instruction du Prince de Parme, Oeuvres de Condillac*, 23 vols., Paris, 1798

Condorcet, J.A.N.C. de, *Esquisse d'un tableau historique des progrès de l'esprit humain*, Paris, 1971

Constant d'Orvillé, ed., *Dictionnaire universel, historique et critique des moeurs, loix, usages & coutumes civiles, militaires et politiques; & des cérémonies & pratiques religieuses & superstitieuses, tant anciennes que modernes, des peuples des quatre parties du monde*, 4 vols., Paris, 1772

Coyer, F. G. (Abbé), *Dissertation sur le vieux mot Patrie, Oeuvres Complètes de M. l'abbé Coyer*, 7 vols., Paris, 1782-83, vol. 1

——, *Dissertation sur la Nature du Peuple, Oeuvres*, vol. 1

——, *Bagatelles Morales, Oeuvres*, vol. 1

——, *Plan d'Éducation Publique, Oeuvres*, vol. 3

Crévier, J.B.L., *Difficultés proposées à Monsieur de Caradeuc de la Chalotais sur le Mémoire intitulé Essai d'éducation nationale ou Plan d'études pour la jeunesse. Presenté au Parlement 24 Mars 1763*, Paris, 1763

Delandine, F. A., *Couronnes Académiques, ou Recueil des Prix proposés par les Sociétés Savantes, avec les noms de ceux qui les ont obtenus, des Concurens distingués, des Auteurs qui ont écrit sur les mêmes sujets, le titre & le lieu de l'impression de leurs Ouvrages*, Paris, 1787

Démeunier, J. N., ed., *Encyclopédie méthodique: Economie*

politique et diplomatique, 4 vols., Paris and Liège, 1784-88

Diderot, D., "Plan d'une université pour le gouvernement de Russie, ou d'une éducation publique dans toutes les sciences," in J. Assézat, ed., *Oeuvres complètes de Diderot*, 20 vols., Paris, 1875-77, vol. III

——, "Essai sur les études en Russie," *Oeuvres*, III

——, "Réfutation suivie de l'ouvrage d'Helvétius intitulé *De l'Homme*," *Oeuvres*, II

Durey de Noinville, J. B., *Table alphabétique des dictionnaires*, Paris, 1758

Durosoy, J. B. (Abbé), *Philosophie sociale ou Essai sur les devoirs de l'homme & du citoyen*, Paris, 1783

Formey, J.H.S., *Traité d'éducation morale Qui a remporté le prix de la Société des Sciences de Harlem, l'an 1762, sur cette Question: "Comment on doit gouverner l'esprit & le coeur d'un Enfant, pour le rendre heureux & utile"* Liège, 1773

Fourcroy de Guillerville, J. L. de, *Les enfans élevés dans l'ordre de la nature ou abrégé de l'histoire naturelle des enfans du premier âge à l'usage des Pères & mères de Famille*, 2nd ed., Paris, 1783

Fréron, Elie, et al., *L'Année littéraire et politique*, 292 vols., Amsterdam, 1754-90

Furetière, et al., *Dictionnaire universel de Furetière françois et latin vulgairement appelle Dictionnaire de Trévoux*, 8 vols., Paris 1732

Gibbon, Edward, *Autobiography*, D. A. Saunders, ed., New York, 1961

Goyon de la Plombaine, H., *L'Unique moyen de soulager le peuple, et d'enrichir la nation françoise*, Paris, 1775

Grimm, M., Diderot, D., G. Raynal, et al., *Correspondance littéraire*, M. Tourneux, ed., 16 vols. Paris, 1877-81

Grivel, G., *Théorie de l'éducation, ouvrage utile aux pères de famille et aux instituteurs*, 3 vols., Paris, 1775

Guyot, P.J.J.G., et al., *Grand vocabulaire françois*, 30 vols., Paris, 1767-74

Guyton de Morveau, *Mémoire sur l'éducation publique avec le prospectus d'un collège, Suivant les Principes de cet Ouvrage*, n.p., 1764

Helvétius, C. A., *Oeuvres complètes*, 14 vols., Paris, 1795

————, *De l'Homme, de ses facultés intellectuelles et de son éducation*, 2 vols., London, 1773

Hohenzollern, Frederick II, *Lettre sur l'éducation*, Berlin, 1770

Holbach, P.H.D. d', *Ethnocratie, ou le gouvernement fondé sur la morale*, Amsterdam, 1776

————, *Système social, ou Principes naturels de la morale et de la politique avec un examen de l'influence du gouvernement sur les moeurs*, 3 vols., London, 1773

Jaubert, P. (Abbé), *Des causes de la dépopulation et des moyens d'y remédier*, London, 1767

————, *Eloge de la roture dédié aux roturiers*, London, 1766

Joly, J. R. (Père), *Dictionnaire de morale philosophique*, 2 vols., Paris, 1771

Krauss, W., ed., *Est-il utile de tromper le peuple? Ist der Volksbetrug von Nutzen? Concours de la classe de philosophie spéculative de l'Académie des Sciences et des Belles-Lettres de Berlin pour l'année 1780*, Berlin, 1966

La Chalotais, L.R.C. de, *Essai d'éducation nationale ou Plan d'études pour la jeunesse*, Paris, 1763

Lefebvre de Beauvray, P., *Dictionnaire social et patriotique, ou Précis raisonné des connoissances relatives à l'économie morale, civile & politique*, Amsterdam, 1770

Le Mercier de la Rivière, P. P., *De l'instruction publique ou Considérations morales et politiques sur la nécessité, la nature et la source de cette instruction, Ouvrage demandé pour le ROI DE SUEDE*, Stockholm, 1775

Lezay-Marnesia, C.F.A. de, *Le bonheur dans les campagnes*, Neufchatel, 1785

Mathon de la Cour, C. J., *Discours sur les meilleurs moyens de faire naître et d'encourager le patriotisme dans une monarchie, Qui a remporté le prix dans l'Académie de Châlons-sur-Marne le 25 août 1787*, Paris, 1787

Mauduit, F., *Utrum vulgo Plebeiorum liberos humanioribus litteris excole oporteat*, Paris, 1773

Meerman, J., *Discours presenté à l'Académie de Châlons-sur-Marne en 1787. Sur la question qu'elle avoit proposée: Quels sont les moyens d'exciter & d'encourager le patriotisme dans une monarchie sans gêner ou affoiblir en rien l'étendue de pouvoir & d'exécution qui est propre à ce genre de Gouvernement?* Leiden, 1789

Mercier, L. S., *Tableau de Paris*, 12 vols., Amsterdam, 1783-88

Montlinot, C.A.J.L. (Abbé), *Discours qui a remporté le prix à la Société Royale d'Agriculture de Soissons en l'année 1779: Sur cette question proposée par la même Société: Quels sont les moyens de détruire la Mendicité, de rendre les Pauvres valides utiles, & de les secourir dans la ville de Soissons?* Lille, 1779

Navarre (Père), *Discours qui a remporté le prix par le jugement de l'académie des jeux floraux en l'année 1763 sur ces paroles: Quel seroit en France le Plan d'Etude le plus avantageux?* n.p., n.d.

Necker, J., *De l'importance des opinions religieuses*, London, 1788

Perreau, J. A., *Instruction du peuple, divisée en trois parties*, Paris, 1786

Philipon de la Madelaine, L., *Vues patriotiques sur l'éducation du peuple, Tant des villes que de la campagne: Avec beaucoup de notes intéressantes*, Lyon, 1783

———, *De l'éducation des collèges*, London, 1784

Richelet, P., *Dictionnaire de la langue françoise ancienne et moderne*, 3 vols., Paris, 1728

Rivard, F. D., *Recueil de Mémoires touchant l'Education de la Jeunesse, Surtout par rapport aux Etudes*, Paris, 1763

Robinet, J.B.R., ed., *Dictionnaire universel des sciences morales, économiques, politiques et diplomatiques; ou Bibliothèque de l'homme d'état et du citoyen*, 30 vols., London, 1777-83

Rolland d'Erceville, B. G., *Compte Rendu aux Chambres As-*

semblées par M. le Président Rolland de ce qui a été fait par MM. les Commissaires, nommés par les Arrêts de 6 Août & de 7 Septembre 1762, Paris, 1763

————, *Compte Rendu aux Chambres assemblées, Par M. Rolland, des différens Mémoires envoyés par les Universités sises dans le Ressort de la Cour, en exécution de l'Arrêt des Chambres assemblées, du 3 Sept. 1762, relativement au plan d'Etude à suivre dans les Collèges non dépendans des Universités, & à la correspondance à établir entre les Collèges & les Universités*, Paris, 1768

————, *Discours prononcé dans la grande salle de l'hôtel de ville, à la séance publique de l'Académie des sciences, belles-lettres et arts d'Amiens, le 25 Aout 1784*, Amiens and Paris, 1788

Rousseau, J. J., *Emile ou De l'éducation, Oeuvres complètes de Jean Jacques Rousseau*, vol. iv, B. Gagnebin and M. Raymond, eds., Dijon, 1969

Rousseau, Pierre, et al., *Le Journal encyclopédique ou universel*, 302 vols., Bouillon, 1756-93

Thélis, C.A.P. de, *Idées proposées au gouvernement sur l'administration des chemins. . . . Terminées par un Plan d'éducation citoyenne & militaire, relative à leur confection*, n.p., 1777

————, *Moyens Proposés pour le Bonheur des Peuples qui vivent sous le Gouvernement Monarchique*, n.p., 1778

————, *Plan d'éducation nationale, En faveur des pauvres enfans de la Campagne*, n.p., 1779

————, et al., *Mémoires concernant les écoles nationales*, Paris, 1781-89

———— and Charost, *Reglement concernant les écoles nationales*, n.p., 1780

Thiebault, *Nouveau plan d'éducation publique*, Amsterdam, 1778

Thomas, A. L., *Epître au peuple. Ouvrage présenté à l'Académie françoise en 1760*, n.p., 1761

Tissot, S. A., *Avis au peuple sur sa santé*, 2 vols., Paris, 1779

Turgot, "Mémoire sur les municipalités," in G. Schelle, ed., *Oeuvres de Turgot*, 5 vols., Paris, 1913-23, vol. IV

Vauréal, *Plan ou Essai d'Education générale et nationale ou La Meilleure Education à donner aux hommes de toutes nations*, Bouillon, 1783

Verlac, B., *Nouveau plan d'éducation pour toutes les classes de citoyens,*, Vannes and Paris, 1789

Voltaire, *Dictionnaire philosophique*, J. Benda and R. Naves, eds., Paris, 1961

———, *Oeuvres complètes*, Beuchot, ed., 97 vols., Paris, 1828-34

Young, Arthur, *Travels in France during the Years 1787, 1788 and 1789*, J. Kaplow, ed., New York, 1969

SECONDARY SOURCES

Agulhon, M., *La vie sociale en Provence intérieure au lendemain de la Révolution*, Paris, 1970

Allain, E. (Abbé), *L'instruction primaire en France avant la Révolution, d'après les travaux récents et des document inédits*, Paris, 1881

———, "Les questions d'enseignement dans les cahiers de 1789," in *Revue des questions historiques*, XXVIII (1885)

Ariès, P., *Histoire des populations françaises et de leurs attitudes devant la vie depuis le XVIIIe siècle*, Mulhouse, 1971

———, "Problèmes de l'éducation," *La France et les français*, M. François, ed., Bruges, 1972

———, *Centuries of Childhood*, R. Baldick, trans., New York, 1968

Armogathe, J. R., Besse, G., et al., *Images du peuple au dix-huitième siècle*, Paris, 1973

Artz, F. B., *The Development of Technical Education in France, 1500-1850*, Cambridge, Mass., 1966

Aulard, A., *Le Patriotisme français de la Renaissance à la Révolution*, Paris, 1921

Babcock, R. W., "Benevolence, Sensibility and Sentiment in

Some Eighteenth-Century Periodicals," *Modern Language Notes*, LXII (1974)

Babeau, A., *L'Instruction primaire dans les campagnes avant 1789 d'après des documents tirés des archives communales et départementales de l'Aube*, Troyes, 1875

——, *L'Ecole de village pendant la révolution*, Paris, 1885

Bahner, W., "Le mot et la notion de 'peuple' dans l'oeuvre de Rousseau," VS, LV (1967)

Baker, K. M., "Scientism, Elitism and Liberalism: the Case of Condorcet," VS, LV (1967)

Barnard, H. C., *Education and the French Revolution*, Cambridge, 1969

Becker, C. L., *The Heavenly City of The Eighteenth-Century Philosophers*, New Haven, 1959

Bellanger, C., Godeschot, J., et al., *Historie générale de la presse française*, vol. I, Paris, 1969

Blanc, M., *Essai sur l'enseignement primaire avant 1789*, Forcalquier, 1954

Boss, R. I., "The Development of Social Religion: A Contradiction of French Free Thought," JHI, XXXIV (1973)

Braudel, F., and Labrousse, E., eds., *Histoire économique et sociale de la France*, vol. II, Paris, 1970

Brissenden, R. F., *Virtue in Distress: Studies in the Novel of Sentiment from Richardson to Sade*, New York, 1974

Buisson, F., ed., *Dictionnaire de pédagogie et d'instruction primaire*, 4 vols., Paris, 1882-93

Burguière, A., "Société et culture à Reims à la fin du XVIIIe siècle: la diffusion des 'lumières' analysé à travers les cahiers de doléances," AESC, XXII (1967)

Champion, E., "L'instruction publique en France d'après les cahiers de 1789," RIE, VIII (1884)

Chartrier, R., Compère, M. M., and Julia, D., *L'Education en France du XVIe au XVIIIe siècle*, Paris, 1976

——, "Les élites et les gueux: quelques représentations (XVIe-XVIIe siècles)," RHMC, XXI (1974)

Charvet, John, *The Social Problem in the Philosophy of Rousseau*, Cambridge, 1974

Chaunu, P., *La Civilisation de l'Europe classique*, Mulhouse, 1970

Chaussinand-Nogaret, G., *La Noblesse au XVIIIe siècle: de la féodalité aux Lumières*, Paris, 1976

Chisick, H., "Bourses d'études et mobilité sociale en France à la veille de la Révolution: Bourses et boursiers du collège de Louis-le-Grand (1762-1789)," AESC, xxx (1975)

——, "Institutional Innovation in Popular Education in Eighteenth-Century France: Two Examples," FHS, x (1977)

——, "School Attendance, Literacy and Acculturation: *Petites écoles* and Popular Education in Eighteenth Century France," *Europa*, iii (1980)

Choulguine, A., *Les Origines de l'esprit national moderne et Jean Jacques Rousseau. Annales de la Société de Jean-Jacques Rousseau*, xxvi, Geneva, 1937

Coats, A. W., "Changing Attitudes to Labour in the Mid-Eighteenth Century," *Economic History Review*, 2nd series, xi (1958)

Cobban, A., *In Search of Humanity*, New York, 1960

——, *Aspects of the French Revolution*, London, 1971

Cognet, L., *Le Jansénisme*, Paris, 1968

Compayré, G., *Histoire critique des doctrines de l'éducation en France depuis le 16e siècle*, 2 vols., Paris, 1904

Crocker, L. G., "Rousseau and the Common People," in John Pappas, ed., *Essays on Diderot and the Enlightenment in Honor of Otis Fellows*, Geneva, 1974

Darnton, R., *Mesmerism and the End of the Enlightenment in France*, Cambridge, Mass., 1968

——, "The Grub Street Style of Revolution: J. P. Brissot, Police Spy," JMH, xl (1968)

——, "The High Enlightenment and the Low-Life of Literature in Pre-Revolutionary France," P&P, no. 51 (1971)

————, "Reading, Writing and Publishing in Eighteenth Century France: A Case Study in the Sociology of Literature," *Daedalus*, no. 100 (Winter, 1971)

————, "In Search of the Enlightenment: Recent Attempts to Create a Social History of Ideas," JMH, XLIII (1971)

Dautry, J., "La révolution bourgeoise et l'Encyclopédie (1789-1814)," *La Pensée*, nos. 38 and 39 (1951)

David, M., Duby, G., et al., *Niveaux de culture et groupes sociaux*, The Hague, 1971

Davis, D. B., *The Problem of Slavery in Western Culture*, Ithaca and London, 1975

Delvaille, J., *La Chalotais, éducateur*, Paris, 1911

Depauw, J., "Pauvres, pauvres mendiants, mendiants valides ou vagabonds? Les hésitations de la législation royale," RHMC, XXI (1974)

Durkheim, E., *L'Evolution pédagogique en France*, Paris, 1969

Edelstein, Melvin, "Mobilité ou immobilité paysanne? Sur certaines tendances conservatrices de la Révolution française," AHRF, XLVII (1975)

Fairchilds, C. C., *Poverty and Charity in Aix-en-Provence, 1640-1789*, Baltimore, 1976

Ford, F., *Robe and Sword: The Regrouping of the French Aristocracy after Louis XIV*, New York, 1965

Francastel, P., ed., *Utopie et institutions au XVIIIe siècle: Le Pragmatisme des Lumières*, Paris and The Hague, 1963

Frijhoff, W., and Julia, D., *Ecole et société dans la France d'ancien régime: Quatre exemples: Auch, Avallon, Condom et Gisors*, Paris, 1975

Furet, F., et al., *Livre et société*, 2 vols., The Hague, 1965 and 1970

Furet, F., "Pour une définition des classes inférieures à l'époque moderne," AESC, XVIII (1963)

Gagliardo, J. G., *From Pariah to Patriot: The Changing Image of the German Peasant 1770-1840*, Lexington, 1969

Garden, M., *Lyon et les Lyonnais au XVIIIe siècle*, Paris, 1975

Gay, Peter, *The Party of Humanity*, New York, 1964

————, *The Enlightenment: An Interpretation*, 2 vols., New York, 1966-69

Geoffroy, A., "Le 'peuple' selon Saint-Just," AHRF, XL (1968)

Gerbi, A. (trans. J. Moyle), *The Dispute of the New World: The History of a Polemic, 1750-1900*, Pittsburgh, 1973

Geremek, B., "Criminalité, Vagabondage, Pauperisme: la marginalité à l'aube des temps modernes," RHMC, XXI (1974)

Godechot, J., "Nation, patrie, nationalisme et patriotisme en France au XVIIIe siècle," AHRF, XLIII (1971)

Goldmann, L., "La Pensee des 'Lumières,'" AESC, XXII (1967)

Gontard, M., *L'Enseignement Primaire en France de la Révolution à la loi Guizot 1789-1833*, Paris, 1959

Goubert, P., *Cent Mille Provinciaux au XVIIe siècle: Beauvais et le Beauvaisis de 1600 à 1730*, Paris, 1968

—— (trans. Anne Carter), *Louis XIV and Twenty Million Frenchmen*, New York, 1970

Gourdon, H., "Les Physiocrates et l'Education nationale au XVIIIe siècle," RP, XXXVIII (1901)

Groethuysen, B., *Philosophie de la Révolution Française*, Paris, 1956

—— (trans. Mary Ilford), *The Bourgeois: Catholicism vs. Capitalism in Eighteenth-Century France*, London, 1968

Grosperrin, B., "Faut-il instruire le peuple? La reponse des physiocrates," CH, XXI, 1976

Guillaume, J., "Le Chevalier de Pawlet, et l'Ecole des Orphelins Militaires (Documents nouveaux)," RP, XIX (1891)

Guillaume, P., and Poussou, J. P., *Démographie historique*, Paris, 1970

Gusdorf, G., *Les Principes de la pensée au siècle des lumières*, Paris, 1971

Gutton, J. P., "A l'aube du XVIIe siècle: idées nouvelles sur les pauvres," CH, X (1965)

——, *La Société et les pauvres en Europe (XVIe-XVIIIe siècles)*, Paris, 1974

Hampson, N., *A Cultural History of the Enlightenment*, New York, 1968

306 · BIBLIOGRAPHY

Hazard, Paul (trans. J. Lewis May), *The European Mind: 1680-1715*, Cleveland and New York, 1967
——— (trans. J. Lewis May), *European Thought in the Eighteenth Century: From Montesquieu to Lessing*, New York, 1969
Healey, F. G., "The Enlightenment View of 'Homo Faber,' " VS, xxv (1963)
Hertzberg, A., *The French Enlightenment and the Jews: The Origins of Modern Anti-Semitism*, New York, 1970
Honour, H., *Neoclassicism*, Bungay, 1968
Hufton, O. H., *The Poor of Eighteenth-Century France 1750-1789*, Oxford, 1974
———, "Begging, Vagrancy, Vagabondage and the Law: an Aspect of the Problem of Poverty in Eighteenth-Century France," ESR, II (1972)
———, "Towards an understanding of the poor of eighteenth-century France," in J. F. Bosher (ed.), *French Government and Society*, London, 1973
Huxley, J., "A Factor Overlooked by the *Philosophes*: the Population Explosion," VS, xxv (1963)
Hyslop, B. F., *French Nationalism in 1789 according to the General Cahiers*, New York, 1934
Janvier, A., "Esquisse biographique sur Jacques Sellier," *Bulletin de la Société des Antiquaires de Picardie*, XII (1876)
Jones, M. G., *The Charity School Movement: A Study of Eighteenth Century Puritanism in Action*, Cambridge, 1938
Kaplow, J., *The Names of Kings: The Parisian Laboring Poor in the Eighteenth Century*, New York, 1972
Kempton, A.C.L., "Education and the Child in Eighteenth Century French Fiction," VS, CXXIV (1975)
Kors, A. C., "The Myth of the Coterie Holbachique," FHS, IX (1976)
Labriolle-Rutherford, M. R. de, "L'Evolution de la notion de luxe depuis Mandeville jusqu'à la Révolution," VS, XXVI (1963)
Laget, M., "Petites écoles en Languedoc au XVIIIe siècle," AESC, XXVI (1971)
Lamy, M. F., "Jacques Sellier et l'école des arts," *Mémoires de*

l'Académie des Sciences des Lettres et des Arts d'Amiens, LXVII (1925)

Landry, A., "Les idées de Quesnay sur la population," *Revue d'histoire des doctrines économiques et sociales*, II (1909)

Lebrun, F., *Les Hommes et la mort en Anjou aux XVIIe et XVIIIe siècles*, Paris, 1975

Lefebvre, G. (trans. E. M. Evanson), *The French Revolution From its Origins to 1793*, New York, 1967

Legagneux, M., "Rollin et le 'mirage spartiate' dans l'éducation publique," in J. Proust, ed., *Recherches nouvelles sur quelques écrivains des lumières*, Geneva, 1972

Leith, J. A., "French Republican Pedagogy in the Year II," *Canadian Journal of History*, III (1968)

———, "The Hope for Moral Regeneration in French Educational Thought, 1750-1789," in Paul Fritz, ed., *City and Society in the Eighteenth Century*, Toronto, 1973

———, "Modernization, Mass Education and Social Mobility in French Thought, 1750-1789," in R. F. Brissenden, ed., *Studies in the Eighteenth Century*, vol. II, Toronto, 1973

———, "Nationalism and the Fine Arts in France, 1750-1789," VS, LXXXIX (1972)

Leroy, M., *Histoire des idées sociales en France: de Montesquieu à Robespierre*, Paris, 1946

Lichtenberger, André, *Le Socialisme au XVIIIe siècle: Etude sur les idées socialistes dans les écrivains français du XVIIIe siècle avant la Révolution*, Paris, 1895

Limonas, "Eloge de M. Scellier," *Mémoires de l'Académie des Sciences des Lettres et des Arts d'Amiens*, LI (1904)

Lough, J., *The Encyclopédie*, London, 1971

———, *The Encyclopédie in Eighteenth-Century England and Other Studies*, Newcastle-upon-Tyne, 1970

Mackrell, J.Q.C., *The Attack on 'Feudalism' in Eighteenth-Century France*, London and Toronto, 1973

Mandrou, R., *Introduction à la France moderne (1500-1640): Essai de psychologie historique*, Paris, 1961

———, *La France aux XVIIe et XVIIIe siècles*, Paris, 1970

Marion, M., *Dictionnaire des institutions de la France aux XVIIe et XVIIIe siècles*, Paris, 1969

Martin, K., *French Liberal Thought in the Eighteenth Century*, New York, 1963

Mathiez, A., "Pacifisme et nationalisme au XVIIIe siècle," AHRF, xiii (1936)

McLaren, A., "Some Secular Attitudes toward Sexual Behavior in France: 1760-1860," FHS, viii (1974)

McNulty, P. J., "Adam Smith's Concept of Labor," JHI, xxxiv (1973)

Mirot, M., *Manuel de géographie historique de la France*, Paris, 1970

Morizé, Andé, *L'Apologie du luxe au XVIIIe siècle et 'Le Mondain' de Voltaire: Etude critique sur 'Le Mondain' et ses sources*, Paris, 1909, reprinted Geneva, 1970

Mornet, D., "Les Enseignements des bibliothèques privées: 1750-1780," *Revue d'histoire littéraire de la France*, xvii (1910)

———, *Les Origines intellectuelles de la Révolution française*, Paris, 1967

———, *La Pensée française au XVIIIe siècle*, Paris, 1969

Mortier, R., "Diderot et la notion du 'peuple,'" *Europe*, nos. 405-406 (Jan.-Feb. 1963)

———, "The 'Philosophes' and Public Education," *Yale French Studies*, no. 40. *Literature and Society: the Eighteenth Century*

———, "Voltaire et le peuple," in Brumfitt, Barber et al. *The Age of Enlightenment: Studies Presented to Theodore Besterman*, London and Edinburgh, 1967

Mousnier, R., "Les concepts d'ordre, d' états, de fidelité et de monarchie absolue en France de la fin du XVe siècle à la fin du XVIIIe," RH, ccxlvii (1972)

Orcibal, J., "Qu'est-ce que le jansénisme?" *Cahiers de l'association internationale des Etudes françaises*, iii (1954)

Palmer, R. R., *Catholics and Unbelievers in Eighteenth-Century France*, Princeton, n.d.

———, "The National Idea in France before the Revolution," JHI, i (1940)

Payne, H. C., *The Philosophes and the People*, New Haven, 1976

——, "Elite Versus Popular Mentality in the Eighteenth Century," *Historical Reflexions*, II (1975)

Ponteil, F., *Histoire de l'enseignement en France: Les grandes étapes, 1789-1964*, Sirrey, 1966

Poynter, J. R., *Society and Pauperism: English Ideas on Poor Relief, 1795-1834*, London and Toronto, 1969

Proal, L., "Les causes de la dépopulation et ses remèdes d'après Jean-Jacques Rousseau," *La Grande Revue*, CII (1920)

Prost, A., *Histoire de l'enseignement en France 1800-1967*, Paris, 1968

Proust, J., *Diderot et l'Encyclopédie*, Paris, 1962

——, *L'Encyclopédie*, Paris, 1965

Raymond, A., "Le problème de la population chez les encyclopédistes," *VS*, XXVI (1963)

Reinhard, M., "Elite et noblesse dans la seconde moitié du XVIIIe siècle," *RHMC*, III (1956)

Richet, D., "Autour des origines idéologiques lointaines de la Révolution française: élites et despotisme," *AESC*, XXIV (1969)

Rigault, G., *Histoire générale de l'institut des frères des écoles chrétiennes*, 5 vols., Paris, 1937-53

Rihs, C., "Les Utopistes contre les Lumières," *VS*, LVII (1967)

Roberts, Warren, *Morality and Social Class in Eighteenth Century French Literature and Painting*, Toronto, 1974

Robin, R., *La Société française en 1789: Semur-en-Auxois*, Paris, 1970

Roche, D., *Le Siècle des Lumières en province, Académies et académiciens provinciaux, 1670-1789*, Thèse pour le doctorat d'état, présentée à l'Université de Paris-Sorbonne, sous la direction du professeur A. Dupront, 1973

——, "Encyclopédistes et académiciens," *Livre et société II*

——, "Milieux académiques provinciaux et société des lumières," *Livre et société I*

————, "La diffusion des lumières. Un exemple: l'Académie de Châlons-sur-Marne," AESC, XIX (1964)

Rocquain, F., L'Esprit révolutionnaire avant la Révolution 1715-1789, Paris, 1878

Rohan Chabot, A. de, Les Ecoles de campagne en Lorraine au XVIIIe siècle, thèse de 3e cycle, Paris, 1967

Rothkrug, L., Opposition to Louis XIV: The Social and Political Origins of the French Enlightenment, Princeton, 1965

Roustan, M., Les Philosophes et la société française au XVIIIe siècle, Paris, 1911, reprinted Geneva, 1970

Sée, Henri, "Les classes ouvrières et la question sociale à la veille de la Révolution," Annales Révolutionnaires, XIV (1922)

Shackleton, R., "Jansenism and the Enlightenment," VS, LVII (1967)

Shafer, B. C., "Bourgeois Nationalism in the Pamphlets on the Eve of the French Revolution," JMH, x (1938)

Silver, H., The Concept of Popular Education: A Study in Ideas and Social Movements in the Early Nineteenth Century, London, 1965

Silvy, M. A., "Les collèges en France avant la Révolution," Bulletin de la Société d'économie sociale, IX, 2e partie 1895

Snyders, G., La Pédagogie en France au XVIIe et XVIIIe siècles, Paris, 1965

Soboul, A., La Civilisation et la Révolution française: I. La Crise de l'ancien régime, Paris, 1970

Spengler, J. J., French Predecessors of Malthus: A Study in Eighteenth Century Wage and Population Theory, Durham, 1942

Stone, L., "The Educational Revolution in England 1560-1640," P&P, no. 28 (1964)

————, "Literacy and Education in England 1640-1900," P&P, no. 42 (1969)

Talmon, J. L., The Origins of Totalitarian Democracy, New York, 1970

Taton, R., ed., Enseignement et diffusion des sciences en France au XVIIIe siècle, Paris, 1964

Tavenaux, R., "Jansénisme et vie sociale en France au XVIIe siècle," *Revue d'histoire de l'église de France*, LIV, 1968

Thénard, J. F., "L'enseignement populaire sous l'ancien régime: Témoinage de Turgot," RP, XXIV (1894)

Van der Byl, F. V., *Le Chevalier Pawlet: Educateur Oublié*, Paris, 1934

Vissière, I., "Le peuple d'après Condorcet: Classifications et images," *Structure et fonction du vocabulaire social dans la littérature française*, Halle, 1970

Vyverburg, H., *Historical Pessimism in the French Enlightenment*, Cambridge, Mass., 1958

Wade, I., "Poverty in the Enlightenment," *Europaische Aufklarung. Studies Presented to Herbert Dieckmann*, H. Friedrich and F. Schalk, eds., Munich, 1967

Walter, E., "Sur l'intelligentsia des lumières," *Dixhuitième siècle*, V (1973)

Weintraub, K. J., "Toward the History of the Common Man: Voltaire and Condorcet," *Ideas in History: Essays presented to Louis R. Gottschalk*, R. Herr, ed., Durham, 1965

Young, D. B., "Libertarian Demography: Montesquieu's Essay on Depopulation in the *Lettres Persanes*," JHI, XXXVI (1975)

Index*

* The index was compiled by David Gradowitz.

education (*cont.*)
  tality on, 203; as cohesive force,
    214, 238; power of, 239-43; *see*
    literacy
  elites, 73, 279
  elitism: of Enlightenment, 34, 58n,
    262-64; of academies, 37; of
    seventeenth century, 245
  empiricism, 6, 100
  encyclopedias, 49, 70, 196n, 256
  Encyclopédie: Philipon's drawing
    on, 15; and Jaucourt, 25; and en-
    lightened community, 36; and
    bourgeoisie, 37n; article
    "Peuple," 48n, 56, 58, 68; am-
    bivalence toward lower classes,
    70-71; and Formey, 105; and
    Journal de Trévoux, 117; and
    Grivel, 145; article "Population,"
    189, 191n; article "Patrie,"
    207n-208n, 222; and poor, 223n
  Encyclopédie méthodique, 145, 185,
    189, 190, 208
  encyclopedist, 31, 37, 69, 100, 103,
    105, 148
  England, 190, 281
  enlightened community: basic be-
    liefs of, 5-6; definition of, 18;
    mentality of, 33-34, 38, 289; so-
    cial composition, 33-36; role of
    academies in, 36-38; interest in
    education, 41-45; attitudes to
    lower classes, 48, 254-55, 257-58,
    262-63; on popular education,
    76-78, 121, 139, 145, 148, 153-
    54, 156, 273-74, 277-79; on de-
    mography, 192; patriotism of,
    221; and beneficence, 234; on
    power of education, 242-44; at-
    titude to old regime, 266
  Enlightenment: values of, 5-6, 117;
    as intellectual movement, 12, 18;
    attitude of mind, 33, 117; elitism
    of, 34, 261-73; epistemology of,

38-39, 242; Gay on, 73; and
    classics, 74; and religion, 96,
    114n, 117-18, 220; demography
    of, 177; population theory of,
    196; patriotism of, 206-10, 223;
    beneficence in, 225-26; exten-
    sion into nineteenth century,
    285; and popular education,
    277, 288-90
  epistemology, 6, 40
  état, see state
  Europe, 35, 43, 141, 186, 190, 194,
    202, 255, 279
  Expilly, 189, 191-92

  Fabre, 54, 57n, 68
  Farlan, 136
  Fénelon, 257n
  Ferlus, 19, 28, 216, 220, 222, 224,
    256
  feudalism, 124
  Fillassier, 228
  Flaubert, 281
  Fontenelle, 271
  Formey: career, 19, 27-29, 105;
    danger of educating people,
    107-109; blends Enlightenment
    and religious outlooks, 117-18;
    on power of education, 239; on
    people, 246-47, 255, 259, 262;
    on equality, 265
  Fourcroy, 16, 19, 26, 179-81, 187,
    192-94, 216
  Fourier, 281-82
  France: population of, 61n, 184,
    187-89, 192; as aristocracy, 73;
    under feudalism, 124; na-
    tionalism in, 131, 206n, 212-14,
    217-23; in crisis, 204-205, 238;
    industrialization of, 272
  Franklin, 141
  Frédéric de Castillon, 246, 262
  Frederick II, 27-28, 40-41, 104,
    166

Frères de la doctrine chrétienne, 91
Fréron, 22, 94, 149, 151, 215-16,
   237, 248
Furetière, 50, 51, 56, 68, 72

Gay, Peter, 32, 73, 77, 116, 263
Genlis, Madame de, 280
Gibbon, 96
Giddy, 280
Gosselin, 19, 64, 211
Gourdin: career, 19, 24, 27; on
   need for popular education,
   129, 145, 153, 264; education
   relative to social standing, 136;
   priests as teachers, 165, 213; occupational instruction, 172-74;
   physical training, 175; on population, 186n; on towns, 195,
   196n; on self interest, 199-200;
   on luxury, 201; on patriotism,
   219; on power of education,
   240; on lower classes, 247, 253,
   254n, 258-59
Goyon d'Arzac: career, 19, 23, 26;
   and Academy of Châlons-sur-
   Marne, 10, 14-15; on lower
   classes, 131-32, 246-48, 251-53,
   259-61, 264; on popular education, 133, 158; on literacy, 137-
   41; on religion, 159, 220; on occupational instruction, 169; on
   physical education, 177, 180-81;
   on depopulation, 187; on
   swaddling, 194n; on luxury,
   200; on state control of education, 210, 214; on power of education, 240
Goyon de la Plombaine, 19, 202,
   204
Granet: career, 19, 26, 105; unde-
   sirability of educating lower
   classes, 109-10, 264, 277; popular instruction, 139; on depopulation of countryside, 195; on

corruption, 198; on power of
   education, 239; on condition of
   lower classes, 252-53
Grégoire, Abbé, 17
Grimm, 43, 61, 90n, 93, 100n,
   102-103, 155
Grivel: career, 19, 26, 29; on popular education, 145, 168; on
   power of education, 167; on
   physical education, 176, 180; on
   swaddling, 194n; on corruption,
   196n, 198; on town and country,
   259-60
Grotius, 24
Gustave III of Sweden, 41, 214
Guyton de Morveau: career, 19,
   26, 104-105; as participant in
   essay contest, 14n; on enlightenment, 105-106; on popular education, 106, 273; on nation's control of education, 208,
   212; on patriotism and Christianity, 219; on power of education, 239; on condition of lower
   classes, 253; elitism of, 262

Hampson, 33
Helvétius: career, 20, 30; on ignorance, 9, 146-47; as source for
   Philipon, 15-16; as *philosophe*, 29;
   on academies, 38; on sensationalist psychology, 39; and
   enlightened despots, 41; on
   power of education, 240
Henri IV, 201
Herodotus, 72
Hodgson, 280
Holbach: career, 20; on ignorance,
   9-10, 147; as *philosophe*, 29; as an-
   tisemite, 74; on lower classes,
   136, 250-51, 260-61; on secular
   morality, 164; on infant mortality, 192n-93n; on population,
   196-97; on corruption, 198; on

Library of Congress Cataloging in Publication Data

Chisick, Harvey, 1946-
    The limits of reform in the Enlightenment.

    Bibliography: p.
    Includes index.
    1. Education—France—History—18th century.
2. Enlightenment.   I.   Title.
LA691.5.C52   370'.944   80-7512
ISBN 0-691-05305-7

The Author

*Harvey Chisick is a Senior Lecturer in the Department of General History
of the University of Haifa in Israel. He is the author of a short monograph
and several articles on the social history of education under the old regime
and is currently engaged in further research on the Enlightenment.*